1991

D1519923

Covered Wagon Women

Covered Wagon Women

Diaries & Letters from the

Western Trails

1840-1890

edited & compiled by
KENNETH L. HOLMES

Volume X
1875-1883

THE ARTHUR H. CLARK COMPANY
Spokane, Washington
1991

LIBRARY OF CONGRESS CATALOG CARD NUMBER 82-72586
ISBN 0-87062-145-9 (complete set)
ISBN 0-87062-211-0 (volume 10 only)

The Arthur H. Clark Company
P.O. Box 14707
Spokane, WA 99214

Contents

Illustrations

Introduction to Volume X

In this, the tenth and final volume of text in the series (to be followed by a volume containing the series index, bibliography and other reference materials), we again find ourselves using words such as "poignant," "moving," and "touching," as we seek to unlock the innermost feelings of these women as they traveled from the Missouri/Mississippi heartland to the Pacific slope states.

The emotional reactions which these women experienced in the face of both triumph and tragedy on the western trails has been a source of unending fascination. Our intent in presenting these materials has been to expose a broad audience to the original source material compiled by women on the overland trails. We have left to others to analyze the data and interpret it. We preferred to let the women speak for themselves.

Travel was faster in the 1870's and 1880's than in previous decades. Horses and mules predominated, rather than the oxen so relied upon in earlier migrations. This was made possible because there was plenty of grain available at farms and towns along the way. Some of them drove cattle, but none of the diarists published herein used oxen for wagon power. When towns were not near at hand, there were railroad stations along the way, which were often used as camping grounds. The travelers often followed the Union Pacific line westward. Communication along the route was greatly improved, and the travelers could often send and receive mail at stopping places.

We want to thank especially John W. Evans, Librarian at Eastern Oregon State College in LaGrande, who has been kind enough to copy and edit the original diary of Sarah Collins. He plans to donate this diary to the Oregon Historical Society in Portland.

For those who have not read the introduction to the first volume of this series, we reiterate some salient points which have been used to guide the editorial hand. It is a major purpose to let the writers tell their own story in their own words with as little scholarly trimming as possible. The intent in this publication of primary sources is to transcribe each word or phrase as accurately as possible, leaving misspellings and grammatical errors as written in the original.

Two gestures have been made for the sake of clarity:

1. We have added space where phrases or sentences ended and no punctuation appeared in the original.

2. We have put the daily journals into diary format even though the original may have been written continuously line by line because of the writer's shortage of paper.

There are numerous geographic references that are mentioned over and over again in the various accounts. The final volume in the series will include a geographical gazeteer, in addition to an index and bibliography to aid the reader.

The scarce and unusual in overland documents have been sought out. Readily available accounts are not included, but they will be referred to in the final volume along with the bibliography. If the reader knows of such accounts written while on the journey, please let us know. Our goal is to add to the knowledge of all regarding this portion of our history—the story of ordinary people embarked on an extraordinary experience.

KENNETH L. HOLMES

Monmouth, Oregon, 1991

The Diaries, Letters, and Commentaries

A Letter from the Arkansas Valley, 1875

℘ Annie Brigham Mitchell

INTRODUCTION

This is a version of the "Arkansas Mining Association" by a participant in that wagon train. The party was led by Anson W. (Grizzly) Callen from Junction City, Kansas, to Prescott, Arizona Territory. It is told in a column in the Junction City *Union*, in its issue of August 7, 1875, telling of events experienced up to that date. The writer of the letter was a young school teacher, Angie Brigham Mitchell.

We first saw the letter in the Sharlot Hall Museum in Prescott. The clipping had neither date nor place. These facts were supplied for us by the staff of the Kansas State Historical Society in Topeka.

Angie Mitchell was born on October 5, 1854, which means she was 21 years old at the time of the overland journey. Her father, Daniel F. Mitchell was a civil engineer and a surveyor. His first task upon arrival in Prescott was to survey the new town. Angie went to work as a school teacher, some say the first in Arizona. She had anticipated teaching in the new territory and had brought with her a collection of books and maps. She had attended the college in Manhattan, Kansas, now Western Kansas State College.

Prescott was a rip-roaring mining town at an altitude of 5346 feet, in Yavapai County. There is a note in the Sharlot Hall Museum that when Angie Mitchell began to sing at the Union Sunday Church, all the gambling houses closed up "tight shut" for that hour and the miners and gamblers put on their best clothes and attended church, often putting a generous handful of money in the contribution box "and went back to open up the most prosperous and lucky games of the week."

It was on April 20, 1881, that Angie Mitchell was married to a prominent citizen, a member of the legislature named George E. Brown. She moved to his large ranch on the Agua Fria (Cold Water) River. There they ranched and farmed for many years. Brown also served as a deputy sheriff, and deputy United States Marshall. In his late years he was Superintendant of Irrigation for the Pima and Maricopa Indians.

Angie Mitchell Brown died on December 23, 1909.

We are grateful to the Sharlot Hall Museum in Prescott, Arizona, for use of the Angie Mitchell/Brown papers in their collection as references for the life of this interesting lady.

ANGIE BRIGHAM MITCHELL'S LETTER

Camp on the Plains, July 28, 1875
To the Editor of the Union:[1]

Knowing the interest you take in the Argonauts, I send you a few lines from headquarters. We are camped about four miles from Sargent.[2] Came here Monday p.m.; expect to remain till Friday, the 30th, to recruit the stock previous to hard traveling. Yesterday being a bright, sunny day, the wagons were unloaded, everything inspected, aired and repacked. Our camping ground is on a high prairie, smooth and level, covered with the short buffalo grass. Grass and water for the stock are abundant and excellent at this point, but good drinking water was not to be found, so a party turned out to dig a well. Struck water at about five feet. This proved to be too strong with alkali. Another was dug; this did

---

[1]The editor of the Junction City *Union* in 1875 was Noble L. Prentis. He was a native of Illinois and a Civil War veteran. Harold C. Evans, editor, *Kansas, A guide to the Sunflower State* (New York, 1949), p. 124.

[2]Sargents, Colorado. A postoffice would be established there in 1880 and named for Joseph Sargent, a rancher, and first postmaster. Frank Dawson, *Place Names in Colorado* (Denver, Colo., 1954), p. 45.

not prove satisfactory, but a third yielded an abundance of good water.

For several days we have been traveling through the valley of the Arkansas with the river on the one hand and the A.,T. & Santa Fe R.R.,[3] on the other. Though for days we have not seen a house, except when we passed through the railroad station, we have felt that we were not entirely removed from civilization, for twice a day the railroad train has passed us.

The Arkansas valley certainly does not deserve the title of "drouthy," for ever since we entered it we have had one or two showers every twenty-four hours, many of them accompanied with high wind, and with vivid lightening and loud peals of thunder. The greater part of the showers come in the night, and sometimes catch us unprepared. At such times there is a general gathering up of beds that have been spread in the open air, and a hasty retreating to the "big tent." The camp resounds with calls of "Turn out boys, make the tents fast!" "Cover the wagons!" etc., and then echoes of mattocks and tent-pins, and shouts can be heard for a long distance. Last night we had three showers, but our canvas houses afforded an excellent protection, as the wind was not high. To-day is very warm, little air stirring, and the clouds warn us that to-night we may look out for our usual shower.

We have been expecting to go to Las Animas,[4] but the leaders of the party have decided to cross the river at Grenada [Granada],[5] Col., taking a route that has been laid out within a couple of years, thus saving fifty miles of travel, and getting better grass and more water, though less wood. We shall

---

[3]Atchison, Topeka and Santa Fe Railroad. A good short treatment is found in Howard R. Lamar, *Reader's Encyclopedia of the American West* (New York, 1974), pp. 61-62.

[4]Named by the Spaniards for the river, "El Rio de las Animas Perdidos in Purgatorio," "The River of the Lost Souls Lost in Purgatory." Dawson, *op. cit.*, p. 31.

[5]Granada, Colorado. Spanish word for "End of the Road." It was the end of the railroad for a period. Dawson, *op. cit.*, p. 24.

strike the old route again about four miles from Fort Union,[6]
New Mexico. It is said there is a little more danger from
Indians on this route, but we have no fear of them, as our
train is large and well-armed, and we do not propose to be
caught napping.

We are about 2,600 higher than Junction City, and find at
this early day quite a difference in the atmosphere, it being
clearer. Sounds can be heard at a greater distance, and one
becomes sooner wearied by exercise.

Last Sabbath we camped near Old Fort Aubry,[7] now in
ruins. This consisted of a few adobe houses, situated on one
side of a spring of clear, cold water, and upon the other a
roofless one-story house 20x30 feet, the walls of which are
perforated with loop-holes. It is situated so as to command an
extensive country, and probably was the stronghold against
the Indians.

Much of the scenery has been fine. The Arkansas river is
full of small islands and these with the dancing, rippling
waters in the sunshine, the deep blue of the sky, and the
distant hills all go towards making a pretty picture. We have
seen a few new and beautiful flowers, and a variety of snakes,
among them, some good-sized rattle-snakes, several having
been killed that had from seven to twelve rattles. Abundance
of antelopes have been seen, but our hunting parties have not
been successful in obtaining any, for they have been hunted
so much by the emigrants passing along this route that they
are very shy and watchful.

On the morning of the 15th there was great excitement in
camp. About sunrise a buffalo made its appearance near
camp, and a general "hurrah boys" ensued. Shouts of

[6]Today there are the ruins of an abandoned fort eight miles north of Watrous, New
Mexico. T.M. Pearce, *New Mexico Place Names* (Albuquerque, 1985), p. 59.

[7]This fort, established in 1866 and abandoned in 1867, was named for a French
trapper and guide, Francis X. Aubry. Evans, *op. cit.*, pp. 389-90.

"Buffalo! Buffalo!" resounded, and there was running to and fro. When the call was first made it was not generally believed, for we had so often been called out to see the game, but after a little there was a general stir, not a few reaching the spot just in time to see the dark object rolling off over the hill. Hunters, both horse and footmen, were soon in motion, but the footmen after a two miles' chase returned to breakfast. Mr. Callen and three others followed the game four or five miles before killing it, then returned, triumphantly bearing the tongue to convince the skeptical. A wagon was unloaded and sent for it, and for a few meals we luxuriated on fresh meat. At Dodge City[8] we learned that this was the first buffalo of the season.

We are camped near Spirit Mound.[9] This is a terraced, oval mound, of shale rock, a hundred feet or more in length by Sixty or eighty feet in width, and is at present about twenty feet in height. It is supposed to be at least a hundred years old, and at one time it must have been and extensive mound, as the prairie about it for quite a distance is thickly covered washings from it. Originally there must have been five terraces, as they are now distinctly marked, though only three are perfect. It is called Spirit Mound because the Indians came here at the full of the moon to consult the spirits of departed braves, hold their war dances, and perform various ceremonies. It is an open question whether this mound is artificial or natural. Public opinion is about equally divided upon it. One thing is certain—it is composed of entirely different material from anything about it, and if natural is one of nature's singular freaks. The bluffs back of it seem to be of sand, intermixed with clay and a variety of stone, while the tops are thickly strewn with all shades of quartz,

---

[8]Located on the Arkansas River. It is dubbed by Harold C. Evans "the metropolis of southwest Kansas." Evans, *op. cit.*, pp. 177-184.

[9]This became Dodge City's "Boot Hill." *ibid.*, p. 180.

from milky white to a rose so deep that it is almost black; and spar, flint, such as the Indians use for arrow heads, small sand-stones, nice [gneiss], mica, and now and then a clear agate.

We have seen many places and things of interest, among them Kit Carson's table rock. This is a soft shale limestone of mushroom form, three miles from Old Fort Harker.[10] It is covered with names of people, from all parts of the Union. Also Pawnee rock,[11] near Pawnee, where the Indians of former days held their councils. But most of the places are familiar to your readers, so I will not describe them.

At Grenada [Granada] Judge Austin and Mr. Trott leave us, much to the regret of the whole company. In a few days they will be at home and doubtless will give graphic pictures of camp life. All are well and happy.

July 29.—About nine o'clock last night a severe storm broke upon us—it literally poured down. The water ran in from the hills back of us and in less than an hour our camping ground was five or six inches under water. The "big tent" was blown down, and a general rush was made for the wagons, where the rest of the night was spent. Though every one was more or less wet and uncomfortable, not one bit of grumbling was heard but merry jokes, ringing laughter and gay songs resounded. This morning the sun is shining brightly, the air is pleasantly cool, the water all gone, and everybody is busy drying bedding and clothing. Some look a little "wilted," not having slept much, but all are in good spirits.

The hunters of yesterday met with good success, and to-day we have antelope for dinner. Would you not like to dine with us?

A.B.M.

---

[10]Had been established in 1864 and abandoned in 1873. The town of Kanopolis grew up on the site. *Ibid.*, p. 358.

[11]Pawnee Rock is now a Kansas State Park.

Iowa to Oregon, 1878

ℐ Mary Riddle

INTRODUCTION

One of the most remarkable collections of primary documents in any Oregon collection is to be found in twelve ledgers that make up the diary of Mary Riddle. These volumes are in the Astoriana collection in the Astoria Public Library. They are carefully preserved, and an accurate typewritten transcript has been made of the entire collection for the use of researchers. The first entry in her diary was made on May 8, 1878, in Dow City, Crawford County, Iowa, the first stop after leaving their home in Coon Grove. They traveled in a small covered wagon drawn by a span of mules.

Between the first date in her diary, told above, and the last entry 45 years later on July 19, 1923, were recorded twelve ledgers of day-by-day personal experiences.

We are grateful to Bruce Berney, Astoria Public Library Director and to several members of the Clatsop County Historical Society for giving us access to the diary and for aiding in our search for information.

Another rich source of information about our diarist and her diaries has been an article in three parts detailing events in the life of Mary Riddle and her family. This is Vera Whitney Gault's "The Diary of Mary Riddle of Svensen," recorded in *Cumtux, the Clatsop Historical Quarterly*, Vol. 4 (1984), No. 3, pp. 2-14; No. 4, pp. 22-36; and Vol. 5, No. 1, pp. 20-31. *Cumtux* is Chinook Indian jargon for "to know," or "to inform." Svensen, the little town near which the Riddle family lived, is about eleven miles up the Columbia River from Astoria, on the Oregon bank of the "Great River of the West."

We have extrapolated the following information from the Clatsop County, Oregon, Federal Census for 1880:

Riddle, Moses Wm   45   Farmer   b. Ohio
       Mary   40   Keeps House   b. Indiana
       Henry L.   15   Son   b. Pennsylvania

The children were adopted.

Mary Riddle lived a long rich life. She was 38 years old when she left for Oregon. Her last entry in her diary was made on July 19, 1923: "Now I think I will write the last lines that I will ever write." She suffered from blindness and deafness. It was on April 20, 1929, that Mary Riddle's body was found among the flowers in her garden, her favorite spot on earth. She was nearly 89-years old.

The donor of Mary Riddle's diaries to the Astoria Public Library, Bruce Endicott of that city, did not include Volume I. He did allow the libary staff to make a typescript of the original, and he has given us permission for its use here.

MARY RIDDLE'S DIARY, 1878
COON GROVE, IOWA, TO ASTORIA, OREGON

May 8, 1878, Wednesday night.   Now I intend to write a diary of our trip to the far West. I intend to write each days travel at the end of the day of all that we see and do. And now to begin with I just say that we are in Dow City to-night and as I know the whole camp is a happy one. We started this morning from the dear old home.[1] How very sad it is to brake up one's home and leave the good friends behind to go out and seek a better place. So many of the dear old friends came this morning to say the last good-bys—the yard was just full of our friends when we started to drive off. How hard it was to look back at the weeping ones that we was leaving—but it has to be parting and meeting and meeting and parting in this life

---

[1]Their home town was Coon Grove, in Crawford County, in west central Iowa. A post office had been established there in 1875. G.R. Ramsey, *Postmarked Iowa* (Crete, Nebr., 1976), pp. 108-110.

MARY RIDDLE
From *Cumtux: Clatsop County Historical
Society Quarterly*, Summer 1984

—now here we are in Dow City seven miles from home. We come out here and camped so our friends from all around would come into camp to visit us which they are doing—the whole camp is like a swarm of bees moving about from camp to camp. We have so many friends for miles around. It is some like last night at home so many coming and going. Last night we never put out our lamps the whole long night—lots of our friends staid up all night. I laid down once just a little while. Moses never went to bed at all. There is a dark threatning cloud laying off in the West—it looks like we may get a drenching before morning. Now I must go and call on Jennie Coubern for the last time maybe in life.

May 9th, Thursday.   We got up early this morning to find all in good shape—everybody full of life—we did not get started out of camp very early for the friends come around to get a last word. When we got to Dunlap, Will Galbreath was out with a livery team to go a ways with us—Frank and Henry come on to Dunlap last night to stay with Will. He drove until we stopped for dinner then eat his dinner with [us] before he went back. He took a queer way to eat his dinner—he would not set down with any one of us but just went from one lot to another taking a piece from all saying he must eat with all the last time—poor boy, he felt so very bad to say the last goodby—oh, it is heart braking any way to be leaving so many dear dear friends. After dinner we drove on west on our way fast leaving all the familiar seanes behind us. We drove through Logan and drove three miles out and camped for the night in a nice grove to timber—we made up a grate camp fire to cook our supper by—everybody is visiting from camp to camp. As I sit writing by the camp fire Johnny keeps piling on sticks to see them burn. Henry is setting on a camp stool saying Oh dear, I belive I'll die of joy. Indeed we are all happy as can be.

May 10th. When we got up this morning we found everything covered with frost—it was very cold—there was ice froze on our water pails. Every green thing was froze down to the ground. We have traveled all day through such a lot of beautiful farms but all are blackened by the hard frost. Ada took the first ride on Nelly but she turned the sadle off and Ada too then Maggie tried to ride her—she turned the sadle with her too. Then I tried to ride her—she laid down and roled me off then she was rid of us all for the day. We camped for dinner by a little country store—afternoon we went on through Crescent City out by Terry's fine nursery—it is all black with frost. We got into Council Bluffs about five o'clock— drove on out about a mile and camped for the night. Got our water out of the railroad tank—we got supper early so the men could go back into town to see what they could see. Albian C. Smith came back with them making our camp lively for awhile. Later in the evening Billy Grader and his wife come out from the City to see us. She brought us a gallon of milk. She said she thought we would like a last taste of old Sally's milk as we had sold her to them back at the old home last fall.

May 11th. We got up early to cross the Missouri River. We crossed over on the cars—drove all the teams rite into closed cars and went over—every one staying in their own wagons. We then drove out two miles and a half from the river and camped to fix things in better shape for traveling (we are beginning to learn that we are not ready to travel). After dinner a lot of us went back into Omaha to do some trading. I bought some green onions for supper. In the evening Albian Smith come in to camp again lively as ever. The young folks are having a dance on the grass Mr. Smith joining with them all having a good time.

May 12th. Sunday. We are all in the same camp—we have

more or less fixing to do—everyone has something to do. I
had to take off both our wagon covers and mend them—the
horses tore them all to pieces last night. Johnny Gilbreath
helped me mend them—he and Maggie are still with us
putting off the going back from day to day—dreading the
parting. Nearly the whole day we have heard a fine band of
music back in the grove and after we all got our camp work
done we went to see what it was ment for. We come out into a
Dutch Beer garden all drinking and dancing for dear life.
This evening Louie Dewolf come into our camp. Mr Smith
come and staid all night in camp—these are some of the old
home friends still hanging on to us yet—Maggie and Johnny
have been with us all the way from home having a good time
every hour.

May 13th.   We got up early to let Johnny get off for home
on the morning train but they were too late and missed the
train—this afternoon a lot of us went in to the City to see
things— then in the afternoon hitched up and drive back
into town and got our stoves and tents and a general outfit for
camping out then drove out to the old emigrant road and
camped ready to start on trip in earnest—here we found a
family camped waiting for a company to travel with—he
joined our train making nine waggons on our train (this
family was Mr. Sloops family).[2] In the evening a lot of us
went back into town—I bought me a watch and a revolver.
Moses bought him a fiddle.

May 14th.   We got up early again to let Johnny and Maggie
get off on the morning train—then came the hardest parting
of all—it was breaking the last link that bound us to home
and friends. Johnny, Maggie and Louis Dewolf all bid us
good-by and started back home while we started on our

---

[2]The Daniel Sloop family were the Riddles' neighbors in Coon Grove. They would
also settle near Astoria. Mrs. Helen R. Sloop of Monmouth, Oregon, is descended from
them.

westward way. We now begin to realize that we are leaving home in earnest—up to now we have had no rain—the weather has been nice—it has been like some nice pleasure trip—but now we are on our way for certain just our little company alone among strangers. We drove till noon and camped for dinner out in the open prairie then drove on to Elkhorn River and camped for the night We tried to catch some fish but it was too cold for them to bite—it has been very cold all day—windy from the north.

May 15th.   We started at six o'clock from the Elkhorn river. In about a half an hour drive we come to the little stream where the boy was skinned alive some years ago for shooting an Indian. This part of the country is perfectly level—we can see for miles and miles around us. There is some very fine farms but no fencing. Farms lay open along the road just the same as the wild prairie—no timber but the groves that are set out on the farms which in time will make good timber and a grate wind brake which this country needs. We drove through Fremont City about three o'clock. About three miles out from town we come up with Doctor Croppers train in camp. We stopped and ate our lunch with them then we drove three miles the rain pouring on us all the time. We camped in a little grove near by a man's yard. The rain kept up a steady poore down—this is our first rain since we left home.

May 16th.   We got up early the rain still pooring down— after we had our breakfast it stopped raining. The men all went fishing but got none but Mike Riddle he got one little one. George Sold[3] found a ducks nest—he gave me three of the eggs. I made a cake with them for dinner. We started on after dinner—the country is perfectly level—we traveled along the railroad. We stoped at a farm to buy horse feed. I

---

[3]The George Sold family was from Turner County, Iowa. They would settle as neighbors to the Riddles near Astoria, Oregon.

bought some pie plant for our supper. We are camped to-night
by the side of the grate Platt River—it is a big muddy
stream—nearly every body went fishing but got none. All our
camp are well and as happy as can be. There is just 24 persons
in our train.

May 17th.   We got up early but it was raining—it stopped
about nine o'clock then we hitched up the teams and started
about eleven—it began to rain again a fearful pourdown. We
saw all the beauty of a Nebraska storm—it rained and hailed
and blowed—we could not find any kind of shelter out of the
storm till about four o'clock we drove down into a farmer's
grove and camped. It makes pretty good shelter—this was a
fearful storm—just one continual flash of lightning. There is
no fencing all along the road—the farmers stake out their
milk cows—I even saw a sheep staked out to-day.

May 18th.   When we got up it was still raining—our
beding was all wet but the whole camp was in good spirits
considering the weather. We had fish for our breakfast for the
first time. We are eight miles of Columbus City. We spent the
day in camp drying our beding. Moses went into Columbus
City to get oil to spear fish with to-night. I have been out
awhile to the lake to see them spear fish but I got tired of
it—its too windy and cool for me. The lake is a beautiful
thing—just a deep basin in the level prairie. There is a skift
on it to go out to spear fish—now its nine o'clock—I'll go to
bed—some of the women are in bed—some are out by the
lake.

May 19th.   When we got up it was fine—clear and warm.
We hitched up and drive to Columbus City and on through
about a mile and come up with Dr. Cropper's again in camp.
They had passed us some way by some other road. We went
into camp with them and got our dinners then spent the rest
of the day visiting around the other camp getting acquainted

with our new neighbors and they will join our train and travel together—we are now 17 wagons and tents—68 people all as jolly as can be. Harve Dale come to our camp yesterday. He has come from the old home on the cars and overtook us. It came up a fearful black cloud this evening but did not rain.

May 20th.   We started all in line—Moses drove out in the lead. The first thing was to cross the Loup River on a bridge a half mile long. We drove through the little town of Jackson at ten o'clock—went five miles farther on and stopped for dinner. Just as we were hitching up to start the sheriff of Platt County come into camp and arrested Harve Dale and started him back to old Crawford [County][4] again—he has tried awfly hard to get away from justice at home—he felt very bad to have to go back after trying so hard to get away. We drove on to Silver Creek. Here we got our first letters from home— what joy to get mail on our way. We got four letters and the Review—oh, what a treat. I got throwed off Nelly about four o'clock this after-noon and I fear that I am hurt very bad—I can't stand on my feet at all—they had to lift me out of the wagon—I'll not give up unless I have to. The Doctor says there is no bones broken.

May 21st.   We started at ten o'clock this morning. It rained all the afternoon on us. We ate our dinner rite on the open prairie in the pooring rain but it stopped raining before night. We are camped out on the open prarie to-night. I think likely it will be open prarie from now on westward. I am very soar—I can't stand or move only as Moses lifts me. I have suffered more to-day than tongue can tell—just terrible. Ada has a bad sore finger to make things worse for us—it is hard to get our work done but Frank helps all he can. Henry and him can do lots of it. We find no wood along now—every

---

[4]Crawford County, Iowa, was their home county. Denison is the county seat.

chip or cob we see we pick up to do our cooking with. Henry
finds lots of chips and trash along the railroad—he don't let
one thing pass him.

May 22nd.   This morning the Cropper train drove out in
the lead—our part of the train in the rear. We drove through
Grand Island—here Dr. Cropper sold his monkey—it made
them too much trouble in camp. Mrs. Cropper could not get
her work done for the bother of the children around her tent
playing with it. It has been fearful hot to-day by spells and
hard rain showers by spells. How I suffer riding and jolting—I
have to lay down in the wagon all the time. Moses lifts me out
and in the wagon. We are camped by the little town of
Chatman [Chapman] and it is threatning a hard storm.

May 23rd.   When we got up this morning we were wet from
top to toe—the storm last night was terrible hard—it blew all
through the tents and wagons. Frank and Henry got soaked
all through—they sleep in one of the wagons and it blew right
through the cover. We drove till noon and stopped and tried
to dry our bedding. We are camped to-miles of Harny
[Kearney] Junction on the railroad. We are still traveling over
perfectly level country—not a brush of timber or hardly a bite
of grass for our teams. They buy hay whenever they can get it.

May 24th.   We drove into Harney Junction and camped for
the day. Moses got both our teams shoed and Nelly too. I am
very lame and very weak—can hardly bear my pain.

May 25th.   We started out early—drove sixteen miles and
stopped for dinner. I've drove all afternoon over fearful rough
roads. I have suffered awful this afternoon. I can't stand
alone yet. The captain (Mike Riddle) of the train will not
stop and let me get better. He wanted this morning to leave at
Harney Junction till I'm better then take the train and catch
up with them. I will not be left alone—if I die then they can
leave me behind. Some of our train want to stop till I do get

better and some will not stop. Moses would stop with me but
the captain of the train will not let him—they say they must
keep together so for fear of the Indians. We do hear frightful
news about the Indians on further west. I think our crowd is a
little mad and divided to-night. They elected another captain
(Dr. Cropper) this morning. Now we have two captains—both
are a little mad to-night. Water is very hard to get along here
now. With the water so hard to get and two captains
everybody feels mad—one captain wants to drive fast the
other wants to drive slow—so tonight Mr. Solds folks and
Charley Bowens and Mike Riddle folks are camped ahead of
us and we don't know what they mean by it till we catch up
with them if we ever do.

May 26th.   We didnt catch the fast crowd until noon. We
eat our lunch and drove on ten miles and camped by a school
house—there is a little settlements here around. We saw our
first jack rabbits to-day as we come along. The men are out
hunting them now—one come running into our camp just a
spell age—the dogs run it in. It is used to running under the
schoolhouse but the children and dogs made it pretty lively
for it. I can only set in the tent door and look out—I can't
stand alone yet. I have wrote a letter this evening to send
back home.

May 27th.   Now they have made a rule to drive in the lead
by turns—one man one day then all the next day that one will
drop back behind the train and so on until all have a lead a
day. We stopped to eat our dinner by the railroad station and
to-night we are camped on the Platte River. This makes our
third camp on the same River. We are traveling near along by
it for several days. They tried fishing but got none. We have
seen strange and wonderful things all day—It is well worth
the trouble of traveling to see the strange and new things.
Henry got me some beautiful flowers to-day—he rode off on

the pony   is a great comfort to the children to ride for a
change (if she did nearly kill me she was not to blame). They
have the side sadle or Henry's sadle on her every day—sometimes change the sadles two or three times a day.

May 28th.   We have traveled all day close along by the Platt
River—the road has been perfectly level—the River on our
left hand—the high stony bluffs off on the rite. To-day we
have seen our first sand—we have expected to find sand on
our way before this. The grate sandy plains that we have
heard about is nothing to dread or at least we don't find it so.
We camped by a school house—got water out of the well. We
sometimes now find it hard to get good camping places for
water and grass is scarce.

May 29th.   We got up early and just as we were starting an
antelope come near by our camp. Nearly every man got his
gun and began to shoot at it—the bullets flew after it like hail
but no one hit it. They kept up the shooting until the little
thing was a mile off. Poor thing it was scared nearly to death.
It was the first antelope we have seen. We stopped to eat our
dinner to-day by the railroad. We used water out of a hole by
the side of the track made by grading the road. It was just a
pudle hole of dirty water but it was all we could get. We
camped at night by Antelope Station. Just before we stopped
for night Henry was off from the road a ways and Nellie and
he catched a little young antelope. Its a little beauty. About
four o'clock this afternoon as the cars was passing by us
Harve Dale stood out on the platform moved his hand and
went on. We found him at the station waiting for us—he got
off from the sheriff some way.

May 30th.   We started out early. Henry gave the little
antelope to the woman at the station. We could not keep it for
want of milk or we would have carried it along for a pet. We
traveled sixteen miles by noon drove off the road quite a way

to get water to get our dinner. Just after we got back on the road Charley Colwell killed a antelope. It set our men wild. About a half dozen of them took their guns and went hunting and got behind so they had to walk ten miles to catch up which they did after we had went into camp. We are having more or less quareling now every day. Some want to drive fast and some want to drive slow. I am sure we are driving far too many miles a day for the good of our teams when food is so scarce and the water so poor—hardly fit to give the horses or to cook with. We are still following the grate Platt River valley. The road is very level and smooth now. We are also following rite along the railroad. The railroad is a fine place to walk on when they get tired of the wagons—sometimes there is as many as twenty people out walking at one time. I am getting better now every day—I can begin to stand and walk. We are camped by the railroad. There is not a stick of timber in sight anywhere. We just pick up what we can find along— every old cob where teams have been fed we pick up every chip and every big big stalky weed. Them that rustles most get the most stuff to cook with. We have always had enough yet to do well enough.

May 31st.   We have traveled 28 miles. The road is perfectly level. We have seen antelope all day on every side of us—we camped by the railroad. The roads are getting very dry and dusty—we are getting too.

June 1st.   We have traveled very hard to-day—the road was very dusty. Not a brush or tree anywhere to make a shade. Nothing but sage brush and prickly pears. We see anough prickly pears now each day to pave all the streets of Denison. The sage brush helps grately in our wood—we can cook quite well with it—it is something like a weed. More like a woody brush shrub. It will burn green by cutting it up fine. Just before we stopped for dinner and camp Mike Riddle killed an

antelope. Moses drove a mile off the road to get water to get
our dinner. We had some of Mike's antelope for dinner.
Then we drove back onto the road and two miles further on
to a railroad station so we could get water out of their tank.
This is Saturday night. We will stay in camp over Sunday
and rest for we need it—so does the teams. We are in
Colorado Teritory now.

June 2nd. Sunday night.   Now of all the bad storms that I
ever seen last night beat them all. Just at evening the grate
black cloud began to draw nearer over us. It had been laying
off in the west all afternoon. Everybody began to fix things
up for a hard wind storm. Frank and Henry would keep
fixing things—our tent a little better as the storm gathered
and come closer over looking more fearful each minute. Just
as the dark came on so did the storm. I never seen such hail
and wind. Its very noise was enough to scare us and our
horses to death. Frank and Henry held down one of the tent
posts—Ada and I held down the other one—how we cried
and screamed I'll not try to tell—even the boys cried. We did
not care so much for the storm as we did to know that Moses
and John Church was out in the dark and storm in this
strange wild country. They had gone late evening to hunt
awhile. We was sure that the Indians had got them. After the
storm was over they come in very beaten up with hail. When
we got around to see how the storm had done for the camp
every tent had blowed down but Doctor Croppers and ours.
Everybody was wet and cold. The horses was nearly scared to
death—it was all the men could do to manage them. There is
not one bit of grass left standing. We have spent the day
drying our things and mending what the wind tore up last
night. We started early in the morning and here we left the
grate Platt valley.

June 3rd.   We turned more northward. Traveled all day up

a small stream called Pole Creek. The road is still level only the valley is not so wide as the Platt River valley. The hills are closer to us now. They are all stone hills and pretty to look at. Our spie glasses come in good play every minute—all around the camp want take a turn a looking. We can't deny any for it is a grate pleasure sure. We have traveled out of the track of the hail but there is no grass to amount to anything now. There is not as much feed on one hundred acres as there is on one acre in Iowa.

June 4th.   We heard this morning that Mr. Adams crowd is only one day ahead of us. We drove very hard. Passed through Sidney (Colo) [present Nebraska] bought more horse feed than drove on and made a very short nooning. We are getting very tired and some are as mad as fury at the fast driving. Just before we stopped at night Moses killed a antelope. One will not make a mess for the whole camp now. There is 15 teams of us now. We are camped on Pole [Lodgepole] Creek. We are very scared of the Indians now all the time. We corell the wagons every night and keep a gard out. Two men stay up at a time half night at a turn. We have 21 men in camp. We have the company of a pet antelope in camp to-night—it is fine fun for the children to play with—it is real pretty.

June 5th.   We got up early and it was raining. Our pet antelope was still in camp. It belongs to a house nearby. We traveled on in the rain—cleared off by noon. We are camped on Pole Creek again only we had to drive a little off the road to get to it for water. The prickly pears are very thick all around—the sharp stickers go through thin shoes. The poor little bare foot children suffer awfully in them. Some went fishing and some went hunting. An awful storm came up at evening. We tied our tents to the wagons. It all had to be done in five minutes for the storm came on so quick. Moses had gone out hunting again but when the storm began to come on he hurried back to camp. He had not forgot Julesburg.

June 6th.   We drove ten miles and stoped for lunch. Can see jack rabbits on all sides of us and antelopes are very plenty everywhere. We drove ten miles after dinner and camped on the same little creek. I don't know why they call it Pole Creek for I'm sure there is not a pole on it large enough to pole one hill of lima beans tho there might have been one day a brush or two on it. I'm sure it is the longest little stream I every saw.

June 7th.   We traveled 28 miles up this same little stream. We done without our dinner and we camped at an old camping ground. There was lots camped here when we came up and we camped near by them. Some of our own crowd have not come up at all—they are so very mad about the hard driving—it seems that we are driving hard enough to kill our teams and the people too. We are getting very tired. I am getting most well now and I can walk when I want to.

June 8th.   We got up early and drove to Sheyane [Cheyenne] (Wyoming). Stopped about four hours to buy feed and our provisions. Here we had lots of trouble—so many are mad at the fast driving—there is grate danger of a general out brake in camp. Mike came around to our camp saying he will not go any farther with such a crowd but after a lot of talking and fussing they drove on until night together each captain agreeing to take day about bossing the train. We camped here where five teams are already in camp.

June 9th. (Sunday)   We staid in camp all day resting. We surely need rest and we have a nice camping ground. The country is wild and beautiful—nice to look at—but too wild to ever be of any use to mortals only for the wild beasts to roam over. A good many done out washing to-day. I didn't do any.

June 10th.   We started out early the five teams joining us.

Now we are twenty teams in our company. We began to come in to the mountains about ten o'clock. The mountains are the most beautiful sights that we have seen on our trip. The grate rocks are piled up in all shapes and ways. One grate pile of rocks was piled in such a way that it looked as tho a man might with one hand push them over but not so for they have withstood the hard winds and storms for years and years and will I suppose for ages yet to come. Nearly every woman and child—yes and even the men was out walking gathering flowers new kinds that we had never seen the like—everything strange and new—the little wild flowers are the most beautiful that I have ever seen before. The nicest thing of all to me is the spice smelling goseberry bush that is just in bloom. Its all covered with little pink sweet smelling flowers. What a grand place to have a picnic. Many was the bunches of flowers that was gathered to put in letters to send back to the friends at home. We stopped at noon by a little farm rite in between two high mountains of stone—the small pine trees seem to just grow rite out of the rocks—they come out of every crack and hole wherever a seed could find a lodging place for there is not one bit of dirt or ground to be seen on these rocks. Everybody went out over the rocks after dinner to see the strange sights that is so fine a change after passing over so much wide level dry plains. Things are really pretty. We passed tons and tons of snow all afternoon and it looked so cool and pretty. We camped at night by a grate bed of snow. The young folks have played snow-ball to their hearts content. We have a roaring big camp fire (for the second time since we left home). The pine wood burns very nice. It seems so good to have a good camp fire. It looks good besides it is good for it is real cool—too cool for comfort. It is raining some too. Some of the men climbed up on the mountain so high that to look at them they looked like small boys. Everyone is hunting for something new and strange.

June 11th.   We got up early and as we got up higher into the mountains we passed snow on all sides—snow from one foot to six foot deep—the snow water running every where making it very muddy and slipery. Very very muddy. We got to the summit of the mountains about ten o'clock. Nearly everyone got out to walk to see if it made any change in the walking in the light mountain air but none could walk but a little way until all out of breath. There is no mistake—there is a difference in the air—even the teams felt the change. They could go only a little way until they had to stop and rest. We then come out on a high level plain then began to go down hills again. The western slope is much shorter than the east side and not so much rock or trees. In fact the trees are all behind us at noon. We got down the mountains and into Laramie City about one o'clock. We got our dinner and bought provisions and horse feed. We bought water kegs for now we are getting into the alkalie country where the water is bad. We can smell the alkalie as we pass along—they tell us that we will have to haul water along now for awhile till we get through this belt of alkalie country. While the men bought feed and things a lot of us went through the territorial prison which was near by our camp. It is a sad sight to see so many men in prison shut off from liberty and sunshine. There is some nice looking men in there as any of our doctors or lawyers or editors. What a shame that men can't do what is rite and then there would be no need of these places. There is seventy eight in the prison—some black negroes—there is seven women in it too.

June 12th.   I will have to write a little more about yesterdays travel. We drove 20 miles yesterday afternoon after we left Laramie City—we did not go into camp till nine o'clock at night—some awful mad about the late hard driving—there come being a near rebellion in camp—some declare they will not travel so hard killing the teams and the people too. We can't certainly stand this kind of travel long. This morning they all got together and talked it over. All concluded that it is best to try to keep together for more protection from the Indians which we are hearing so much about now all the time. We did not get started very early for it took so long to get peace in camp. This morning was clear and real cool for we are so near the snowy mountains. We traveled all day up a high level plain—the grate Laramie plains we have heard so much about—I have heard about the grate Laramie plains since I can remember—it is all alkalie on every side—the snow covered mountains are on our rite and left hand. We are traveling to the northwest between them. It is cool even when the sun shines out bright and clear. We camped at four o'clock as there was such a fearful looking cloud coming up it passed along the mountain range and only rained on us a little. The men went out hunting—they killed four antelope and three jack rabbits. We see them thick every day on all sides of us. Their meat makes a nice change in our eating.

June 13th.   The first thing this morning was the crossing of the worst mud hole of our whole trip. It was a deep hole of alaklie mud so sticky that our teams could hardly get through. The whole day was muddy roads till just about night we come out onto a piece of rocky road—such a rough road I never seen. In some places our wagons would jump down nearly two feet at a time—it was awful. I thought that I was about over my hurt but I felt this afternoon drive very badly. Just before camping we had to cross a deep ugly stream—it was real dangerous it was so deep and swift and the rocks so bad and high in the bottom. We just drove upon the bank and made our camp. It rained a little all day and such wind as it has been. Once we had to turn our wagons all around with the

back end to the wind to keep from upsetting our wagons. The
teams don't like such storms—they are hard to manage when
the wind blows so hard. They killed one antelope today. Its
fearful cold to-night. The gards have their overrcoats on.
This is the worst camping to set our tent on—the sage brush
smells so bad when we are brushing around it.

June 14th.   When we got up this morning it was clear bright
and cold—our breakfast steamed on the table like a winter
morning back home. We could see the horses breath all over
our camp. We are rite along the side of the great Elk
mountain   its a grate bank of snow. At noon we camped for
dinner down in a narrow valley. There was a lot of dry brush
and we made a grate camp fire and hung up quilts to shelter
us off from the cold winds. It was very cold—we really
suffered with cold. The afternoon was warmer but very
muddy—the snow water running every where soaking up the
alkalie mud. I never seen such sticky mud—several teams
got stuck in the mud through the day. We crossed the
Medicine Bow River and some of the men was behind
hunting. When they come up to it they had to wade it. The
water was deep cold and swift.

June 15th.   We drove until noon on quite level ground—it
got some warmer by noon. We have seen antelope on all sides
to-day. We traveled 24 miles to-day. The road was more or
less muddy. We are camped on a little stream near the Platt
River. We could have drove on further but the ferryman said
if we would wait till to-morrow he would put us across the
Platt for a half dollar less on each team—thats worth waiting
for. We are very tired anyway. We are driving awful hard
every other day—one captain drives fast when it is his day
and the other drives slow.

June 16th.   We got up early and began to cross over the
river—it took five hours to put us all across. We paid $2.50

for each team. The man said he had run the ferry eight years and that one of Moses teams was the largest horses he had ever put over the river. Fort Steel[e][5] is rite on the west bank of the Platt river—here is lots of soldiers stationed to protect the country from the Indians. Our two teams got put across nearly the first so we had a good time watching the soldiers drill and train. When all was across (it only took one team at a time) we drove one mile out of town and camped the rest of the day. We had a lot of visitors out from the Fort. Our big team seemed to be a grate wonder to them all. The young folks have been having a happy day—they are happy or seem to be for all have been gathered in groups making things ring with their singing. Well, let them be happy as they can for us old ones have to bear the burdens. One man went back into Fort Steel and sold his team and wagon so he can go on the cars. He is afraid of the Indians but so are we all for that matter.

June 17th. We drove on to Rollins [Rawlins] and stopped to eat our dinner. Here we heard bad news of the Indians. We are rite in their country now. We drove hard all afternoon. There was a fearful wind storm came up—we had to turn the teams square around to save our wagons from tipping over. We are camped down between two high mountains. The water is very bad alkalie. We could only let the horses have a half pail apiece—its poison. They have tied up all the horses to keep them from drinking and kill themselves. There is scarcely any grass anyway. Our teams are having it hard— with the hard driving and bad water and scarce feed they are failing.

June 18th. We drove twenty-eight miles without stopping

---

[5]This was Fort Fred Steele, so named at its founding on June 30, 1868, by General G.M. Godge. It is in Carbon County, Wyoming. General Frederick Steele was a Civil War hero. The fort was an important trading center and military post until it was abandoned in 1886. Mae Urbanek, *Wyoming Place Names* (Missoula, Mont., 1988), p. 70.

for dinner—it is enough to kill all the teams and people too this way. We crossed the sumit of the Rocky mountains to-day—now we begin our downward course towards the Pacific slope. Camped at night by the grate Sulphur Springs. This little creek is called Mud Creek—the water is very bad. Oh dear, what would I give for a good drink out of the old pump at home—this is awful.

June 19th.   We got up early to start on but there was several sick in camp. We are rite in the mountain feaver range—the doctor said there was seven people very sick. Henry is sick a little but not very bad. We staid in camp all day. Charley Colwells baby is very sick—the doctor says it will die. A lot of the folks went to the sulphur springs to get some of the water to drink—the doctor advised them to. At these springs there has been some kind of a battle fought in the years gone by. There is a wall or rocks built up and ditch cut down to the water so to get the water without being seen. We don't know what has happened here at some by gone day. There is graves where the dead are buried. Oh, I hope none of our company will have to be left on the road side. We see graves all along the road. This is my birthday. Twenty three years ago I was traveling from Illinois to Iowa. Now it is from Iowa to Oregon or some other place. Then I was young and as happy as the happiest of young folks—not a care on my mind to bother me. My poor mother had all the care then on her shoulders the same as I have it now while my children are happy and care free. Mrs. Colwells baby is very sick.

June 20th.   All the sick are getting better now. I set all last night with Mrs. Colwell in her wagon to help her with the baby. We watched every minute of it to die all the fore part of the night but as the morning come on we could see a change for the better and by the time the camp began to make a stir it was surely better so we had lots of hope for it and when the doctor came around he said it was all rite and safe so we began to travel again. (P.S. Here in this camp is where we came in company with old Mr. Barrows, James McComber and Sam Elison.) They came into camp this evening we did only a few hours later. Little did we think then we would be neighbors in after years.

June 22nd.   Now I did not write last night for the very reason that I could not—we drove on and on hoping to find water. After driving forty miles and until eleven o'clock at night we had to camp down without water or supper—very sad and sick. By daylight this morning June 22nd we began to get out on the road again in hope of finding water. At ten o'clock we came to a little stream called Bitter Creek. It was very bad alkalie water—we tried to use some of it to make tea and bread but we could not eat our bread after it was made. We drank a little tea made very strong. We had some fresh elk meat that Mose had killed back in our Mud Creek camp and we all fried some of that and eat with our tea. They give the horses a half pail apiece—a full pail would have killed them. We drove on after dinner and about ten o'clock we met a hurd of Oregon ponies on their way east for sale. The men told us where we could get water ahead by driving two miles off the road for it. We drove on eight miles then off the two miles. We was all willing now to drive fast for once to reach the water. We got to it about five o'clock. Them that got to it first came running back along the line of wagons with water for the rest as they come along up. No one knows how to enjoy a drink of water till they want it as we did. The weather is hot and the dust so blinding the poor teams suffered more than the people did. This spring is the nicest water we have seen—the children played and paddled in the little stream that ran off from the spring. They are surely happy in it as tho they are afraid to leave it for fear the same old thing happening to them.

June 23rd.   We drove back onto the road again and traveled
12 miles and stopped for dinner on a little stream of pretty
good water. Afternoon we drove 15 miles and camped for the
night all tired out and mad as hornets. We did not get into
camp till dark. There is some very mad people in camp
to-night—we cant live this way long—we could hardly get
our supper in the dark. I do pity the tired women that has a
lot of children. I will not complain for myself for I have it so
much easier than lots of them. This afternoon we met a train
of people on their way back from Oregon. They tell us such
hard tales about that country it is enough to scare us out and
turn us on the backward track but we have got too far to go
back now and they tell us some fearful bad Indian news. It is
bad—we are really afraid to go on. We may have trouble with
the Indians before we get through our journey. We are all tired
and out of heart and nearly sick after the last few days of hard
traveling in the heat and dust and bad water. All the afternoon
we traveled down between two high mountains. We passed by
a large cave under the mountain of rock—some one has lived in
it for years and years by the signs of the place. There is
hundreds of names written on it on all sides and overhead. It
looks like a den of robbers that we read about in novels (it is a
robbers den maybe) it looks like they might have lived in
there 20 years—I would just like to know who did live in
there. Henry rode Nelly right into it and wrote his name as
high as he could sitting on her back. This little valley is so
narrow and the mountains so high on each side that it makes
it quite dark along the road. There is just bearly room for the
road in the bottom of the valley—a little stream runs down
it—we have crossed it 20 times I think. The road was very
bad. At night we came out to where the valley is a little wider.
We camped by a house here and a little patch of garden. It
looks nice after so long traveling over rocks sand mud and

snow and dust. The man here is a cattleman. He keeps his cattle in these mountains on the bunch grass. The spring of water is nice. A little stone house is made around it and the little stream that runs off from it makes all the stock water that is needed. Here we met a family coming back from Union County Oregon. They don't like any of Oregon—they give it a hard name. They would discorage us if they could but we will go on now and see for our selves then we will know.

June 24th.   We staid in camp all day resting. Some done out some washing and some done baking. I wrote letters nearly the whole day. There must have been nearly one hundred letters written in camp to-day. The young folks had a dance in the house to-day. The two young men herders that live here was so pleased to see some young people here in the mountains. They just sat and looked and smiled. I do believe they thought our young girls are prettier—than cattle. They could not be persuaded to take a dance with them. This evening Mrs. Dorsey Cropper and me climed the highest mountain that was near us. We got up about three hundred feet high. It is just grand to get up so high and look back down on our camp wagons and teams look small from so high. It was quite level after we got up on top—there was lots of shelly rocks and grate cracks in the rocks. It was well worth our trouble of climbing to see the grand sight off down the valey.

June 25th.   We got up and started out again—the roads was very rough and full of diches and some spots of sand. I had no idea that sand was so hard to travel in—it tires the poor horses so to walk in it. It gives way under their feet and they get very tired when we pass over the sand patches. We drove very hard and late. A good many are swaring like sailors—so mad at the hard drive. Just about every other day we make a long killing drive. One captain is fast the other slow. It is

killing on us in this dry hot dusty weather. We are all getting
very tired. Mose and Frank don't get in to any of their
squables—they just take it as it comes. Mose is sure that his
two teams can stand it as long as any teams in the crowd. He
can go fast or slow just as the train has a mind to go but he
would rather go slow on account of the people getting so tired
by hard late driving.

June 26th.   We drove all day till four o'clock without
stopping for dinner. This is not so hard on old folks but the
little children suffers so for so long a drive without stopping.
The poor mothers too has it so hard to keep them still in the
wagons. We are camped one mile out from Green River City.
The men went in to town and bought provisions—a delivery
wagon brought the stuff out. There is a fearful fuss in camp
to-night. I am so tired of so much fussing and quarling all the
time but as long as Mose and I keep out of it we can bear it.
We have to anyway. We have not had a word in any of the
quarels yet and we hope not to. Frank is a good boy too—he
keeps out of it all he can for our sakes. There is not one
partickle of grass on the ground now—we have buy hay for
the teams. We are rite on the bank of Green River. We will
cross over in the morning.

June 27th.   We crossed the river this morning and drove
out five miles and camped for dinner. The road is right along
by such stacks of high rocks—they are pretty to look at. We
make out to see the beauty of the seanry as we pass for all we
are so tired. We drove ten miles this afternoon and found a
fine camping ground by a good clean stream of water but we
are all tired out and such a lot of mad ones to-night. I fear we
will have a real rebelion in camp soon—the train is likely to
brake up and devide at any time.

June 28th.   We traveled very hard to-day. It has been very
warm—the road is very dusty and it raises up and settles all

over us in the wagons so we are all covered with it so when we move it will poore off our clothes. It is a funny sight to see each one all covered with dust. The women have nice gray mustash all the same as the men (made of dust) and all the hollow sunken cheeks are loaded with it. If things keep on this way we will all be hollow sunken cheeked so we will all carry an even shair. It is enough to sink the cheeks and hearts and spirits of all. The horses is having it real bad. We hope for something to better our troubles before it comes to a real brake up.

June 29th.   We drove hard and stopped for dinner down in a little valley. Found some wood and made a fire—it was real cold. Here some of the crowd dropped behind. They have rebeled at last. Now we are a small train—only three teams more than when we started from home and the other captain has the big crowd. We camped for to-night down in a little reviene—its very cold. We have found wood and have a camp fire. We had to carry water three quarters of a mile. After we were in camp the other part of the crowd came up and passed by us and went on two miles further on and camped.

June 30th.   When we got up this morning it was the coldest that we have been on the road. Ice was froze in our water pails half an inch thick. We was all real cold—realy suffering we were so cold. We started out and passed the other part of (us) before they was ready to start. We got to Eveston [Evanston] and across the Bear River and stopped to eat our dinner then the other part of the crowd came up and passed by us—all as mad as fury. Its too bad we have got such trouble in our journey. Its hard enough at best. We only drove about three miles and camped for the day. Both trains camped in one hundred yards of each other. They all are afraid of the Indians so they are afraid to get too far apart but too awful contrary to keep together.

July 1st.   We let the other crowd get started out of camp
first but by nine o'clock we passed them by again. Its too bad
to hear them sware at each other. We made a hard drive—it
was very windy. Doctor Croppers cariage blew over and broke
the top all to pieces. This morning some of the young folks
was out walking on the railroad and they didnt notice that
our road was leaving the railroad. They walked on so did we
travel on and when we stopped by for noon they had not come
up yet. We came back to the railroad just at noon. We
stopped but no young folks was in sight yet. Moses and Frank
started back along the road and met them a mile or two back.
They were nearly give out. The girls was just about gone.
Moses took Ada and nearly carried her—she was nearly
ready to faint down when he got to her. The boys was helping
the girls along the best they could when he met them. Moses
took one arm of Ada and Frank the other and nearly carried
her along. Her feet is nearly one solid blister. We camped for
the night in the head of the grate Echo Canion—we have
passed some very pretty scenery to-day but all are too tired to
enjoy the sights as we pass them but it is grand and strange and
we are all excitement about our separation. It is a bad thing
and will do neither party any good.

July 2nd.   We staid in camp all day to let the other crowd
get one days travel ahead of us to save trouble. It is too bad to
have to pass and re-pass them when all are so mad they cant
pass without saying some disagreeable thing to each other.
Some find out just as we are passing that their teams need
swaring at. They want others to know that they can sware if
need be and some sware when I cant see the need of it. Moses
and Jake Solds went hunting—killed three deer. This is a
wild rocky country—grand and awful looking. We are rite by
the railroad station. There is only one family living here. We
are in Utah territory. Here we have seen the first of polygamy

among the Mormons. A little way down in the valey we went
to buy some milk and butter. He keeps a lot of cows and
makes butter and cheese to sell to the movers that pass. He
lives in a grate long house—one room joined on to each other.
Each wife and her children living seperate from each other.
Each have a front door coming out into the same yard. It
reminds me of our hog pens back home where we build a row
of pens and an old hog and her pigs in each pen and realy the
family did not seem to be much more than mere hogs. They
dont seem to be bright or inteligent but of corse they have no
chances here to know much. The man seamed to be all rite
and had some education but the women and the children
dont know nothing that they ought to know. They say each
wife has her own room but all eat and work together. He had
three wives here and two out on another ranch. Such a way of
living is not human or civilized either and had ought to be
stopped entirly.

July 4th.   Now we let the crowd get two days ahead of us so
this morning when we got up we talked it over about where we
would go to spend the Fourth (either to Denison or Dow
City this time) but we come to the conclusion that either was
too far away so we started on down Echo Canion. To look
ahead down the canion it seemed that we wouldnt have room
to go through. The mountains come right down together at
the bottom with a small stream of water running along the
narrow bottom—the railroad and wagon road and a little
stream go winding down crossing and re-crossing each other
at every turn. The wind blew a gale rite down the canion
whirling dust and fine sand over us so we could not see the
teams ahead of us at times. This days travel has been a
wonderful day to see strange and odd things. Such piles of
queer looking rocks. This road itself is a wonder—the railroad
and wagon road and a little stream. I wish I had counted how

many times they crossed each other. We passed the mouth of
the tonel where the railroad goes under the mountain. Some
of the crowd walked through it. The mountains seem to be
rite strait up on our right and left—some places the road is
made rite through solid rocks. Just blasted of enough off the
side of the mountain to make the road. The little bottom is so
narrow there is bearly room for the roads. If it had not been so
fearful hot and the dust flying so bad we would have had a
grand days travel—the sights have been fine and wonderful at
times. We passed by what they call the Devle Slide. There is
two rows of rocks. They seem to be about ten or twelve feet
apart—rock set up edge ways and end ways into strait rows
up the mountain side making a grate ditch. At night we come
out where the bottom is a little wider where there is some
little patches of garden growing—the stuff looks rank and
fine. There is a railroad station here and a few houses—and
some stores. Everybody seemed happy. They had been having
a Fourth of July celebration. Just before we camped for the
night we passed John Rickman howing potatoes by the road
side. He had stopped to earn some money to go on with. He
started a month before we did. He came with his wife out to
our camp and spent the evening. They were very glad to see
some one from the old home. Here we see some more of
Mormanism. I went to a house to get some milk. There was
two sisters living in the house the wives of one man. They had
eleven small children—none looked to be over nine or ten
years old. They had just come in from the picnic. They were
dressed well and seemed to be just as happy as could be (God
firbid such a way of living). Mrs. Bowen went in where there
was five wives and the whole houses full of children. They
seem to be doing well in here. They are all dressed well and
seem to be intelligent enough in this settlement.

July 5th.   We had a wonderful days travel all through.

Every day things are getting more wonderful grand and nice. We are not so tired and worried as we have been. We forget the past weeks of hardships when we are looking on such strange and beautiful sights—we just enjoy it all as we pass. We are out in the Weber Canion tonight. Things are far more fine and wonderful looking than in Echo Canion which we got out of early this morning. Every one is amaized at the rock and mountains and the river and the road. This road is a grate piece of work to make it through sollid rock in places. One place the road was just wide enough to drive along with only two feet to spare—rite along the high mountain side three hundred feet above our heads. On our left hand is the Weber River down below about 50 feet the water rushing down over the rocks so swift that it is dashed into white foam. I never seen a stream run so fast as it does but I never seen a stream that went down hill so fast—it has a grate fall to every yard of it. We have just wound along the bank of it for ten miles nearly every yard of the road dangerous to drive over. We came out of the valey into a high open prairie just a little down hill for five then down into a valey and come out to Ogden City and here we came up with our other crowd and they had camped just outside the City. We are camped in town on a vacant lot. We stopped about four o'clock. We had not stopped for dinner at all. I got six letters here. What a joy to get our mail along the trip. This is a fine town and the country around is a splendid farming country. The crops are fine. They raise everything by iragation. It dont rain here in summer. Such fine fruit orchards. I think I would like to live here if we had a farm. We hear bad Indian news. It seems dangerous to go on. Oh, I wish we was back home again.

July 6th.   We got started about nine o'clock. We had to buy feed and provisions. The other crowd got started first and passed us in camp but when we got up into the main part of

town there we passed by them again. I do wish that them (or
us) was off the road. It is so disheartning to see so much
trouble and contrairyness (I say real meanness) its a shaim for
men to act as they do. We traveled nearly strait north untill
noon—passed by some very fine farms. Stayed in a lane for
dinner. This seems more like sivilisation again. We had new
potatoes for dinner. The other crowd came up and passed by
us while at dinner. We then started on and passed them at
their dinners (this is terrible). This afternoon we have passed
by some fine Morman homes. Some farms look like a small
town—so many houses to keep their many wives in. We
passed by an artifishal fish pond. It had been scraped out and
filled with water from a small stream. It was a grand sight.
The water was so clear we could see fish only an inch long in
it. We passed over a little stream coming down from the foot
of a grate mountain about 20 rods off to our rite hand. The
stream was hot so our teams would hardly go over it—the
spring at its head is boiling hot. We camped for the night in
an open prarie in between two farms—not one speck of grass.
We have to carry our water two miles. Its bad salty stuff when
we do get it. We are going around the grate Salt Lake
now—we can see it all the time off on our left hand. We can
smell it too.

July 7th.   We started out early. We got into Corim [Corinne]
at nine o'clock. Here we found a lot of folks come in from the
country—all scared in by Indians. We didnt know what to
do—some were scared to bad to talk about. They realy was
too scared to talk. Some thought we might get on to Kelton
[Utah] all safe and then stop if need to if it was not safe to go
on but we drove ten miles and stopped for dinner. We went
strait west along the railroad and long side of Salt Lake. We
stopped at the foot of a grate high mountain. We could not
get a drop of water nowhere. There was plenty of grass but it

was all shining with salt. The grass was just in one spot of a few acres—all the rest of the country was just one grate white plain of alkalie and salt. There was nice clean salt lieing on the ground—a nice clear little stream of water running by it but it was pure brine. We could not use it or give it to the horses. We camped for the night a half mile from a cattle ranch. We have passed by all the farming country now. The water is very bad but we can make out to use it. The grass is pretty good.

July 8th.   We traveled hard all day. The whole day has been over grate white plains of alkalie and salt beds. I geathered up some pure salt nice enough to use. I want to send it home in a letter. One place we had four miles in the strait string of alkalie mud—the worst I ever saw. Team after team got stuck and had to be helped out. We drove till dark before we could find any water that we dare use. All are tired this night.

July 9th.   We drove into Kelton by noon. Here we had another Indian scare—its enough to turn one gray headed to hear the storys they tell us. Some of our train wanted to stop—some wanted to go one road and some another road. Some want to sell our teams and go on the cars but we heard that there was some other emigrants camped out a ways waiting for some other train to come up so they could travel with them. We bought provisions and drove on out to them in the afternoon. Just before we stopped we saw our other train coming up but they stopped in camp behind us. It is a wonderful camping ground. There was eight teams of the movers and six teams of freighters in camp here.

July 10th.   We staid in camp all day. We all are very glad to rest and have good water which is fine—such a nice spring. Our other crowd came up about nine o'clock and camped rite near by. All use water out of the same spring. Us women meet and visit as friendly as we used to do. We have never had any trouble with the women part of the crowd. We always speak and smile as they are passing for we all know its pure contrariness to act so.

July 11th.   We started on—four of the freight teams joining us. We drove hard all day. Didnt stop to get any dinner and camped at night down in between two high mountains. We have good wood here to make a camp fire. They have put out extra gards to-night. I'm more afraid to-night than I have ever been—it realy looks scary—more so than any camp we have made. Its quite cool down in here to-night.

July 12th.   We traveled hard all day over bad roads. Very rough and very hot and dusty. We stopped for dinner a few minutes—not over 20 minutes. Here the other crowd passed us again. This is getting to be perfectly rediculous foolish silly simple. No sense at all. In the afternoon we had to pass down through a deep narrow canion. The freight men said that this was the most dangerous part of the road for Indians. They were seen here last week watching this part of the road. Here we was scared in good ernest. The canion was so deep and narrow there was just room at the bottom for the wagon road. On each side was steep brushy mountains. The men walked before and behind each wagon with their guns in their hands—the women driving the teams Not a word was spoken or hardly breathing while we were passing through but we saw no Indians (glad of it too). We came out on a level open prarie and camped by a little stream of good water but no grass at all. Our other crowd ws here in camp before us. There is a kind of fort made here. Its made of sods and sage brush. The wall is three foot thick and six foot high and one hundred foot square. We did not camp in it. Some of the men took the horses up to the foot of the mountains to herd them on the grass but they came running back into camp frightened until they was just wild. They staid around the camp and

done without food. They must have seen or smelled Indians
up there.

July 13th.   We started on at eleven o'clock—the four teams
stopping again so we went on with our own small train. We
are such a small crowd now that we are realy afraid to go on
alone. We drove 18 miles and camped for the night by a fine
spring of water but no grass. There was a few teams camped
here when we come up. This is a wild looking country all
along.

July 14th.   We got up early this morning before the sun
rose. Just a little way off from our camp we saw 21 teams in
camp—they had come up in the night and camped. Henry
went over by the camp and come running back telling us that
Mr. Adams folks was in that train. Sure enough Mr. Adams
that had started a week before us from home was there in a
crowd behind us. We started early—some of that train
joining us. Now we are a larger train we are not so afraid. I got
in to Mr. Adams wagon and rode all day visiting. This day
was the worst dust of the whole trip so far. Everybody was
covered with dust. I never seen the like of it. We drove hard
all day without dinner—this is no good way to get fat or even
take comfort. We camped on Rock Creek. There is 30 teams
in camp to-night—they was here when we came up.

July 15th.   We got started by daylight all in a hurry to get
across the river. Our mad train was ahead of us here. They
was just swaring mad. A new trouble had come up they
declaring that they would beat us across Snake River or kill
all their horses. So they did beat us across but I fail to see anything smart in it anyway. We crossed at noon and just stopped
a few minutes for dinner and drove on to the Malad River
and camped for night. Here we come up with our mad crowd
again. All camped near together. We are traveling through
dangerous ground. We have seen all day the houses with the

windows taken out and walled in with stone for safety against the Indians. At noon while we was crossing the river two teams came up loaded with goods that had got togeather up where the Indians had killed the freighters and scattered the goods.

July 16th.   We got up early. Was afraid to go on and afraid to stay where we was but we made a hard drive and at noon got to a stage station. The stations have little stone forts made to go in in case of need. We got on to another station at night and camped. After we had camped our other crowd came up and camped near by us. They had a little boy dead in their train. He had died about three o'clock. Poor little fellow he had been sick all the way. I went to see him this morning before we left camp. I didnt think he would die to-day but its best for him. Oh dear, if we was only off this fearful trip. Here at this station the Indians took the stage horses all away from the men only three weeks ago and distroyed all his garden stuff and took all his provisions away from him. He hid himself while they done it. There is no women at any of these stations nor at the few farms we pass by.

June 17th.   We got up very early before sunrise. Mrs. Sold, Mary Bowen and I set up last night with the dead boy but no one can begin to tell the awfull dreariness of setting up with a corps in a tent in a wild country. It is so sad and lonesome to set and hear the silent gards keep up their steady tramp around the camp. It is more than I would like to do again if I could help it. The men made a grave and just after the sun came up they buried him and then started on. God help the mother that had to go on and leave him alone there in that spot by the road side. We have traveled very hard over rough stony roads. We passed by one stage station and camped at night by a little ranch—here is just one lone man staying. He had a little stone fort made for safety.

July 18th.   We have had a fearful bad day of dust. Sometimes we couldnt see our horses heads for dust. Its about six inches deep. We didnt stop for dinner. Camped for night by a small ranch. One man stays here alone. Here is another little stone fort. here we hear more bad Indian news. its enough to make one crazy with fear.

July 19th.   We started early. Our other crowd was ahead of us. They said they would beat us to Boyce City or bust but we passed by them while they was yet in camp. They just hollered goodby as we passed. Said now they would give it up. We drove hard and got in to Boyce [Boise] City. We drove through to the north side of town and camped. The others come up and camped on the south side. We staid in camp the rest of the day. We hear more bad news of the Indians and we are afraid to go on. There is lots of soldiers here.

July 20th.   We drove three miles out of town where we could get water and feed for the teams. Here we found lots of teams camped waiting for better times to go on. This is a nice place—water fine and the grass good.

July 21st.   We staid in camp all day. Its very hot here. We cut brush and made a shade over our tent and in front of it. It made us more cool and comfortable. This is such a nice resting place—we are taking comfort sure. I wrote several letters home. Some done out washing.

July 22nd.   We are still in camp. Some of the men went into Boyce to hear the news. it is no more favorable now than when we stopped. We are enjoying this place. We are getting rested. There was more teams come in to camp to-day.

July 23rd.   Still in camp. We cant go on yet—the news is no better. Some of our crowd has got tired of doing nothing so they have gone to quarling (making good the old saying that

Satan can find something for idle hands to do). Our own little
home camp are very happy and resting more every day.

July 24th.   Still in camp. Some men went back to the city
today again to hear what news there is. There is nothing new
so they have made up their minds to go on. So all have
something to do to pick things up and get ready to move
again.

July 25th.   We got up early. The whole camp was called in
to council to see who was willing to go on and who were not or
would rather stay in camp yet awhile. The larger number was
in favor of going on—then they elected another captain for
the train—an old frontiersman who had been over the road
before. (P.S. this was old Mr. Barrows)[6] so we got started on
again to the relief of many. We started out with 35 teams. We
drove hard all day and camped at night at the little town of
Midleton [Middleton, Idaho]. Here some more teams come
up and joined us. This valey is a good farming country. The
crops are nice.

July 26th.   We drove 15 miles and stopped for dinner.
Afernoon we drove 8 miles and camped at a stage station—
here some more teams come up. Now we are 44 teams. Quite a
good army if it was not for the women and children. All
things go on smoothly under the rule of our new captain.

July 27th.   We traveled hard. Started early. The road was
over a dry dusty sage brush plain. We crossed the Payett
[Payette] River and soon camped for our lunch. The river
was deep but we foarded it—the water run in our wagons. We
had left a man behind in the morning hunting for his horse.
He did not come up by dinner time so we waited for him until

---

[6]This was probably Henry Barrows, a Californian, son-in-law of the notorious trapper,
William Wolfskill, partner of Ewing Young. He had recorded the story of his father-in-
law's life in a famous article in the Wilmington, California, *Journal*, on October 20, 1866.
Kenneth L. Holmes, *Ewing Young, Master Trapper* (Portland, 1967), p. 153.

it was too late to go any further. When the stage driver come up he told such frightful Indian stories that we are nearly scared to death. They have run the wagons in to a stronger correll than common and put out an extra number of gards to watch. Moses and Frank are both out tonight for the first watch. Every tent is stretched inside the correll of wagons but ours and Mr. Sloops. The horses are always tied on the inside. I am more afraid of the horses if anything should scare them to make them brake loose. Our tent is rite by the wheels of our wagon so we can run in to the correll if need by.

July 28th.   We have been afraid all day. We drove hard without stopping for dinner. We camped for night by a stage station. There is lots of soldiers here to keep the Indians from crossing over the Snake River. The scouts come in this evening and say that they had seen the Indians over on the other side of the River. We took our glass and could see the streak of dust from them where they were going south about 15 miles off but the River is between them and us and the soldiers are here but all are excited and afraid. A lot of the men have took the horses all out to the foot of the mountains to keep them there all night. They will hurd them out there away from camp.

July 29th.   We got up and found all alive and well for all the grate scare last night. We drove out a little way to come to another squad of soldiers watching a crossing on the Snake River to keep the Indians from crossing. We drove very hard and came to the fery across the Snake River—about ten o'clock. Begin crossing and by two o'clock all was over. Then we was in Oregon the wonderful land (Oregon) that we had been traveling and toiling over long weary miles of sand dust and stony roads rain hail and winds heat and cold to reach. Just as we got over there was an eclips over the sun that cast a shade over all for a few minutes. There had been so much talk of Oregon Oregon all the while that when the men began to yell out Oregon little Mike riddle stuck his head out the side of the wagon cover and said Ma, where is Oregon—I cant see it. We camped between two high mountains—a beautiful place—the water is so nice. The grass is good and our poor teams need it.

July 30th.   We have traveled hard all day. Our road has been a little down hill all day. Very high mountains on the right and left. The canion is deep and narrow at the botom. We eat our dinners in the hottest place I ever seen—the mountains so high and rocky—the sun beating down—not a breath of wind. We camped at night at a stage station in 25 miles of the whole Indian army. This is getting a little worse than I like—its fearful scarry. I am getting very tired but I have it so much better than many of the others in camp I ought not to complain.

July 31st.   We have drove hard all day. Didnt stop to eat any dinner—was awfully afraid all day and to make it worse Mr. Adams team begin to give out. Moses took nearly all of his load into our wagon to lighten his load and took all his family to ride with us so if possible he might keep up with the train. We camped at night by the Virtue mines[7] seven miles from Baker City rite in the open prairie—a very rough hilly country.

August 1st.   We got up early —got breakfast then called together all in council to see who of them wanted to go by Baker City and who wanted to go strait on to Uniontown. All decided to go on to Union all but six teams—our two teams

[7]One of the richest gold lode mines in Oregon was the Virtue Mine near Baker City. It was named for James W. Virtue, resident of Baker County and one-time sheriff. Gold was discovered there in 1862. In 1878 the mine was purchased by George W. Grayson, an entrepreneur from San Francisco. From 1862 to 1907 some $2,200,000 worth of gold was produced. Albert Burch, "Development of Metal Mining in Oregon," *Oregon Historical Quarterly* XLIII (March 1942), pp. 110-111.

Mike's two Mr. Adams and Jake Sold. So here was the final separation of our fellow travelers so the train will be broken up at different camps now for they will be stopping off to see for each ones self which place they like best. Each will choose his best place to stop. I see very plainly that what will suit one will not be the best place for another. All cant see alike but they are in Oregon and they will begin to stop and look about for something. We drove on to Baker City. Got there at ten oclock. We stopped outside of town for fear of the diptheria that was raging. Mike went up in town to see if John Tillett might be in town. He found him in Baker so we drove out to his place 3½ miles west from Baker City. We got out and camped by noon. Here is the end of our journey for the present and I am very glad of a little rest after three months of hard travel.

EDITOR'S NOTE

The Riddles spent the winter of 1878-79 in Baker City. The men worked in the gold mines. Their second winter (1879-80) was spent in La Center, Washington, where they stayed with Mary's parents, who had homesteaded in that location. Moses searched the valley of the Columbia River for a spot of land to be homesteaded. He finally decided to settle on a 160 acre claim in the dense rain forest on the southern bank of the Columbia River. They cleared over the years that followed first land for a dwelling to be built, then a more expanded territory for a farm. Mary wrote of their first home in Clatsop County, "We now every one of us went to work in real earnest to fix a place to make [our] house. . . . We now named our new home Forest Home and a forest home indeed it was. . . . Now this is the end of over two years wandering about trying to get into the best place but if this is the best I do pity the worst."

Journey in a Prairie Schooner, 1878

§ Lucy Ide

INTRODUCTION

Nowhere in the literature of the overland trail is the contrast of the diaries of the 1840s and the late 1870s better shown than in this record of a journey in 1878. We counted her references to towns along the way and find the names of thirty-five settlements between Omaha, Nebraska, and Dayton in eastern Washington. Nowhere were they stranded for lack of the possibility of buying wagon parts, other supplies, and feed for the teams.

Although the Union and Central Pacific Railroads after 1869 made travel much more rapid and easier on the overlanders, many still preferred to travel by wagons. J. Orin Oliphant, in his introduction to the printed version of Lucy Ide's diary points out that Walla Walla newspapers of the 1870s contain numerous references to overland parties of emigrants who passed through Walla Walla on the way to localities farther north in eastern Washington.

We choose to call the party with which the Ides were associated the Mondovi train because they and their fellow travelers were from that town in western Wisconsin. Chester and Lucy Ide gave that name to what is now a cross-roads some thirty miles west of Spokane in Lincoln County, Washington.

The family was made up in 1878 of the father, Chester Dean Ide, age 47 years, and the mother and the writer of this daily diary, Lucy Allen Ide, age 39 years. There were three children: Clarence W., age 18; Earnest W., age 11; and George LaVergne, age 7. There was another much loved person, their maid: Lucinda

Hessler, age 27. It has been noted by several other travelers that Lucinda kept a diary, but we have not been able to find it. The family settled in eastern Washington, living over the years in several communities, but they eventually moved to Spokane, where they lived out their later years.

Lucy Ide was quite interested in social welfare. She was for several years president of the board of the Spokane Home for Friendless Children. Her husband, Chester, became active in the life of what was then called Spokane Falls. His first work was as a carpenter, then as a builder of new homes, finally as a real estate developer. The Ides were active Baptists and supported the First Baptist Church of Spokane both with their presence and with their money.

There are numerous typewritten copies of Lucy Ide's diary and one printed copy. All of them are inaccurate, some slightly so, others in the extreme. We have gone directly to the original, which is in the Eastern Washington State Historical Society Library in Spokane. We are grateful to the Society and to its archivist, Edward W. Nolan, for giving us access to the original.

Several other persons have been most helpful in our pursuit of this very special resource: Barbara Veltrie of Oregon City directed our attention to the Lucy Ide document. She introduced us to R.L. Olson of Lodi, California, who has published in typescript a number of primary documents relating to the Ide family. His book entitled *In a Prairie Schooner* is a rich source and indispensible to the scholar. He has searched out newspaper stories, letters before and after the journey, and other persons' reminiscences of the overland trip. Especially helpful is his publication of "George Baker's Recollections." Baker was a member of the Mondovi wagon train. Mr. Olson has been a great help and enriched our understanding of Lucy Ide's diary beyond measure.

THE DIARY OF LUCY A. IDE, 1878

May 1st   Our company start today from Mondovi [Wisconsin]   I am at my fathers at Gilmanton   Shall start tomorrow and meet them at Mr Bailey's where they camped tonight

May 2nd   Commenced my journey to the far far west. The hardest of all is bidding farewell to my near & dear friends many of whom I fear I have seen for the last time on earth. We stopped to Mrs. Baileys to bid her good bye   she gave me some butter and a cheese   God bless her   We went as far as Robert Henrys and stop in front of his house beside a small stream and strike our tents for the first time   everything new and strange but little sleep visit our eyes this night. N.K. Fisher and wife came as far as this with [illegible]   here they turn back.

May 3rd   We start as early as we can get under way but as everything is new to us it takes some time   Here we part with Mr. & Mrs. Fisher also Mr. Claflin comes out to bid us good bye and I sincerely hope it is all the old friends I shall have to part with   It is almost more than I can bear. May the Lord spare them to meet again but who can tell. We go as far as Winona and cross the Ferry over the Mississippi River went through town. While passing through Winona the people thought it was a circus and we occupants of the wagon the wild animals I guess for we do not feel very tame as it is very cold and snowing   We camp on the fair grounds and make qute a display. some of our company show the white feather by going to a hotel but not I   I have no idea of stopping at hotels all the way through   Lucinda[1] & I get our supper as well as we can with half frozen fingers and tumble

---

[1] Lucinda Hessler was the Ide family's maid. She continued to live with the Chester D. Ide family after their arrival in Washington.

ourselves into the wagon and cover up and then we are warm

May 4th   It snows it blows but we make the best of it and comfort ourselves with thinking over the old adage "a bad beginning makes a good ending"   our tents are very comfortable & so are our wagons   we start as early as we can get together and only travel five miles   we camp tonight in a gentlemans pasture   got our horses into the barn and a nice spring of water near us

May 5th, Sunday morning   it has cleared off very pleasant indeed but we stop over Sunday here to get a good fresh start tomorrow

May 6th   We start this morning in the rain   did not rain long   we went as far as Enterprise 12 miles from where we started this morning   stopped for dinner   Chet picked dandelions greens and Lucinda and I looked them over as we rode along and we cooked them for dinner   they were good We start again and travel about 10 miles to stop to a farm house owned by a man named Hevath   a beautiful place and a very nice grounds   we pitch our tent by the side of the road and get our supper & go very tired to bed.   we have passed some beautiful farms but very bad roads on account of the recent rain

May 7th   Started this morning at 7 oclock   rode over some very rough roads & passed some nice farms   stopped at Chatfield and got our dinner   A little town set between two rows of hills but very nice when you get to it   had beefsteak & all the accessories bread potatoes & etc   We started after dinner went out about 12 miles and camped for the night

May 8th   Started at seven oclock   went 12 miles over about the same looking country as yesterday   some good looking country and some not so good and stop to get our dinner. Started at half past one and traveled 14 miles and camped for the night

May 9th   We traveled until we came to Mr. Eager's a brother of L. Eager. We stop here overnight and wash   start at noon and travel 14 miles and camp on the bank of Cedar river

May 10th   start 7 oclock & travel 29½ miles today   We are now in Iowa two of our teams got stuck in mud Eager & Hunter but got out with very little trouble   have not seen a hill for two days   a perfect dead level   it is very cold   has been for two night   a heavy frost   almost every farm in Iowa is advertised for sale

May 11th   Just got our breakfast and started   travelled as far as Mason City and camp within about a mile of the city   the crops through Iowa look very backward

May 12th   Attended church today at the Baptist church an excellent sermon was preached by one of Spurgeon's[2] scholar   the church was nice and the town looks very pretty as we pass through it   it has about 3000 inhabitants. we have today had a great many callers from the city

May 13th   Traveled from Mason City to Clear Lake   a very nice small town with a lake   one side of it covered with sail boats   came 18 miles from Clear Lake and camped   a little warmer traveling today

May 14   Mr. Eagers mules left last night and we are waiting for them to be found   We wash a little and along comes a peddler   bought some dried peaches. The mules were found back toward Clear Lake 12 miles and now at noon we are ready to start   we went 4 miles past a little town called Belmond and camped near a little lake   a very pleasant place

May 15th   Started this morning at 7 oclock   passed through a little village called Clarion   One of our teams &

---

[2]Charles Hadden Spurgeon was a famous Baptist preacher, pastor of the Metropolitan Tabernacle in London. His sermons and autobiography were published and were read and quoted from by every aspiring evangelical preacher of his day.

one of Eager are down axle deep in the mud   got out with
little trouble   We travelled 23 miles today & tonight camp
in a nice place   good wood water & grass

May 16   Rains this morning and makes it rather hard
travelling but we are ready to start and are going rain or no
rain   our wagons do not leak to trouble us.   hard time
today in marshes   had bridges to make   some fun considerable hard work but many hands make quick work so bridges
are built and we move on   are now 10 miles from Fort
Dodge   get our dinner & on we go   camp at Fort Dodge
across the Des Moines river on the bank in a very pleasant
place   coal mine near by   the boys amuse themselves with
collecting it and burning it in our stoves   it burns nicely but
makes a very hot fire and burnt biscuit is the result of that
experiment   Ford Dodge is a nice city of 6000 inhabitants
and some as elegent buildings as you ever saw

May 17th   Staid here until noon   some washed some baked
and now we are ready for a start 12 oclock sharp   well we
made a wrong start   went about a mile out of our way but
turned about and come only about six miles and camped
about 4 oclock   obliged to camp here on account of wood &
water   rained all night   the hardest thunder shower I ever
saw I think   all night it wet us through & through beds
bedding children and grown folks.   well well this is not so
romantic   thoughts will stray back (in spite of all our at-
tempts to the contrary) to the comfortable house that we left
and the question arises in my mind is this a good move but
echo answers now a word—but still we move breathe & have a
being and we are most truly thankful for that

May 18th   Faces rather long this morning   found other
wagons had leaked and other people look blue so that cheers
me up and I am now ready to laugh at the rest   feel more
like it than I did about 12 oclock when Ernest & Varney were
crying because the water was running down their beds.   but

now we proceed to strip our wagon dry our beds & bedding   for this purpose we stop here until afternoon   This is Lizzard creek   The worst travelling that ever was I guess *mud mud*   Stop at about 6 miles from Lizzard creek

May 19th   A Beautiful Sabbath morning but we are obliged to travel on account of want of wood and water we are almost six miles from   Camped at 5 o'clock 7½ miles from Lake City   rained a little today

May 20   Pleasant again this morning   start at the usual time   a little better road but we have seen a hill and felt like kissing it   give me a few hills.   stop at Lake City to bait our horses

May 21st   a little better roads & pleasant weather

May 22nd   Rain again but we start about 11 oclock   went 15 miles and camp   rained thunder & lightened all night again but did not wet into our wagons so bad

May 23rd   Started at eight oclock   it cleared off pleasant we have travelled through a very beautiful country today passed through Dennison & Dowville   stopped at Dowville had a horse shod   camped a short distance out of town in a pasture near the R.R in a pleasant grove

May 24th   Started out this morning at ½ past 7   it is a most glorious morning   everything looks pleasant and so of course we all *feel* pleasant   2½ miles are quickly passed and we arrive at a quite a nice little town called Dunlap.   a nice little church and some very handsome residences.   stopped had another horse shod   bought a few supplies such as oats codfish pickles & etc   started on again through nice looking country and passed through a town called Woodbine stopped just outside of the town for dinner near a farm house   a Lady kindly offered us all the mustard we was a mind to pick for greens   we thankfully accepted the offer and had a most excellent dinner

May 25th   Camp on the banks of the Boyer river   we follow this river all the way to Omaha   a few ripe strawberries but not many   a very nice day

May 26th   Come out 11 miles   passed a little south of the village of Logan, looked nice as we saw it at a distance. another nice day and we are passing some nice looking country   we are now only 25 miles from Omaha   camp for noon   start again and go ten miles   go into camp for Saturday night

May 27th Sunday   a nice day   here we rest ourselves and teams and think of our distant friends at this time attending church—

May 28   Start at 7 oclock for Omaha   stopped 1½ miles east of Council Bluffs to get our dinner   we have passed through part of the state of Iowa that has the appearances of being and old settled country nice large shade trees but only through the western part does it look as nice.   now we start   we cross the great muddy looking Missouri river in box transfer cars into Neb. and here we are at Omaha   now for our mail—it is received and eagerly read   the first news from home   I rec'd letters from mother sister—Alice Cochrone Mrs. N.K. Fisher Mrs. Adams also lots of papers—it almost seems that we have been back on a short visit but all pleasant things must end so does our letter reading   so now we must get our supplies and westward go   we bought oysters[3] (a case) lobsters flour sugar crackers horsefeed & etc and start out five miles & camp for night   We have plenty to talk about as all have had more or less mail and the news one hears is soon imparted to the rest for we all have a common interest in dear Mondovi—

[3]George Baker, in his "Recollections," says "According to Aunt Lucy Ide, it was there [i.e. in Omaha] we had oysters, lobsters, etc., on our menu, giving quite an 'Oscar-of-the-Waldorf' effect which must not be taken as an indication of our daily fare, but which made a real 'Bat' of our Omaha stay." p. 22.

May 29   rained last night but it has cleared off and we are busy getting ready to start   travel 13 miles and camped on the banks of the Elkhorn for night   a cheese factory is in good working order here with only one house in sight but the workmen told us he had the milk from 160 cows but we wondered where they were

May 30th   Start at 7 oclock   go as far as Fremont and camp on the common at one end of town at eleven oclock for dinner   here we done a little shopping   bought wollen stocking yarn for 80 cts a lb, and from here Cushman Hunter takes the cars for Cheyenne   he was bleeding at the lungs and it was thought best for him to go by rail—start at two oclock and go out 13 miles and camp near the Platte River thunder and lightening & rain all night not a moment cessation it seemed   if this is the style in Neb I do not care to stop here long

May 31   clear this morning   start at eight oclock   passed a little town called North Bend and on we go to camp on the Banks of the Wonderful Platte River   it is a large muddy looking river   as you look at it as it flows along through such a dead level as Neb is you almost seem to look up to see it   all along we follow the river

June 1st   Start at 7 oclock   sun shines very hot today passed through a town called Schulyer   it is a nice little town   Came on as far as Columbus a *large dirty foreign* looking place   we stop and buy what is needed and while we stand here a few minutes saw two men taken to the lockup   I should judge by just glancing around that about 4/5 of the people ought to go there   they tell us here that we cannot go any farther on account of Indians but the story is not credited so we shall proceed to pass through this interesting town and camp on the banks of the Loup river   clouding up again for another Southwester—and at sundown it has opened on us

its batteries hail thunder & lightening rain and wind a regular
gale   blew H. Hunter tent down but there were but few in it
the ladies being in the wagon   it rained a little all night

June 2   pleasant this morning   cool and nice   it is a feature
of this state we are told the storms are mostly in the night
Laid over for to-day is the Sabbath   we have many callers
they are urging us very hard to settle here   it is a nice
looking country but oh those thunder showers   *I think we
will pass on*

June 3rd   Start at ½ past 7   it is pleasant and cool—

June 4   travel 22 miles   passed Silver Creek & Jackson
small RR towns   saw a man from Wis named Fox   camp
three miles from Silver Creek

June 5   pleasant   travel 22 miles and go into camp at
Grand Island at ½ past 3 oclock   rained a little

June 6th   Laid over to wash   this is quite a large place
clouding up again   we may look for another Neb thunder
shower   some of our company are talking about looking land
up in the Loup river valley   I hope they will not stop for we
have been so long together it will be hard parting with anyone
of our train

June 7   All are going on and last night where you saw sad
and tearful faces all are fresh and smiling and happy.   we do
a little trading and start on   we go 20 miles and go into
camp   here we have plenty of room   the whole broad prairie

June 8th   Start at ½ past 7   pass through the same looking
country and about the same distance and took dinner in a
little grove with a house and mill attached dignified with the
title Scapauppville [Schauppsville] Mills (pronounce it to
suit yourself)   we proceed to within 20 miles of Kearney and
camp for night

June 9   start ½ past 7   rained all day a little   saw 6 elk today they were tame ones   did not stop for dinner on account of rain   now we are at Kearney arrived at 3 oclock We are going to stop for tomorrow is the Sabbath

June 10   pleasant day   attended church with Elder Morse a brother of our old pastor and strongly resembles him we think   we heard a good sermon   it does us good for it has been 4 weeks since we heard the last one before 14 of us went today and some went this evening

June 11   started ½ past 7   a pleasant morning   went 28 miles today and camp at night at Overton the place Flora Hollister used to live   a very small town—Mr. Gifford accidentally shot a steer in the leg while out hunting Jack rabbits.   as is likely to have some trouble about it   while we are having fun with him.

June 12   another nice morning and we are all ready to start   go as far as Plum Creek [Nebraska] and go into camp for noon   Mr Gifford is arrested[4] and the Sheriff happens to be a brother of Roll Smith of Durand   we had a first rate visit with him   told him all I could about his brother—he is a nice appearing gentlemen   he showed us the jail and Court house   a lady confined in jail for the murder of her husband and two men in for murder   the lady looked very sad did not look as though she was guilty   had her little girl with her. Mr. Gifford paid 12½ dollars settled up the affair and at two we start on   went 8 miles and camped   two wagon have joined our train from Kansas bound for W.T.

June 13   all ready for a start ½ past 7   looks like rain   Stop

---

[4]George Baker says of this episode, "E.B. Gifford went out hunting jack rabbits, and in taking a shot at a rabbit, the bullet struck the ground, ricocheted, and struck a beef steer, breaking his leg,—and maybe he wasn't joshed by the crowd. We went into camp that forenoon at Plum Creek. Gifford was arrested by the sheriff who turned out to be a brother of Roll Smith of Durand, Wisconsin, an old acquaintance of Gifford's. He took us all thru the jail and courthouse. Gifford finally paid a fine of $12.50, and we had lots of beef instead of jack-rabbit—maybe." *ibid.*, p. 23.

at stop at noon. Mr Gifford has a sick horse but it grows worse and worse and as it looks like rain we hitch up and start on for in the distance we can see a house   we go as far as that and corral for night as there is a terrific storm coming up   we just get in order our wagons chained together and tent firmly staked down and Mr Gifford comes with the news his horse is dead.   but the terrible storm is overhead and such thunder & lightening and wind I never never saw before   we go to bed without our supper only a bite of cracker and dried beef and here let me say I shall always remember with grateful feelings Jacob Bond and his present of a good generous piece of dried Beef and I shall never forget where we ate a portion of it and under what circumstances. It stormed all night   the horses stamped and snorted and but little sleep visited our eyes I venture to say

June 14   well we are all alive and that is about all   the people all look rather blue   I guess that Mr G——— feels as well as any of us. We are going to lay over and let the water dry up   We have heard that the RR track is all washed away   no trains have passed today   where we took dinner yesterday noon a cloud burst and we were just in the edge of the storm   if we had staid there we should have been washed away I guess   I have not a very good opinion of Neb. so far—

June 15   started pleasant this morning   as we pass along we count 25 telegraph poles struck by lightening one after the other   not one skipped   farther on 4 horses side by side dead struck by lightening   camp by the railroad 5 miles from North Platte   could go [no] farther for a bridge is washed away across a creek

June 16   a stray pony came along   proved to be Buffalo

---

⁵William Frederick Cody, "Buffalo Bill," lived in several localities in Wyoming. Seven years later, a town farther north would be named for him in 1895. Today there is a Buffalo Bill Museum in Cody, 50 miles east of Yellowstone National Park. Mae Urbanek, *Wyoming Place Names* (Missoula, Montana, 1988), p. 41.

Bills[5]   Verney rode it and had a nice time   Sunday layover 10 wagons come up today from Missouri   a rather hard looking sett too

June 17   Start   fix the bridge so the horses can get across put chains on the end of wagon tongue and draw over the wagon and it took some time   22 wagons all together   Came 5 miles to the village of North Platte   here we saw the celebrated Buffalo Bill   he owns a ranche near here   passed through the town 12 miles on and passed 7 head of cattle run over and killed by cars   Camped near a section house

June 18   pleasant & cool   travelled over clear prairie nothing but herds of cattle & the Platte river for your eye to rest upon   such a sameness, here let me say that the grass here is very nutricious for cattle   there is 149 different varieties of grass along the Platte[6] and a great many different kinds of cactus   they look very beautiful   the blossom is as large as a dahlia and fully as handsome.   of all colors beside a great variety of other beautiful flowers

June 19   We have today seen vast herds of cattle such as I have read about but never expected to see   as we pass through a town called Ogallala they tell us there is 75,000 head of cattle been driven in from Texas and I should not dispute it for the broad Prairie is one moving mass of cattle driven by the Mexican herder on his pony with his broad rimmed hat on and a bowie knife and two revolvers in his belt   he looks quite formidable   he carries in his hand a short handled whip with a very long lash sometimes 20 feet and some longer even than that and wo be to the unlucky cow that strays out of line for he is sure to hit her with that terrible whip—The Mexican & Texas herders are a very rough class of men   they think nothing of shooting each other on the

[6]Where Lucy Ide got this figure we don't know. The usual number of grasses for the United States and Canada is generally estimated at 1,000.

least provocation   they just had a little shooting scrape as we passed through

June 20   still nothing but cattle & ponies as far as you can see in any direction

June 21   Went fishing   caught enough for supper   they were good   splendid roads like pavement

June 22   start at the usual hour   very pleasant   good roads and the same dead level prairie

June 23, Sunday   stop over   a nice day to read and rest and we enjoy it

June 24   Cushman came out to meet us this morning and brought out our mail

June 25   start ½ past 7   it was pleasant till toward noon   it thundered & rained some   not hard   took dinner at Point of Rocks   on these rocks Kit Carson carved his name   we see it very plainly and a great many other names and we also with the memorable Kit Carson leave our names beside his on this Rocky monument.

June 26   All well this morning & feeling fine—but this afternoon Mrs. Christian was taken sick & we were obliged to stop early—and we saw for the first time those cloud capped snow covered ever to be remembered Rocky Mts.

June 27   Nettie better   we start at 8 ocl   at noon as we stop for dinner we see a covered carriage coming.   the cry goes around Mr. Hunter is coming and sure enough we soon see his pleasant face & right glad are we all to see him and he to see his children   he ttakes the girls and Anna and goes back and we follow on and at an early hour we arrive at Cheyenne—a nice bright lively western city

June 28   Laying over here a few days   went down to Jims and Franks place   saw some of the most elegant horses & carriages I ever saw   Mrs. J. Hunter looks better than I

expected to see her   she seem in good spirits and anxious to
start her journy   thinks it will benefit her health still more

June 29   Still at C waiting for Mr. H—— folks to get ready

June 30   Sunday   rained so we could not attend church

July 1   washed & baked & getting ready to start in the
morning

July 2   Started about nine oclock as soon as they could
ready at Jims—Franks folks & the Chaplin at Fort Russel[7]
(we passed the fort and it looked very nice & clean as all of
Uncle Sams domains do)   went out with us five miles   took
dinner with their friends   the chaplin made a prayer and we
bade adieu to friends and started on our way over the
Rockies   went to the foot of the Cheyenne Pass and stopped
for night

July 3   started up the mts. and as for giving a description of
the beauty and grandeur & wildness rugged rocks beautiful
flowers &c it is beyond my poor powers to tell   suffice it to
say I feel repaid for all the hardships we have as yet undergone.
we camped on the top for dinner   here we found strawberry
blossoms growing within arms length of banks of snow that
have doubtless been there for ages as canyons many hundred
feet deep were filled even full so hard that we walked over
it.   had a game of snowball   had a hard drive in the afternoon   came as far as Laramie City about 50 miles from
Cheyenne   Mrs. H. Very tired indeed as we all are but feel
for her more as she is not strong yet   she is all courage

July 4   Well this seems very little to us like the Nations
birthday—although the cannon at Ft. Laramie[8] wakened us

---

[7] Fort D.A. Russell had been established on July 21, 1867. The site is three miles west
of Cheyenne. It was given the name, "D.A. Russell" in honor of Brigadier General
David A. Russell, who had been killed in 1864 in Virginia. It was a central supply depot
for the area. It is still a viable military establishment, now named the Francis E. Warren
Air Force Base. Robert W. Frazer, *Forts of the West* (Norman, OK, 1965), pp. 184-85.

this morning telling us that such is really the case—Laying over here this forenoon to ascertain the best route   get an early dinner all ready to start at one oclock   hear cannonading all the time at Fort Sander[9] just across the river   went 22 miles and camped near little Laramie river near a ranche commenced raining before we got our tent up   had a hard shower as they often do at the base of the Mts.   it cleared off so we could get our supper and went to bed tired as usual

July 5   started half past 7   got down to the river and crossed all right although the RR Ties are running like mad   the river is full and looks & is dangerous but we are all safely over   stop just the other side   get breakfast as we did not wait for it as we wanted to cross before the ties got so thick we could not   We did not stop for dinner as we had such a late breakfast but camped for night at 3 oclock

July 6   went over a spur of the mountains today   the worst road we have had in the whole trip so far   took 5 & 6 men to keep the wagon right side up and things got a good deal mixed you can judge   we all walked of course as we always do when we have bad roads   we passed an abondoned mine.— did not pay to work   came across Rock Creek a toll bridge had to pay 31 cts a team to cross   these streams are all made up from snows from the Mts and are very wild & rapid   have seen snow every day since June 26

July 7   Today is Sunday   we are laying over   camped at the base of Elk Mt.   it is covered with snow   it looks to be a mile from here to the snow and it is about six

---

[8] Fort Laramie had been a military establishment since 1849. The laying of track for the Union Pacific 70 miles south and the Chicago & Northwestern 50 miles to the north placed the old fort off the lines of communication east and west and marked the beginning of the end. The army abandoned it in 1889. It is now a national monument. Frazer, *op. cit.*, pp. 181-82.

[9] Fort Sanders had been established on July 10, 1866, about three miles south of Laramie. It wa named in honor of Brigadier General P. Sanders, who had died in Tennessee in the Civil War. It would be abandoned in 1882. Frazer, *op. cit.*, p. 185.

July 8th   started this morning over the Mts and came to a toll bridge   they ask .50 a team to cross the bridge   we would not give it so we forded it all right not withstanding the ties were coming down very fast and we had to use great caution so to not break the horses legs and the wagon wheel   well when we got safe over gave three cheers & went on our way

July 9   started another beautiful morning over the plains and far away   come to the Platte and stopped to wash.   don't know how we are going to cross.

July 10   Here we are yet   are to start at noon   we started at noon   some of the teams forded & some crossed on the Ferry   it took until night to get them all across and a storm came just as the last team landed   we went into camp immediately   one of the teams that forded lost off a tire & could not find it at all

July 11   Going to stop burn coal and sett the tire this forenoon so we will not start till noon   it is a beautiful morning after the shower   Started after dinner   went about 14 miles   stopped for night

July 12   Are passing through Bridgers Pass   magnificent scenery   one thing I would mention it is a sand mountain standing between two that are covered with green grass   no trees all about the same height   the sand a leather color   it looks like a picture   it is splendid   we came through the Pass   camped at another toll Bridge   the usual rates .50 a team but after threatening to tear up the Bridge & cross in the old Ford which they had built the Bridge over they decided to let us pass of .10 a team so over we go and camp   we found here a tent pitched   a family living there they had ploughed up a little patch   had potatoes growing peas &c   I can assure you we looked with wondering eyes upon that garden   the first of the kind we had seen weeks &

weeks   there used to be a fort there   used also to be stage
station in the old days before RR crossed these barren wilds
& it was called Sulphur springs & they were truly named for
the water in the springs was poure sulphur   could put your
hand in reach the bottom take large pieces of clear sulphur
they used to come a great distance to these springs and drink
the water & bathe and many sick people cured so they tell us
here—Here also is a little graveyard near the ruined fort and
as I looked at the faded tombstones thought someone mourns
their buried dead likely never knew where they rest   and in
this lonely place among the Rockies looking & the ruined fort
& the tumbling tombstones I think I rather be laid to rest
nearer the friends of my youth and nearer to Civilization

July 13   start at the usual time   our Dakota friends started
on the lead   have given us French leave I guess—we camped
for dinner at a place called Muddy Creek   start at 2 oclock
and now we take the hardest trip we have yet had   travelled
all night   came to Bitter Creek a poison stream   we dared
not stop or use the water ourselves or let the horses have it so
on we go the whole night long   a beautiful moonlight night
but a gloomy mountain road with large rocks standing guard
through deep passes and over little valleys but nothing to be
seen but the great beds of alkali—it gives one food for
thought I can assure you   We stop at 12 oclock midnight
and rest the weary horses and eat a lunch and as we gather
around a little fire some making tea others making a little
oyster soup   some looking very sad   some quite merry   I
can say it is a scene that once seen will never be forgotten for as
we do not know how long and how far we shall have to go
before we reach water & grass for the horses—& to add to the
list one of our horses taken very lame   poor Dolly she can
hardly go but *must*   Got to fresh water this morning

July 14   at 7 oclock got some breakfast the first thing then

took a nap   all are very tired so are teams   it is Sunday   we
came yesterday afternoon and night over 50 miles   this is
what tries mens souls & womens too but now we are resting—
Near us are camped a company of Princeton N Jersey college
students hunting minerals & fossil petrified woods &c and
having a good time generally   we are going down to see their
collection this afternoon   went down   they seem very nice
refined young men   they have some very nice petrified
woods & other specimens of the bones of animal that are now
extinct   one gave me some choice specimens of petrified
wood and beautiful Moss Agate   they related some their
adventures to us and we told them of some of our hardships
altogether it passed the day quite pleasantly and seemed so
strange to meet refined & cultured people here hundreds of
miles in the wildness of the Rockies and likely shall never
meet them again but shall always remember the day passed in
the moutnain on the Bitter Creek I think   Sabbath evening
the student came up to H Hunter tent it being the largest
and had a sing   they singing their old college songs & all
joined in singing some of the songs sung by Sankey & Moody
and I thought it would probably never happen that so large a
company of good singers would make the Rocky Mts echo
the music of Sankey & Moody[10] songs hundreds of miles
from any human habitation

July 15   Started at 8 this morning   our horse very lame and
stiff   got one from Mr. Gifford to use   went as far as Pine
Buttes   camped near a spring just a triffle better than the
Bitter Creek water   went up on the top of the highest
point   was 2 hours going up   got some mossy stone to
remmember the place   found at the top great piles of stone
laid up like a wall to mark the spot   likely for some purpose

---

[10]Ira David Sankey and Dwight Lyman Moody were prominent American evangelists,
who had published two hymn collections, *Songs and Solos* (1873), and *Gospel Hymns*
(1875-1891).

July 16   started on time   went out   the first water we
came to camped   we don't pass by good water now for in this
alkali country it is hard to find   both boys sick—beautiful
scenery high mountain deep gorges and scenery to suit the
most romantic

July 17   Started at the usual time   all in good spirits   our
horse is better   both boys better and all right   pass through
deep canyons by high rocks and rugged roads   go into camp
at 4 oclock   here we get our dinner & supper together and
did not stop at noon as we could only make 18 miles thought
best to make one drive—we visited a cave[11] large enough to
hold 200 people.   carved our names on the side beside the
names of hundreds of others that came by this cave   raining
a little   quite cool   have not seen a doz mosquitoes since we
started and only one very warm night—

July 18   very pleast morning   travelled over very rough
roads up & down over mts through deep canyons on & on
and at last come in sight of the RR again   it looks like an old
friend   we reach Green River after passing the Devils tea-
pot[12] and other noted rocks about 6 oclock   this is the first
town we have seen since coming from Laramie near 300 miles
away   this day closed sadly for us   we came in company two
teams   they were from Utah travelling for the Lady's health

---

[11] This "cave" is really more of an amphitheater than a cavern, about two miles east of
Point of Rocks. Randy Brown, a knowledgable friend, who lives in Douglas, Wyoming,
checked this out for us. This country is aptly described by the W.P.A. writers in
Wyoming, A Guide to its History, Highways, and People (New York, 1952), p. 244:
    "Gray cliffs form a mile-long wall beside the road. They have a strange moth-eaten
    appearance. . . Holes and small caves in the stone have apparently been scoured
    out by wind and rain. Farther west are rusty brown, grayish-yellow rimrocks.
    West of these the buttes are less spectacular. The distant hills look like monstrous
    sand piles, their sides ribbed with light-gray material and dented with darker
    hollows."
[12] It would seem that she refers here to Castle Rock, Sweetwater County, which stands
guard to the town of Green River. It rises 1,000 above the town. Mae Urbanek writes of
it as "a great beetling rock." *op. cit.*, p. 35.

father brother & husband & little boy going to Colorado but
as she came up the mountain she began to fail and as we met
them advised them to get her back home if possible as she was
scarcely able to breathe the light air of the mts   so today at
noon they overtook us on their return   they crossing Green
River we camping the east side as we wanted to get supplies
before going on   they had crossed just turned the horses
loose when they perceived the lady was dying   she only
breathed a few times & was gone   they came over telling us
she was dead   we advised them to hitch up their wagon
come over to us & we would do all we could for them   they
did so   she had no Lady friend with her but her friends did
all they could & seemed almost heart broken   the little child
was only 8 months old but the men cared for it as nicely as a
woman   it was afraid of us so we could not do much for
it   Lucinda & Mrs H Hunter washed & dressed the corpse
she was a nice looking lady   very poor and looked as though
she had been sick a long time—I went to her trunks and got
out her clothes   she had everyting very nice   had suit after
suit of underclothing & one suit beautifully made & laid by
itself I thought especially for just this occasion   it so impressed that I took it   we put it on her & the men went to
town and got a coffin   we put her in   you can scarcely
imagine how sad we felt as we lay camped there by the river
with this strange lady lying dead dressed for burial in a
covered wagon a few steps away   Lucinda Lena & Nellie
Eager sat up by the wagon (occasionally wetting her face) all
night

July 19   staid here with these people to help them bury their
dead   a good many come from town   we buried in the
cemetery which lies at the base of the Mts   the Green River
rushing by in the distance

July 20   got our supplies   started on our way   forded

green River which is rightly named as the water is a beautiful
Green color   quite deep nearly up to the wagon box and
quite wide but all got safely over   had good luck all day

July 21, Sunday   obliged to travel all day as no feed for
horses to lay over   we do not like it

July 22   travelled 18 miles   went into camp early as it
rained   we rather enjoyed the rain as it something unusual
for this section to have rain in the summer

July 23   travelled all day   another shower tonight

July 24   Pleasant   we are now travelling in a very nice
looking country

July 25   reached Evanston [Wyoming] today   saw more
Chinese here than any place yet old young & middle aged—
we stopped to get supplies before going out to camp   while
here another shower hail & rain   it seem to be a nice place
and much business done here   went out 1½ miles   camped

July 26   come 20 miles out into Echo canyon[13]   the scenery
here is beautiful   it is 29 miles through this canyon   one
continuous down down—high mountains either side and the
RR track side by side with us sometime not six feet away

July 27   come down within 5 miles of the mouth of the
canyon to camp & spend the Sabbath   arrived about 1
oclock

July 28, Sunday   it is very nice & we are all resting   this is
a perfect glen   an old saw mill is here all ready to fall
down   was built likely while they were building the RR   we

---

[13] Echo Canyon, Summit County, is a defile into the Wasatch Range from over the
summit just west of the Utah-Wyoming boundary. The north fork of the Weber River
flows through it. There is a railroad station at Echo. There is a trappers' yarn about Jim
Bridger's experience with the echo which was with sharply reflecting stone walls. The old
trapper would tell tenderfeet how he would call our "Wake up, Jim," and eight hours
later the sound would resound back with those words, "Wake up, Jim," just at the
proper time for his arousal. Rufus Wood Leigh, *Five Hundred Utah Place Names* (Salt
Lake City, 1961), p. 21.

can not see the sun here only two or three hours in the middle
of the day   as it is rather warm I do not miss it   a little
accident occurred today to stir us up a little   one of the
horses got entangled in Jim Hunter tent rope   got frightened
started and took one half the tent with it   tore it right in to
in the middle   Mrs H being inside was badly frightened and
Jim did not know what to do for a tent   I told him it could
be fixed   Never said he saw such a rent as that be fixed but I
told Elma to get her needle & I took mine and in about two
hours the tent was up all just as good as ever   it happened to
tear very good to sew up again—

July 29, Monday   all ready to start early this morning   an
eclipse today   Mrs. Gifford and myself went out before
breakfast to catch us a trout   I had the luck to get two nice
ones—We arrived at the mouth of the canyon at a little town
called Echo City   stopped in town   got a little fruit   went
on

July 30   came into Weber Canyon   the scenery here throws
every other place in the shade   it is the wildest place one can
imagine   the Devils Gate is here   one solid rock one side
up hundreds of feet   the other side down hundreds of feet
runs the Weber River rushing madly along over great rocks
one solid mass of foam and you can scarcely hear yourself
speak such rumbling down n such a deep canyon   the road
is just wide enough for a wagon barely that in some places you
rest assured we all walked & I for one kept just as near the
middle of the road as I could   then my head swam so I could
scarcely walk   I think it is a half mile through this gate but I
must say it seemed hours we were passing it   but it looks
very grand indeed after all

July 31   arrived at Ogden about noon or near there   we
camped about 3 miles out so to get a place for the horses to go
in a pasture

Aug 1 st   very warm indeed here   we are resting our horses & washing &c

Aug 2   today we have had an addition to our company Edith Gifford has a little boy to-day born in Utah at the foot of the Washatch Mts—3 miles from Ogden

Aug 3   have been out to Ogden   it is quite a pleasant place but entirely Mormon   beautiful fruit & shade trees but oh the dejected degraded looking women is enough to condemn the Mormon doctrine leave all else out—

Aug 4   Today is the Sabbath   we are still here   had an invitation to attend church at the Tabernacle but declined on account of the excessive heat   Edith quite smart

Aug 5   started this morning at 7 oclock   Stopped in Ogden and got our supplies and went out 15 miles & camped in a very nice place

Aug 6   started at 7 oclock   went out to Boiling spring here there are two springs side by side   one is so hot you cannot bear your hand in it and close beside it is one very cold   it is salt and salt lies all around on top of the ground we washed in the spring drank of it and went on and stopped at Corinne   this is a Gentile town and looks very delapidated and poor as all Gentile towns do through this Mormon country

Aug 7   We are waiting here & trying to ascertain whether we are going to be troubled with Indians   they tell us we can go no farther and some of the train want to turn back & some go on   the decision is to start at noon   Started at 1 oclock travelled 12 miles

Aug 8   travelled in the dust   oh so dusty

Aug 9   travelled 12 miles   stopped at a Mormon ranche man by the name of Dilly   he has two wives   one seems to be a very smart & intelligent woman   The other a very ordinary ignorant German woman and the contrast between the two is enough to convince anyone of the evils of Mormonism

Aug 10   we will stop here this forenoon and sett tires started at noon   went 15 miles & camped at a ranche at a place called the Sink

Aug 11   it is Sunday & some want to travel and some do not but those that do prevail so we start & here we are at night still travelling   we have at Last arrived at a ranche   I rather think we shall rest another Sabbath day

Aug 12   Beautiful day   one of Mr. Eagers horses tired out yesterday   they feel very bad indeed as we all do for them they have just traded off the horse & got two ponies and left some of their load to the ranche

Aug 13   started as usual and come to a creek at early night & camped

Aug 14   come to Marsh Basin [Idaho][14] stop   some had tires sett   The Landlord offered the girls 7 dollars a week to stop and work   some have quite a mind to stop but after a time decide to go on and we start after noon and travel 15 miles

Aug 15   Nice weather but very dusty & over nothing but plains

Aug 16   Here we go again over nothing but sagebrush plains—here we are at night at Rock Creek a very pretty stream and had a little shower   hope it will lay the dust

Aug 17   come 18 miles to Mud Creek right in the Indian Country   had a smart shower tonight with a little hail

Aug 18   Stop over Sunday at a Stage station.   we are now on the stage road and have good roads

---

[14]Marsh Basin, now dubbed Marsh Valley, is in Bannock County, Idaho. It was established in the late 1870s by Mormon pioneers. Lalia Boone, *Idaho Place Names* (Moscow, Idaho, 1988), p. 243.

Aug 19   went down to the Ferry   crossed the snake river
and at this Stage Station we find they have built a ditch
thrown up Breast works boarded up the windows and are
prepared for Indians   still we see none   Elma & I see in
the distance a beautiful waterfall and start to explore it   we
went to the foot first and then had an idea we would like to see
the source so we start alone as it looks like rather hard work to
climb the mtn but we persevere and after many slips & falls
and stops to rest &c we get to the top over 100 feet and as we
look at the little fountains at the top feel amply repaid for our
climb   I think there is at least a dozen fountains that throw
water up 3 & four feet   we have a curiosity to examine them
so we take off our shoes & stockings and wade into the water
it seems like a little shallow Lake not over six inches deep but
as we near the falls we are somewhat afraid although they are
small but fall a distance of 100 feet perhaps more   it is not
more than three ft in width and these little fountains seem to
be holes in the bottom of the pond   we run our hands down
as far as we can but find no bottom they are a curiosity sure
but the teams are going on and we must go or be left so we
take a last view of the Beautiful Bridal Vail Falls & go on as
far as the Miladd River   this River is a great curiosity   it
runs in a deep dark Gorge and at a depth of 300 feet   in
some places the Rocks come up perpendicular   it sounds
almost improble [improbable] but it is so for here I sit on a
rock writing this down and Lucinda sits the other side and we
could reach each others hand if we dared to go near it but it is
an ugly looking place I can assure you   in one place a few
feet from us the water falls quite a distance out of sight then
comes up over the rocks and down again   it is a natural
curiosity to look at this stream   we camp here at Miladd
River at a stage station and here we see Mr Buck from
Winona   came in on the Stage

Aug 20   start at the usual hour this morning   met a wagon train of Soldiers   one of them threw us a hard tack   they are Indian fighters & Scouts   we come out 18 miles and camp at another stage station

Aug 21   Start at eight this morning   went 11 miles & camp at the foot of King's Hill for dinner—well this is a hill sure   four miles in length and the most of us walk the whole distance   pass a freighter   he seems to be having bad luck ten mules and he wants the boys to help drive them up the hill   they help a while but soon give up and go on & leave him swearing at the mules   oh but it is hot but we are up at last and go as far as Cold Spring   camp for night.   they tell us here there is a band of Indians camped about a mile from us and a company of calvalry about a mile from the Indians so here we are in the midst of Indians   well if we are to be killed by Indians we shall not be hung so we have a little consolation

Aug 22   went as far as Rattlesnake Creek & camp   see no Indians

Aug 23   went out 22 miles and did not get to camp till after dark and camp on an old camp the soldiers have occupied rather long faces tonight as it is dark and we get a little supper and lay down to wonder what will come next

Aug 24   well this morning finds all pleasant again   faces bright and they have almost forgotten the trials of the night before.

Aug 24   over stones & hills to within 2 miles of Boise City at a Ranche   the mans name is J.P. Walling[15]   come there 31 years ago with oxen   sold some of his oxen for Beef to Fremonts perishing Soldiers and saved their lives   we are well treated indeed and enjoy it.

---

[15]J.B. Walling was a pioneer settler in the Boise area. He became noted for the contribution he made in setting up an irrigatin system. The "Walling ditch" was named for him. Annie L. Bird, *Boise the Peace Valley* (Caldwell, Idaho, 1934), pp. 201-202.

Aug 25   the Sabbath   shall stop over the day here   have
enjoyed the day very much   have had the privilege of sitting
once more in a house in a Rocking chair—Mr. Chase formerly
from Eau Claire but now the Marshall of Idaho Ter gave us a
call   had a sing

Aug 26   Start for the City bright & early this Monday
morning   quite a nice place—

Aug 27   Here we are laying over till night   we could [find]
a good deal of work here if we wanted to stay   we talk of
staying   can get work in a shop at 2.00 a day and Chet can
get 5.00 per day   as we are out of money we think best to
stop   the train started and we bid them goodbye and left
crying   Mr Eagers folks will stop to & Lena Hunter   But
back comes Gifford & says you are not going to stop   come
along in the store and get your supplies & come on   we were
only too willing to go and we follow along and they all seem
glad to see us   as we stop they rush up and shake hands as
though we had been gone weeks instead of about 15 minutes
well it would have been lonesome to have stopped   I guess it
is all for the best perhaps   Mr. Eagers folks & Lena have
stopped here   while stopping in front of the store we hear
music and find that Bernard's[16] troop of Calvlry have just
come in from fighting Indians and they look as though they
had seen hard work to   dirty & ragged but feeling fine   a
large pack train follows them with their baggage   looks quite
grand

Aug 28   here we are travelling through a beautiful country

---

[16]Captain Reuben F. Bernard, Captain of the First Cavalry during the Bannock
Indian War. This entry into Boie marked essentially the end of that conflict, which
George Francis Brimlow described as "the last major uprising of hostile Indians in the
Pacific Northwest of the United States." *The Bannock Indian War of 1878* (Caldwell,
Idaho, 1938), p. 7. See also George F. Brimlow, Editor, "Two Cavalrymen's Diaries of
the Bannock War, 1878," *Oregon Historical Quarterly*, LXVIII, No. 3, (Sept., 1967),
pp. 221-258; No. 4 (Dec., 1967), pp. 293-316). For a portrait of this colorful soldier see
the December reference above, p. 300.

good Ranches good gardens fruit &c &c all around   looks prosperous

Aug 29   we are on our way at 7 this morning   nice day but warm   we have been 12 miles today   at noon came across the Ferry across the Snake River paid 1.50   we are now in Oregon

Aug 30   went about 20 miles and camp

Aug 31   went as far as McDowells ranche & camp at noon   we have a nice place here   they killed a beef here & we bought some   they branded some cattle here the first we ever saw branded   we think it rather cruel   Verney not very well

Sept 1   Sunday and we are laying over   we are exactly where the Indians have raided & stolen horses & cattle

Sept 2, Monday   started   all well rested for a good days drive & went down Willow Creek & camp in a canyon Vernie very sick all night   it rained the wind blew and lonesome I sat up the most of the nigth with Vernie

Sept 3   crossed the Willow Creek mts   passed a mining camp   have very bad roads   come down where there has been a waterspout & tore up the road and trees by the roots but we pass without any great trouble   we camp at the foot of the mountain at a ranche called Smith's Ranche   here we hear of Mr. Gilkey's sister   she lvies a mile off the road Will Allen went out to see her   she was well and very glad to see him

Sept 4   it is cold & windy   has been for two days so we have to wear wraps and are cold at that   we are in sight of Eagle Creek Mts   very high and covered with snow   it is a nice looking country

Sept 5   we past a quaint mill today   come only 18 miles today

Sept 6   come over the mts today   come 18 miles to a town called Union nice clean little town

Sept 7   come on 22 miles to a town called Somerville   a most desolate run down place at the base of the Blue Mts   we are now camped for night just out of the village

Sept 8   It is Sunday and we are laying over & resting for it is the Sabbath   a minister is stopping here   he & his wife are on their way over the Mts to Walla walla   he came up Sunday eve & gave us a little sermon   seems nice to hear one once more   we are now 40 miles from Wallawalla

Sept 9   we are going up up up but the scenery is grand   nice timber pine fir Hemlock   we camped near the summit overnight   we made bonfires and told stories and passed the evening very pleasant   Mrs Hunter is quite sick

Sept 10   Mrs Hunter no better   we think she is very low indeed   she thinks she will not live through the night   we all fear she will not   she cannot speak aloud   I think best to wring out cloths in hot water and lay on her lungs   it seems to give relief   I do believe she is better. I sat up with her all night

Sept 11   she is a little better but very low but wants to go on   we have made her a bed in her wagon as comfortable as possible and try it   we stop at the first house   get her a cup of Tea   she is refreshed and we go on   camp for noon on the bank of the Wallawalla river   bought a bushel of apples for 25. Sallie is no worse   ate a very little but is very tired

Sept 12   went 14 miles   Sally very tired   we stop at a farm house   had all the watermelons we could eat

Sept 13   Arrived at Wallawalla at noon   camped in a yard to get our dinner   Indian camped in the same place   white men with squaw wives   Sallie improving slowly   she is up and feels better   shall stop overnight

Sept 14   are waiting for some to buy stores   ready to start at noon   Jim got his wife some medicine and she is certainly better   start at noon go out 10 & camp

Sept 15   start at usual hour   go 10 miles   camp for noon on the Touchet river   saw a great many Indians   The Snake Indians are giving themselves up and are coming in in great No's   are dressed in new blankets and look & seem to feel very nice   arrived at Dayton about 5 oclock and were welcomed by Dr Day[17]   he gave us a good hand shaking and ordered beef & flour for us as we were nearly out of money & provision to and went into camp for perhaps the last time   we expect to stay over Sunday and see what next will be done   we expect to stop here   some others will   some will go on into the Palouse   so this is the end of our trials and pleasures for this four months & half

L A Ide

---

[17] At first we thought this was Jesse N. Day, who with his wife, Elizabeth, founded the town of Dayton, Washington. That was not the case, however; the "Dr Day" she wrote of was a homeopathic physician named W.W. Day, whom they had known when he lived in Eau Claire. There is in the Ide papers a letter written by him from Dayton, Washington, on January 23, 1878, to the Hunters. He encouraged them to migrate to the Pacific Northwest and gave that area high praise for the countless variety of crops that could be raised there. Whether it was coincidence that the two families became associated with Dayton or because they were related. Dr. Day had traveled overland in 1871. Good references to place names in Washington are Edmund S. Meany, *Origin of Washington Geographic Names* (Seattle, 1923), and James W. Phillips, *Washington State Place Names* (Seattle, 1971).

EPILOGUE

PERSONS MAKING UP THE MONDOVI WAGON TRAIN
(Information supplied by R.L. Olson, Lodi, California)

	Age in 1878		Age in 1878
Chester Dean Ide	47	Luther Eager	50
(Brother of Sarah/Sally Ide)		Abigail Holden Eager	52
Lucy Allen Ide (nee Loomis)	39	Children:	
Children:		James	24
Clarence W.	18	Nellie (Robinson)	19
Earnest W.	11	Everett	17
George LaVergne	7	William	16
James G. Hunter[1]	50	Harriet (Stafford)	13
Sarah or Sally Ide Hunter	50	Edger	11
Children:		Elihu B. Gifford	47
Cushman[2]	26	Catherine S. (Barrows) Gifford	42
George	21	Children:	
Lena (Rombeau)	18	Charles	18
Elma (Robbins)	16	Catherine (Sisson)	10
Luella (Robinson)	14	Chester	9
James Mason	8	John Gifford (Son of Elihu	21
Henry Hunter	43	and Catherine Gifford)	
(Brother of James G Hunter)		Edith Lewis Gifford	17
Susan Hunter (nee Holmes Senter)	43	Child:	
Children:		Homer (Born in Utah enroute)	
Anna (Baker)	21	Albertus L. Christian	26
Frank	19	Julia Etta Christian	22
Earle	7	(Daughter of Elihu and	
Lelia (Mickle)	5	Catherine Gifford)	
		Child: Gifford	1

SINGLE PERSONS

Lucinda Hessler (the Ides maid)	27	Frank Mathewson	?
D.C. (Clint) Gardner	38	William F. Allen	23
(Wagon train captain)			

---

[1]Mr. and Mrs. James Hunter and their daughter, Luella, left Mondovi by train in 1877 and traveled to Cheyenne, where Jim Hunter's brother, Frank, was living. They rented a house in Cheyenne and Jim went on to Washington, purchased land, then returned to Cheyenne to await the arrival of the wagon train with the rest of his family.

[2]As seen by Mrs. Ide's diary, Cushman Hunter did not make the entire trip by wagon. He became ill in Fremont, Nebraska, and went by train from Fremont to Cheyenne, where he stayed with his parents until the wagon train arrived in Cheyenne.

Missouri to Oregon, 1879

⸸ Laura Wright

INTRODUCTION

L.W. "Pat" Wright of Phoenix, Arizona, is the owner of a typescript of this diary of his great grandparents, William T. and Laura Wright. We have carried on a correspondence and talked by telephone many times about the diary.[1] He informed me that the family had given the original to the Manuscripts Collection of the University of Washington Library in Seattle. A letter to that library brought back a photocopy of the original written on sheepts of separate paper. It was written in pencil. That library has been quite helpful in making information available about this pioneer family.

The section of the manuscript written by William T. Wright is made up of just a few lines written in Missouri, not on the journey. The major part of the diary published here, was written by Laura Wright, the mother. We begin our transcription with the entry for April 19, 1879. The departure from Carthage, in southwestern Missouri, was on April 22.

With them traveled three children: Jennie, who was probably about 12-years-old; Nellie, age unknown; and Charles, also age unknown. However, we do know that he was old enough to drive one of the mule-drawn wagons.

The Wrights settled first in Weston, Oregon, just south of Walla Walla, Washington. Most of their subsequent lives were lived in Milton, Oregon—now Milton-Freewater.

One of the problems with Laura Wright's diary is that she refers to members of their wagon train either by their given names or by their surnames. The result is that we have not been able to identify

---

[1] He also supplied us with portraits of William and Laura Wright.

several of them. One identifiable person is Winthrop (Win)
Dougherty. The Dougherty clan settled in Wallowa County,
Oregon. Martha A. was Dougherty's wife. Some of their descen-
dants still live in the Wallowa area.[2]

One thing we learn from her obituary, published below as
"Epilogue III," is that after the death of her husband, William,
on March 13, 1903, she became the wife of T.L. Childers of
Milton, Oregon.

THE FAMILY JOURNAL OF LAURA WRIGHT

Saturday, April 19th 1879   Well hear it is most a month
since I have writen in my jornal   we have been very busy
geting ready to go away to Origon   we have had company
evrey day most except when we was away to town   theair
hear yesterday   Lidey Butler hear and stayed all night   we
expected to of started to day but when we went to fasten the
wagon covers they was to small so William went to Carthage
[Missouri] to get Some more ducking to finish them out   I
am about worn out   Mrs Hinton has been helping me
yesterday afternoon and this forenoon   I am afraid
Sunday, Apr 20th 1879   I am about Sick to day   I went
over to Hintons a while to day   had good visit   the girls
went with me   We wan to get started to morow if nothing
happens   I am so tired   William got home from Mr Car-
uthers to day   he went down theair last night to See about
note and stayed all night
Monday, Apr 21st 1879   William went to Carthage to finish
up business   Mr Crampton at our house helping Georg fix
the wagons   theair is good many hear to day   Mr Fosdicks

[2]This information was provided for us by John W. Evans, Librarian, Eastern Oregon
State College, LaGrande.

LAURA WRIGHT

WILLIAM T. WRIGHT
Both photos courtesy of L.W. "Pat"
Wright, Phoenix, AZ

and children   Mr Hinton helped me all day   Mrs Crampton helped me fix covers on the wagons   we cooked Some
more   Mrs Stiger washed for me   the wind is blowing
terrible and I am awful tired and about tired out

Tuesday, 22 Apr 1879   We loaded up and got started to day
quarter past 11 o'clock   theair was good many to See us
Start   all of the Hintons and Cramptons and Mr Fosdicks
our teams went all right but the ones we went to lead   we
went up and called at Mr Fullers few minets   we went down
to Berians and took diner   She Sends her respects to Mrs
Leaming   we went to Georgia City and camped on Spring
river[Kansas]   we did not put our tent up and Just as we got
half through eating it coment to rain so we had to first hurey
around and get our things in to the wagon and go to bed

Wednesday 23   we got up as Soon as day light   I rested as
well as could be expected   we got breakfast and got Started
at half past Seven and from theiar to Pittsburg [Kansas] and
then toward Girard and camped on cow creek and camped
within a mile and a half of G[irard]   put our tent up   had
Splendid place to camp   I had to bake bread to night for the
first [time]   my Stove is just Splendid and the tent we could
hardly get along with out for it is raining   it comenced before
I hardley got Super ready   Jenny is Sick to night   She had
light chill and has hard cough   I cant eat any thing hardley
and have the headache teribley and feel awful bad

Thursday, 24th 1879   It rained considerable last night   we
had to fix up things and did not get Started till about 7 o
clock and came to flat rock creek one mile and half of Osage
Mission[1]   the roads very good   had one bad place   I am
not feeling very well   a man by the name of Spencer over

---

[1] A Roman Catholic mission intent on ministering to Osage Indian girls. Its main aim
was educational. Located at present St. Paul, Neosho Co. at the juncture of the Neosho
River and Flat Creek. Louise Barry, *Beginning of the West* (Topeka, KS, 1972), pp. 559,
680.

took us from Jasper Co   he told us of Some friends he had in Baker Co by the name of Sturgill   it is cool to day

Friday, Apr 25   It rained last night again   it is wet and mudy   we left camp this morning 20 min after 8 o clock and past out north of Osage Mission a little or in Sight of the town   there is some nice places north of the Mission   we saw some men from Joplin by the name of McLeland going out on the Neosho River   we crossed Big creek about Sundown and camped out on the Prairie   the other side one mile or more we had hard work to find hay   it has been quite warm most of the day   we are about twelve miles from Humbolt [Humboldt] on the north rode   it is Some mudy they have had so much more rain than what we had down in Missouri

Saturday, Apr 26, 1879   we got up and got breakfast   I feel miserable   it was damp last night an awful dew   we past through Humbolt just after noon   we Stoped in Humbolt and sold some of our loose things So as to lighten our loads   we camped on beyond Humbolt Six miles and had Splendid place on the prairie where their was Some cotton wood trees and some water

Sunday, Apr 27th 1879   We got Started this morning about 8 o'clock and past through Leroy and acrost the Neosho river toward Burlington   we had quite disagreeable time in fore-noon.   it rained and was so cold   we had to cross some big flats on the Neosho river   it was not very mudy but very ruff   we camped between Leroy and Burlington   had a Splendid place to camp in Some timber   it is pleasant tonight but the nights are cold and damp

Monday, Apr 28   We did not get Started very Soon this morning   we past through Burlington and got Some corn and pickles   had a good road past up the Neosho River toward Emporia   we past in Sight of Streams

Tuesday, Apr 29th 1879   We did not get started till awfull late   William traded mules this morning   traded off Jack and Jin for some black mules   I am awfull weak and have no apitite to eat   we camped on the Neosho river to night   have good place to Stop   had good roads all day   we are about three miles of Emporia

Wednesday, 30th 1879   It rained last night till after day light so we did not get up so early this morning   The men had to fix theair locks and now it begine to thunder again. It comenced to rain Soon after we got Started and it blowed and rained awfull hard   we had an awfull day and hard work to find a Sutable place to camp   it is so wet and mudy   we past through Emporia and Americus and went down and camped on Wright creek   we did not stop to much to night

Thursday, May 1st   It is bright and clear this morning   no Signs of rain   This morning it is quite mudy though part of the way   we went to Council Groves to night   William traded off his horse for a Span of big mules but they are quite wild.   he Sold the redd horse for $45 dollars   theair is Some more men camped hear to night an old Dutch man and Some others   theair is a very friendly family living clost by us

Friday, May 2nd 1879   We layed over to day to wash and dry Some of our things that got wet   We washed with a new washer that Mr Vancam had   they wanted us to bye one We have had a very pleasant day   we washed and cooked Some and aired our beds   I am very tired to night   theair was three ladys called to see us to night   We have crossed the Neosho 9 times on steel bridges

Saturday, My 3rd 1879   We left Council Grove in prety good Season and next to Parker[ville] and then to White City   the farm houses begin to get prety Scatering   we camped 6 miles west of White city on a Small Stream clost to a farmers house   had a splendid place to camp   nice water and got fead of him   this is a nice looking country   the praries are roleing and Some high mounds   we traviled 23 miles to day

Sunday, May 4th 1879   It is a very pleasant day   we got Started in very good Season   travialed few miles and took the wrong road came to several houses but no body at home and went through the fields   they had fenced up the road So we had quite a time to find the way out   we finley Struck the main road and went to Enterprise and got Some fead and went out north of town on the river to camp   it is the mudiest river I ever Saw   nastiest   nothing will drink it theair is Some Splendid Stone buildings   they have such nice rock for building   Enter prize is quite a nice place   the rail rode is two miles away.

Monday, May 5th 1879   We got Started in good Season this morning   past through Abalean [Abilene] Soliman [Solomon] city and along the rail rode to within 5 miles of Salean [Salina]   it is cool to day   we Stoped near a farm house So as to get hay and water for our mules   the river is not fit to use and the well water is bad a nuff [enough] for it Smells so bad we cant hardley drink it   we met one man to day going back from Colorado   he Said Since he left Pueblo he had kept count of the teams that had gon on to Colorado and he had counted 865 teams

Tuesday, May 6th   We came to Salean [Samina] this morning   10 teams passed us befor we got Started   it is quit cold this morning   we Stoped in Salean a while to go to the P. Ofice and get letters   I put Postal Card in ofice yesterday to Hellen   we passed west along the Side of the railrode our teams dont care any thing for the cars   after leaving Salean we came to Bavaria   took diner before we came into the town.   the town is most Ohio folks some from Cleaveland

the water is better   from theair we came to Brokville [Brook-
ville]   got Some hay and Oats and waterd our mules at a well
then passed on through town out to Spring creak and camped
for the nigth   Grain and fead is hier   the farther west we go
the Emigration have used up all the Grain in the country
corn is 40 cts and hay 40 cts a hundred lbs this is quite a rail
rode town   they have large round house hear and considerable Stock is Shiped from hear but the town is Small with hills
all around it   rent is very high hear $12 for comon house   we
Saw man hear last night that advised us to take another rout
Wednesday, May 7th 1879   It was rainey this morning and
we did not Start out till after noon   we passed one Small
Station and went about 12 miles and camped on Small branch
in the prarie   Soon after we got Started we came to larg mud
hole where a team was Stuck   they got out and our teams
went through all richt   the girls and I got out and walked
around on the rail rode   the country is quite hilly and ruff
but our road passed around through the valey along the rail
rode   we are 209 miles west of Kansas city this after noon
they had to comence to graze out the horses to night for the
first [time] we could not get hay any more
Thursday, May 8th 1879   we have passed over Some ruff
country this morning and passed through fort Harker[2] but it
is not used for a fort now but a more diserted looking place I
never Saw   we passed by a larg high rock on the top of a
hill   befor we came to the fort we came to Elsworth [Ells-
worth]   it is quite larg place and looks very well   from
theair we went toward Wilson 13 miles and camped for the
night   theair is Some very pretty country and nice farming
country

---

[2] Fort Harker had been established in 1864 on the bank of the Smoky Hill River to
protect the Santa Fe stages. It was three miles east of the present town of Ellsworth, KS.
It was named for Brigadier General Charles G. Harker. It had been abandoned in April
1872. Robert W. Frazer, *Forts of the West* (Norman, OK, 1965), pp. 53-54.

Friday, May 9th 1879   One of the mules waked me up about
4 o clock   George got up and went to See them and two was
gon   the men got up and comenced to look for them and
they hunted all around and could not find them   I was So
uneasy   I was afraid they was Stolen   William Started
back and found them about three miles away   Some one had
caught them and tied them up   he paid them $1 dollar and
got back about 9 o clock   we got redy as Soon as we could
and Started   passed through Willison [Wilson] and Bunkerhill   camped near a low place about three miles and a half
from Bunkerhill where the rail rode turns to go north west
Some men saw thre Antelope to day   it is not settled up
much between Willison and Bunker but from theair is considerable Settled   the wheat is very nice hear   the hail cut
it off   this is pretty dry country and bad water

Saturday, May 10   We went through Russell   got Some
fead and turned north at Russell and went toward Osborn[e]
we went with a farmer out as far as Paridise creak and camped
theair   it is a nice place   Small Stream with timber   it is
refreshing after crossing over the hills and praries   it has
been so warm and I was so dry I was So glad to get hear   this
Stream was named by Some travilers who had traviled Some
distance without water and it Seamed like paridise to get hear

Sunday, May 11th 1879   We did not Start very early this
morning   it is quite pleasant day   we traviled over hills and
prarie   most of the houses are Sod houses but little water
the old farmer yesterday took us off from the rode to Osborn   took us to far to the west so we wont go to Osborn but
to Bulls city   we havent Seen a town to day   nothing but
nacked praries   We crossed one Small Stream and theair was
two good houses and then we came to Medicine creak to
camp   it is a beautifull Stream So clear and nice   I Saw
School of nice fish playing around

Monday, May 12th 1879   We are going north west for
Kirwin   we passed through Bulls city   it is Small place just
a few houses   I dont think much of this country   it is to
hilly   the houses are mostly Sod houses except in town   the
country is very dry and kneed rain bad   the wheat looks
bad   they raise mostly wheat   it looks like rain tonight
they are having big Storm off to the north east   we did not
get to Kirwin   had to Stop in a Sag on the prarie   the wind
blows awfull   theair hapend to be a Spring or pool of water
near us and we had brought wood with us   we carie Some
wood all the time for it is very Scarse.

Tuesday, May 13th 1879   we loaded up our things and went
about three miles to the river and Stoped and went into
camp   the wind blows So hard we cant travial   we got a
very good place to camp in the valey under the bluff next to
the river   I got diner wrot Sevral Postal cards and letters
the wind does blow teriable hard   William went down to a
mill and got Some choped rye feed for the mules   they had
an earth quake through hear about the 20th of April   Shook
Some Stone buildings in Bulls city So as to leave cracks in
them

Wednesday, May 14th   We went through Kirwin   Stoped
and mailed Some letters one to Mrs Leaming one to Hintons
one to [?] one to Hellen. Kirwin is quite lively place and it is
better looking country around hear   we went out north west
acrost Plum creak twice and then took a divide between two
Small Streams north and west toward Republican city   we
Stoped on Small Stream or Sag with little timber   We
traviled about 25 miles to day   the wind did not blow So
hard to day but it was cool   we did not See but three homes
this afternoon and they was Sod and but very little broke up

Thursday, May 15th 1879   We came to Republican river
crossed it and came to Republic city [Nebraska]   Stoped [a]

while   turned west up the river   we passed through Alma
then on toward Orleans and camped in Sight of town   the
country through hear is quite livley   they are Surveying out
a rail rode up the river   it has been cool to day   we passed
Some very nice locations on the river that Some day will make
a nice place   they are Setting out quite larg groves of cotton
wood trees

Friday, May 16th 1879   It looks very much like rain this
morning   we hurryed and got redy to Start   we Started half
past Seven   came to Orleans   watered our horses   We are
30 miles Arapaho[e]   this is a very prety country along the
Republican river   it Slopes So nicely and is So eaven and
then there is So many nice Streams flowing into the Republican from one mile to three 4 and Some five   the bridge was
gon from over one of them and we had to go away up around
to the bluff and we got out of our Some   we are camped
about 5 miles from Arapaho on one of the nice Streams   it
comenced to Sprinkle rain before we got the tent up and now
it is raining quite hard but we have got our work done

Saturday, May 17 1879   We went to Arapaho   got Some
fead one mule shod and turned north toward Plum Station we
have good roads theair is no Setlers hardly through hear   we
did not pass but two or three houses   about 4 o'clock we
came to a Sheep ranch where we got Some water and that is all
the water we could find Since we left Arapaho   when we
Stoped for diner we found Some prarie hens eggs and cooked
them for Supper   we passed through one awfull place called
the devils gap   Such an awfull Steap crooked road and Such
awfull breakes I got out and walked over them   just before
night Charlie got out to shoot some prarie chickens and when
he went to get back in the wagon run over it and hurt it prety
bad   we camped about two miles on the prarie and had
about two gallons of water was all   we could not wash our
dishes and had an awfull time

Sunday, May 18th 1879   We went on toward Plum Station we had very good roads   we Stoped on plat river on a bridge   the river is full and the bridge is one mile long   I was thankfull when we got acrost   we are about two miles from town and before we got to town theair came up a fearfull Storm   it rained and hailed   our team would not Stand So William put on his over coat and got out to on hitch them   he finley got them on hitched and around to the Side of the wagon and gave me the lines to hold but the Storm got so bad and they began to pull and hurt my hand prety bad   Wiliam got the lines just before they got away but he could not hold them   they got away but did not go far   the girls was driving one team and he had to atend to them   The hail most knocked him down and it would if it had not of been for a piece of carpet I put over his head   Georges team Stood it very well but Such a fearfull Storm I never Saw   My wagon did not get wet much but the things in Charleys and Georges got prety wet   after the Storm abated we went on up to Plum Station[3] and got in to a livrey Stable and put the mules up and cooked Some Supper on theair Stove   the ground is all covered with hail Some of them very large and the ground is all aflout with watter

Monday, May 19th 1879   We did not get Started till 10 o'clock   We got supplies at Plum this morning and went out few miles and Stoped for diner and about 4 o'clock theair came up an awfull Storm   We drove as fast as we could and got in to Cozad before it got So bad   the girls and I stoped at a house till it Slacked up raining   they put the horses under Shed and the wagons up Side of building   we Stoped at a hotell all night   cooked our own vitles   got one bed for us women to Sleep in   our things got Some wet again

---

[3]Plum Creek, Dawson Co., was organized in 1878. The name was later changed to Lexington. Lilian L. Fitzpatrick, *Nebraska Place-Names* (Lincoln, 1960), p. 51.

theair was an awfull Storm east and South of us   it hailed hear but not So bad as it did east

Tuesday, the 20th 1879   We got Started awfull late   drove along the rail rode and Stoped near Station house   got water theair and wood from the rail rode   I dont know what we would do for wood if it was not for the rail rode   the folks was very kind where we stoped last night   Theair names was Rigs from cincinnati   they are fixing up a hotell at Cozed   the place has run down awfuly   hardey a house fit to live in for they leak so bad   it looked like rain again to night but it did not rain

Wednesday, May 21st 1879   We passed through one or two Small stations on the rail rode   Some times clost to the river   The roads were prety bad to day   we crossed the north plat river on a rail rode bridge about one half mile long and came to Plat City [North Platte, Nebraska] & was Surprised to see Such a larg place and Such nice buildings we camped west of town little ways on the prarie   got water from a house   theair is not much farming going on hear mostly stock raising

Thursday, May 22nd 1879   We got started early this morning went west along the rail rode   theair is no houses except small stations and only two or three at them   there was sevral trains passed us to day   we stoped early for diner and turned our mules out   we had hard rain last night and the wind blowed so hard I could not Sleep   the young men that Stoped with us dug a hole in the ground and got water but not enough to water the Stock so we went on to a Water tank on the rail rode and watered our mules and filled our keg   we Saw some folks hear that was going to Origon   we will wait for them at Jules burg [Julesburg, Colorado]   we Stoped to camp on the prairie between the rail rode and the bluff   they are not very far apart hear about one mile   theair is the most

cattel raised hear I ever Saw and nothing but cattle raised
hear. We had quite pleasant time to night   the five young
men that is travaling with us gave us Some musick   they
have a fiddle and guitar and we all Sang Some.   these five
young men are from Iowa   four are clearks from dry goods
Stores and one is a teacher

Friday, May 23rd 1879   We came to Oglaley [Ogallala] and
had to drive prety hard to get hear   one of our mules is prety
tierd or Sick   we went in back of the town between the river
and rail rode   We have nice place   the young men went out
west of town to camp   we are going to lay over to morrow
Some ladies from the Section house was down hear this
eavning

Saturday, May 24th 1879   We washed in fournoon. Some
parties over took us to day little before noon and we are going
to wait for in Julesburg   they washed in afternoon   I was
up to Section in afternoon   I dont think much of the
lady   She had been very kind to us and let us have evrey
thing we need so It is nothing to me   two young men waded
the river to get Some tent poles from Some brush

Sunday, May 25th 1879   This is Sunday morning but it
dont seam so   we had another fearfull Storm last night.   the
first thing I knew the wind awakend me blowing the wagon
thought I was traveling and was going to Some bad place
theair is two other familys camped and going to travil with
us   they have five wagons and 11 head of horses and mules
they had them all in a row and loaded with chains around
theair neck   when the Storm came up two of theair wagons
up Set on to the horses and Such a time as they had to get
them loose   it rained awful hard and it was all I could do to
keep the front curtain down   I dont think theair wagons
wood ov went over if it had not been for the horses pulling
them over. I fixed our wagon Some and then took the Sick

headache and I was awful Sick this evening theair was
sevral ladies from town down to our camp to night the men
had to fix up theair wagons the covers and good many
things Smashed up and broke them all good many men
crossed the river to day horse back they we stock men

Monday, May 26th 1879 We got Started all to gether and
went out through town and traveled very well went about
25 miles camped at night close by the bluffs it looks as
though we would have a bad Storm to night theair is 11
folks in our crowd besides our family I havent learnt all
theair names yet one family is Jonston and one is Dorhety
one man by the name of Win we did not see but three or
four houses to day. We are travaling along the rail rode and
river ever Since we came to Plum creek Station It looks
very nice but I would hate to live hear theair is no timber. I
Saw one tree on an island to day I put Some letters and
cards in ofice that I wrote yesterday one to Mrs. Hicks I
dont feel very well to day but better than I expected I would
after being So Sick as I was yesterday.

Tuesday, May 27th We camp in very good place last
night we past by Burton and then Stoped for diner the
roads were So Sandy we had to travil very Slow we passed
through Julesburg [Colorado] it is a very small place watered
at a tank then we left the Plat river and went up pool creek
along the rail rode it has been very warm all day theair
were 7 other wagons over took us to day they have 27 head
of horses and 16 men and 4 women this prarie is alive this
evening the boys are having big time to night they had
big time having me mark around theair warts to take them
of they think I have some charm about it their is one
felow by the name of Frank that is wide awake felow they
had big time after Some antilopes to day

Wednesday, May 28th 1879 Theair is quite [a] crowd of us

now   the other 7 wagons went ahead of us to the Same old
Storey along the rail rode   the stations are about 18 miles
apart along hear and the Station houses about 8 miles apart
after diner we came to larg mud hole   one of our new
companys teams got Stuick and one of ours got Stuck   a
young man brought his team and helped us out   Mr John-
stons teams got tangled when he was coming out of the mud
but we all got through   in afternoon when the young men
was after an Antalope his horse throwed him and kicked him
in the Side and hurt him prety bad   I went over to see him in
eavening   it looks like rain

Thursday, May 29, 1879   We had another big scare last
night   the wind comenced blowing and I thought we were
going to have another Storm   the men all got up and Staked
down our wagon but Soon Stoped   we all got up earley
before 5 o'clock and Started by 7 o'clock   we got to Sidney
[Nebraska] by 10 o'clock and got Some corn potatoes mollases
and few other things   Went out past Potter Station and
acrost Pool creak   it is a Splendid little stream very clear and
nice   Just before night we came to where the Stream was
under ground   the creak bed is full of Sand   We all camped
clost together to night   our men are afraid of horse thieves
they take turns and Set up all night   the young man that got
hurt yesterday is better so he can ride to day   we are all glad
of it for we expected he would have to lay over.   theair was
great many camped around Sidney mostly freighters   Some
going to black hills Some goin to Colorado   Sidney is quite a
large place   it is the end of one rail rode divishon   it is cool
and pleasant to day

Friday, May 30th 1879   We got a very good nights Sleap
last night   nothing disturbed us   we got up earley   Started
by 7 or before   we went out few miles to where the Stream
runs on top of the ground and watered our teams   theair is

five more teams travaling a little ways behind us   befor we
Stoped for diner it comenced to rain and is raining quite hard
and it is awfull cold   it Seams as if it would Snow.   the boys
Frank and Nieland have built up big fier out of rail rode
ties   We will wait till it Slacks raining and then drive
on.   theair is not So many cattle in Sight   I think they
have taken them down to the plat river to round up and then
mark them.   it comenced to rain about noon and it rained all
the afternoon hard and when we got ready to camp it raind
awfull hard   they put up the tent and the men all got in as
many as could stand up and had big time.   they do have so
much fun   it rained very hard in eavning

Saturday, May 31st 1879   We passed through Bushnell
[Nebraska]   Stoped on pool creak for diner   Some of the
young men that is with us killed an Antilope and gave us
Some   it is Splendid. We came out as far as Pine Bluffs
[Wyoming] or a mile beyond the Station clost to the Bluffs
and watter tank to camp   we have a nice place and talk of
laying over Sunday and untill Monday noon   it is a beautifull
night   the moon Shines bright   the men bring the wagons
in to a circle or corell and Set our tent to one side and bring
the horses in Side and fasten them to the wagons but the other
company that are with us lariet theairs out around and gard
them all night   our men gard theaires   William is going to
Set up till half past 11 o clock   Frank and Nealons or
Killions as I call him Sleep in our tent   I dont know what we
would all do if it was not for our tent   they keep a fier in our
Stove in the tent all night   it is so cold they cant hardly
Stand it

Sunday, June 1st 1879   We all had good Sleep and rest   this
morning Fank and Nealons Started as Soon as light to See if
they could get an Antilope but could not get any   we got
our work done up and got redy to go up on the Bluffs. Mrs

Jonston, Mrs Dorety, Jennie, Nellie, William and I went out
upon the bluffs   we was just going to have a Splendid time
and about the time we got up theair it commenst to rain and
we had to hurry back   Mrs Jonston out run us all   William
run on a head of us to get the umberelly and him and Mrs
Jonston had quite a race   it maid me laugh so that I could
not run So Mrs Dorety and I had to walk   we got prety
wet   it is going to be a raining day   well it has cleared off
and we had a very pleasant time   in the eaving they came in
to our tent or all that could get in and we had Singing till bed
time

Monday, June 2nd 1879   I got up bright and early got our
breakfast and went to washing   we got through twenty five
minets after nine and then we arranged our wagons got diner
and then Started on the rode. I am So tierd for we have
worked as hard as we could Jump all the time   we passed a
lone grave out on the prarie of an old lady that died while
travaling through the country   late in the afternoon one of
the company killed another Antilope. William went out with
one of our mules and helped pack it in So we had Several nice
meals   I am so dizey to night and had to mend Williams
vest so I could not go out to help them Sing   To night all
the wagons formed into a larg circle and had two watchmen
it is clear and pleasant and the moon Shines bright

Tuesday, June 3 1879   We did not go very near the rail
rode   came to a Station at noon by the name of Atkins
[Wyoming] they had hard work to get water   they Let us
have water to cook with and William gave the boy 15 cents
and he let water on enuff for our horses   Some of them after
we went in to camp went and got a gew buckets full for theair
horses   it is very hot and dry along hear   we did not get any
more water till about four o clock and then had to drive off
from the road little ways to creak   We are beginnin to Strike

the foot hills of the Mountains   We came to a Snow Shead
just befor we wattered   to day has been our hardest time for
water we have had So far   we came in Sight of the Mountains
to day with theair white caps and the Black hills to the
north   they are about 100 miles from hear in Colorado   we
got water at a Section house to cook with and Some got
wood   we went a little ways farther and crossed the rail rode
and camped with in one mile of Cheyenne. If we had went one
mile farther we would came to a beautifull lake and better
grass   we have got very poor grass

Wednesday, June 4th 1879   We got up awful early and Soon
as we could went on into Cheyenne to get our horses Shod   it
is pleasant day and is going to be awfull warm. I am writing
while they are waiting to get them Shod   we got all ours
Shod up and got some Supplies   I have been fixing my
travaling dress to day   I got one letter from Hellen   I was
glad to get it   Cheyenne is quite a larg place   Some very
large brick buildings   after we got through trading we went
out through town up along the north side of the rail rode
and Stoped for diner   the Sun is very hot.   we went till four
o clock and then came to a Station and good Spring also a
pond where we Stoped to camp for the night.   before we got
unharnessed theair came up a Storm of rain and hail   we got
Supper   it rained little Showers   theair was man from
depot came in to chat a while.   we can go up on the hill and
look back at Cheyenne   theair is good many Sheep kept hier
about four thousand head   they dont raise any thing much
hear that is vegetable but it is all Shiped in   we Saw cabage
potatoes, ripe peaches and all kinds of fruit in market at
Cheyanne. Theair were two tramps to our camp to night
theair is tramps evrey day

Thursday, June 5th 1879   We started at half past Six this
morning   they get up so early in the morning and then

hurrey So fast to get started   we have been going over hills
to day   the rodes are geting awfull ruff   we came down a
hill to a depot Granet Canon[4] Some of them got water at the
tank   we did not   then went out up a hill   one of our
teams Stoped on the hill   I was awful Scart   Nellie was
driving   She put on the brake as Soon as She could and got
them Stoped   William drove on up and Lafe one of the
young men held them and William went back and drove
them up for him   we went on over the hill about a mile and
camped by a Small Stream for diner   we had very good rodes
this afternoon   crossed the rail rode Sevral times   went
acrost at Buford and turned South to a Small Stream in a
holow to camp for the night   we had good grass at noon and
very good to night but for two or three days we have had very
poor grass and hard work to get water   after Supper we took
a walk up on the mountains and had good time   I had to get
down and crawl in Some places I was So afraid of falling   the
rocks are a red gravil   we had plenty of wood to night   it is
a ruff looking place   I have a card redy to send to Hellen but
dont have time to mail it

Friday, June 6th 1879   We are travaling over the mountains
to day   we have been going up untill we got to Shermin.[5] it is
up hill and down and around   not much timber   once in a
while a scraggy pine but the scenery is beautifull   we can See
Snow tops not more than 20 miles away   we left the rail rode
at Shermin and go a Shorter rout   the rail road turns hear
and theair to get around the hills   the Soil is all gravail and
red Soil   we came to quite a nice valey where theair was a
Sheep ranch and good buildings good grass nice garden and I

---

[4]Granite Canyon, Laramie Co., Wyoming, was a railroad station and postoffice
named for granite rock in the vicinity. It was the main setting for Mary O'Hara's books:
My Friend Flicka and *Thunderhead*. Mae Urbanek, *Wyoming Place Names* (Missoula,
MT, 1988), p. 86.

[5]*Ibid.*, p. 181. Sherman was a railroad town in Albany Co. It is now only a graveyard.

saw house plants in the window   the flours have to be raised
in the house because the wind blows so hard   I saw plenty
Snow Sheds this four noon   we came past Some nice Springs
we got nice camping ground at noon in a holow by a Small
Stream where theair was wood for those that wanted to build a
fier and cook theair diner   we have had better rode to day
than I expected to have over the mountains   We got to
Larima [Laramie] got Some Corn and things to last to Green
River city   went out through town   crossed the rail rode
and over the Larama river and camp between the river and
Semitary on the prarie   we all for got to get wood but Mr
Dorety was back and he brought some old ties So we got along
very well   Some did not have much water   theair was four
other wagons came along to day   they are a distressed
Sight So dirty   they camped beyond us a little   theair is
four diferent camps on this prarie to night

Saturday, June 7th 1879   We have traviated up a vally to
day   part of the way it was Stoney   camped for diner near
the little Larima   after diner we crossed a Small Stream and
then the Larima   it runs awfull Swift and was quite deep
theair was ties runing down it from the Mountains to the rail
rode but we all got acrost Safe then up the valey still we come
to a Small Stream   Oh Such a nice Stream from the Mountains   the water is Soft and cold   the wind blowed awfull
and we had to take our wagon Sheats off   It blowed So hard
and it is quite chilly   to night we are to lay over till Monday
one of our young men Stayed at Larima

Sunday, June 8th 1879   This is a lovley day and the Sun
Shines So bright   most of the camp is very buisey washing
cooking and fixing up   we did not wash nor do much
cooking   the boys that did not have much to do have gon
hunting antilope   We Saw So many yesterday and Some
have gon up to the mountains   in the after noon it comenst
to rain and we could See it Snow on the Mountains   the

boys brought home one Antilope and Some Snow   we all
had Some to eat   Frank Crush was up on the Mt—and it
Snowed awfull hard So he could not See this is a lovley place
to lay over Sunday   Such a lovley Stream in a little valey and
plenty of wood and nice grass   it is very cold

Monday, June 9th 1879   It is very cold this morning and we
had quite a Storm in the night and I was awfull fraid and just
Shook   William would not let me get up   it did not rain
much after all   we left camp and went on over the mountains
the wind blowed very hard and Oh So cold   I wish we had
our winter clothing   we crossed Several Small Streams   I
dont know how many   we had one awfull mud hole   we
Stoped on one for diner and while we was Stoped our Barney
mule took Sick and we had quite a time   they gave him some
midison and bled him So he got better and we went on just
before night we crossed over rock creak on a tole bridge   paid
50 cts a team 5 wagons forded the Stream   it is very Swift
and greait big rocks in the bottom as big as a tub   after
crossing the creak about 2 miles we went on to camp   theair
was Snow in less than one half mile of us to day   the boys
went and got Some   Pery Mills Shot two Sage Hens   he
gave us one and I am cooking it to night and cooking Some
antilope to   theair is 150 teams behind us and 4 ahead beside
small companies

Tuesday, June 10th 1879   We are travaling over the mts to
day   Snow was clost to us   theair was a mountain in front of
us and to one Side most all day   I though we would never
get past it   theair was considerable Snow on   we had awfull
ruff rodes So Stoney and one deep cut and then one cut and
then we came to a tole bridge   It cost 10 cts a team   the
rest all forded it but 2 of Doretys teams and ours   we
camped Soon after we crossed it   not very good grass   in a
few miles we came to a ranch and a Store and quite a daria

[dairy]   we got some butter   theair was Several houses and
a Burying ground   we kept winding around thru the mountains and camped in a holow clost by the road for the
night   had very good water but wood was Scarce   they
finley found Some brush and Some used Sage brush   the
Sage brush is awfull but not very high   I Saw part of an
Indians Skull   It was not quite So cold

Wednesday, June 11th 1879   We left camp quite early and
have been going down the mountain all the four noon   passed
over Sevrall Streams and came to pass creak and filled our
keg of water for we wont get any more till night and then we
expect to Strike the Plat river   we left the Ft Steal [Steele][6]
rode to the right   Some wanted to go that way   we Struck a
more leval country and camped for diner with out water   the
rodes have been very good   the boys have had big times
Shooting Sage hens   they have give us two   we are in Sight
of the river and two men have gon on to See about the ford
where to cross the fery or ford it and the Texas out fit have
over taken us   Some in the train are Sick with chills to day
and Nellie has the tooth ache awfull bad   we waited for
about two hours while Pery went to See about the lower ford
but we could not cross theair So we went on the river and
camped   this is Plat river   theair was three ladies called at
our camp   2 of them live at Ft Steal which is 25 miles from
hear

Thursday, June 12th 1879   We all got ready and went down
to the river to be feried acrost   it was only larg enuff for one
team at a time and three dollars a team   they looked at three
fords to see if we could not ford it but it was to Deep   so we
all feried acrost it   it cost us 9 dollars   we all got acrost Safe

---

[6]Robert W. Frazer, *Forts of the West, op. cit.*, p. 186. Fort Fred Steele was established
on June 30, 1868, by Major Richard I. Dodge, of the 30th U.S. Infantry. He named the
fort for Col. Frederick Steele, who died on Jan. 12, 1868. It was abandoned in 1886. See
also Urbanek, *op. cit.*, p. 70.

and Started over another range of Mountains called the
Snowey range   the rodes was up hill and down and Some
places was prety bad to twist around   it is 35 miles to the top
of the mountains   we traviled till almost night before we got
water   the hills are bare with Some Sage Brush and the
water is alkili   we filled our keg at the Branch and went
about a quarter of a mile and camped on a naked hill and
nothing but Sage brush to burn   the men went about a mile
and found Some grass and took their teams over till dark
their is Sevral Sick to night from drinking the water and I
am afraid one man has the Mountain feaver   he is prety Sick
Friday, June 13th 1879   The men took the Stock over to the
patch of grass and kept them out till after 7 o,clock then we
Started up the mountains   the rodes are about as bad as
ever   no grass   we crossed one or two Streams in four
noon   we passed one Stock ranch just before we Stoped for
noon where the rode come in from Ft Steal [Steele] and about
one mile from their we found a nice camping ground a nice
piece of grass and wood and good water and befor we got
Started it came up a rain and we could not travil this after
noon but we had very good place   they put up the tent
about five o,clock but Oh! how mudy and wet it is   Some
went back to the ranch to get Some fead   they had to pay 3
cts. a pound for Oats
Saturday, June 14th 1879   It is very wet and mudy this
morning   Some of the company want to lay over to day So
they took a vote on it and they are going on   we wound
around over the Mts—and just before noon we crossed the
divided of the continent and was up very high   the old Stage
rout used to go through   at noon we camped in a valey just
over the divide where their was old Stage Stand   their was
a lone grave on the hill of a woman 25 year 4 month Old by the
name of Eliza J Gess   we Soon Struck mudy creak and went

down it up on Side of the mountains   it was awfull Scarey
rode   Some places it was over hundred right Strait down
below   we crossed over mudy creak on bridge and then came
to a ranch where we got Some corn at 3 cts a pound and Some
black tail dear and it was Splendid   we camped about 2 miles
past the ranch   had good water and plenty Sage brush and
the largest I ever Saw

Sunday 15th 1879   We got up and Started early   went
down mudy creak about 10 miles   watered our teams for we
wont get eny more for about 25 miles   Such a baren country
just a few weades and So Sandy   the rodes was very good in
after noon but we are about down the Mts   we Stoped at the
barell Springs[7] and when we got hear we had to dig out the
Springs   it is very alkili but we got Some very good   theair
is quite a crowd camped near us with a drove of horses 11 men

Monday 16   We are travaling over a Sand desert with a
Strange looking wead and Some Sage brush   we passed two
old Stage houses   had to go into dry camp for had a little
patch of grass for our mules   we passed the texas out fit in
morning   while we was eating diner theair came up quite a
rain Storm and maid it quite mudy   we crossed bitter creak
in after noon at an old Stage house   we watered our horses
theair but we had not ought to for it is poison   we went a few
miles into a canion and turned off the rode and went north to
Elk Springs[8] where theair is plenty water, grass and good
Shelter   theair is good Spring hear and another old Stage
house   it is right in a deep canion greait high hills all
around   our Stock men camped in the old house   Soon

---

[7]Mae Urbanek says of the Barrell Springs overland station, "In the vast expanse of
sagebrush was a crystal-clear spring, ice-cold, and much prized by early emigrants who
had to use mostly bitter alkali water. The stationkeeper knocked the ends out of a
50-gallon whiskey barrel, and set it around the springs." *Op. cit.*, p. 11.

[8]Should be Elkhorn Station. It was located nine miles west of Glendo, WY, at the
crossing of the Elkhorn. The locale is marked today by a steel post. Aubrey L. Haines,
Historic Sites Along the Oregon Trail (Gerald, MO, 1981), p. 159.

after we got in to camp the texas folks came in and two other
crouds So theair was thirty teams camped near to night Perry
Mills lost a very nice horse with colic from drinking the water
out of bitter creak   he died Soon after we got in to camp   he
was offered 4 hundred dollars for him in Cheyenne three of
the wagons that came in to night have 21 children we traviled
about 30 miles to day   Nellie Patterson one of our company
is very Sick to night   I think she has Mountain
feaver   I have been giving her Some medison   Mrs Bankey
is Sick to but not So bad

Tuesday, June 17th 1879   We Started very early So as to be
ahead of the rest and just as we was going out of the canion to
get on to our rode that runs west (we was off from our rode
about 2 miles) we met five other teams coming in   they
could not get in last night   theair will be about 40 teams in
theair to night   we camped under very high bluff for diner
we came down Some very Steap hills in fore noon two of them
but in afternoon we had an awfull Steap one   the boys called
it the Elephant and I think it is⁹   I will be glad when we get
over these Sandy mountains   we came to a Spring just before
night but did not Stay   went about 1 mile and got good grass
and water   We have been traveling 8 weeks to day

Wednesday, June 18th 1879   We did not hury off So fast
this morning   fixed up our harness   let the horses eat
went went over hills and wound through mountains   about
ten o,clock we came to a Stream and watered our Stock and
filled our kegs and went on and about noon or before we came
to a nice Strip of grass   this country is all alkali and awfull

⁹The dangers of the overland journey were summed up in this term, "seing the
elephant." See especially John Phillip Reid, *Law for the Elephant*, (San Marino, CA,
1980). See also Peter Tamony, "To See the Elephjant," *Pacific Historian*, XII, Winter
1968, pp. 23-29, and J. Rea "Seeing the Elephant," *Western Frontier*, XXVIII, No. 1,
Jan. 1969, pp. 21-26. Arthur H. Clark Co. published James Mason Hutchings' journal
in 1980 entitled *Seeking the Elephant, 1849*.

drearey   we are about 30 miles Green river city   theair is
few head of Cattle in hear to day   we will Soon be to the
Sumit of the quakenasp [Quaking Aspen] mountain in about
one hours travial   Well we got up the mountain and then
turned and went right down for Sevral miles and went in to
camp by a ranch   we got Some Onions, letise and radishes
and Some milk   we have very good place

Thursday 19th 1879   Well when we got up this morning the
ground was coverd with Snow and it was awfull cold   Mr
Dorty folks and our teams Seprated from the rest of the
crowd this morning   they are going to uper Rock Springs
and then on to Green river   30 miles above Green River
city   from theair to Soda Springs we went to rock Creak
got some potatoes and corn and then up the rail rode to
Green river and camped clost to the fery and clost to the
town   William went up to town and I got Some letters one
from Hellen one from Hickses one from Mrs Leaming, and a
card from cramptons

Friday, June 20th 1879   William went up and laid in Supplies to last to Evinston [Evanston][10] and then we feried
acrost Green River but it was about noon before we got
acrost   we went about 14 miles to Black [Black's] fork
river   theair was Some men ahead of us and they took us of
the main traviled rode acrost the creak but we all turned and
came back to the river and camped   it is in sight of the rail
rode   we dont gard our mules now we lock them up

Saturday, June 21st 1879   we did not make very big drive to
day   we are travaling along the creak but the rode winds

<hr>

[10] Evanston was established as a railroad construction center in 1869 and named for an
official of the Union Pacific, James A. Evans. Mae Urbanek tells in her book, *Wyoming
Place Names* (Missoula, MT, 1988), p. 63, that the famous actress, Sarah Bernhardt,
was held up in 1884 by a landslide that stopped the trains. The stranded passengers were
entertained by Shoshone Indians who rode and stunted with their horses to the delight of
the actress.

around through the hills   we are about 2 miles from Granger Station[11]   the weather is warmer than it had been   the grass is very poor   theair is none on the hills   it is only weads and Sage brush and poor dried up grass along the Streams

Sunday, June 22nd 1879   We changed our minds after enquiring about the route this morning and are going to go by Soda Springs [Idaho]   we went up to the Station and maid Some enquires and then went out a bout a mile acrost Ham fork and then bid Dorteys good by and Started up ham fork alone   it is nearer and better rode and plenty water and best grass and wood   we went up about 8 miles from the Station and camped for diner then went up ten miles farther and camped on the Stream for the night   have good grass and Such a nice Stream of water almost as larg as Spring river and very clear   it is rather loansome travaling alone after having So much company

Monday 23rd June 1879   It has been quite cold to day along towerd night we just Suffered with the cold   we went on up the Stream crossed it sevral times then out over the bluffs   yould think you was never coming on to it again   Georg caught one larg fish in the morning   Charley Shot a Sage hen So we had it for diner and while I was geting diner George caught three more larg fish   one was very large and nice   I cooked them for supper   they are very good   he caught one more to night So we will have e nuff for breakfast we are camped close by the Stream but have not So good grass   we have an awfull place to go up in the morning cross over the Stream past an old Stone hut

Tuesday, June 24th 1879   We got ready to Start and theair was drove of cattle came along and we had to wait till they got

[11]This stage station was named for General Gordon Granger. It was also called Grange. Urbanek, *op. cit.*, p. 85.

through the canion and they had ox team   then William had to fix the rode before we could cross   it was an awfull place to go through clost to the bluff on a dug rode right clost to the Stream of water   after we got over we went up to the Stone hut and to the wigwam then up the Stream a ways about three miles and then acrost the Mts   we camped for diner just before we got to the Sumit and then down the other Side to an awfull deep canion   Just before we went into the canion we came to a Spring that was up hier than the rest of the ground   we Stoped to See about camping and theair was four other teams came un Sight   we went on in the canon and got place to camp and the other teams came up and camped close to us   the bluffs are Straight up on both sides and Such narow rodes in places dug in the Side hill

Wednesday, June 25th 1879   I dont feel very well to day have Such dizzy Spells   we all Started out together throug the canon   prety ruff rode   we met another drove of cattle came to Sevral nice larg buildings but no body living in them   we came to a larg irigation dich going from the Stream in the canon   it went on down into a Mormon farm or Settlement   we got off from our rode and went through the farm and it was awfull late when we Stoped for diner on Bear River   it was nearly three o clock when we got diner ready and then they thought it was not worth while to hitch up So they layed over the rest of the day   we have plenty grass and water but no wood hardly   we got Some acquainted with our niew friends   I like them very well   two families by the name of Parsell and another by the name of Rhodes

Thursday, June 26th 1879   We did not get Started as Soon as the rest this morning   Williams breake was broke and he had to fix it   we passed over Smith fork[12] then passed

---

[12]This was probably a branch of the Bear River named for the famous trapper, Jedediah Smith. Haines, *op. cit.*, p. 275.

through a Settlement on Smith fork theair was tole bridge
theair but we forded the creak   the water was up to the
wagon bed but I dont think it wet any thing to hurt   we
Stoped for diner Soon after on Spring creak   we went on
down bear creak but had to leave it before night   went on to
Toms fork[13] and crossed it and Stoped for the night   had
good place to camp   it is not quite So cold to day   we
passed another Settlement before crossing the creak   evrey
Settlement has erigation dtiches   in the afternoon we met
Sam Bumpus with a drove of cattle   he is going to Cheyenne

Friday, June 27th 1879   We went on down the river   we
came to Phelps ranch and got Some chease   it tasted very
good when we got it but when we came to eat it it made us
Sick   Oh Such Stuff   we got to Montpelier [Idaho][14] in
afternoon   got Some Oats potatoes butter and fish then
went on throug Benington[15] which is four miles from Montpelier and out about one mile and camped on Small creak
they have Splendid water hear and it looks So nice to See the
water runing all along the Streets   the Buildings are all
made of pine logs   Montpelier is the cheepest we passed
through Since we Started

Saturday, June 28th 1879   We passed through George
town[16] before noon and we went about 16 miles before we got a
good camping place and then we had to go off from the rode
Some distance to get to the river   I have a bad headache this
afternoon So I could not hardly set up   We came in Sight of

---

[13]This was Thomas Fork of the Bear River. Haines, *op. cit.*, p. 276.

[14]Montpelier, Idaho, was a Mormon community founded in 1864 by a group of
Latter-Day Saints. It was named for the capital of Brigham Young's native state,
Vermont. Lalia Boone, *Idaho Place Names* (Moscow, ID, 1988), p. 259.

[15]Bennington, Idaho, was named for Bennington, Vermont, where Brigham Young
grew up. Boone, *op. cit.*, p. 26.

[16]This was a Mormon settlement founded in 1870. At first it was named Twin Lakes,
but it was changed to Georgetown by Brigham Young, who named it for a Mormon
leader, George Q. Cannon, who was a delegate to Congress from Utah. Boone, *op. cit.*, p.
153.

Soda Springs and turned off to the hills where we could get
Some grass   theair is a hurd of cattle clost to us to night

Sunday 29th June 1879   We Started quite early and came
into Soda Springs   We all got out and went to See the
Springs   they are a curiosity and they taste just like Soda
and boils up all the time   it comes out Sevral feat higher
than the Stream that runs along below   upon a hill back of
town is a hot Spring and Sevral cold Springs that run over and
runs down the Mountains all the time   while we were all up
theair who Should come out theair but Liviga Taylor   She
has left her folks and is going to Montania [Montana] with
Mr Nobles family   She left hur folks the other Side of Plat
River   She thinks they are about a weak ahead of us   we
left town and went out three or four miles and turned on to
the river and camped for diner   then we went up quite a
mountain and then down quite a hill to a Small branch and
camped for the night

Monday, June 30th 1879   We came on down the mountain
and passed along a Small Stream on a dug rode where it was
just wide enuff for the wagon to pass along   theair was a cave
to the west end of it   Some men had camped in it   we came
on down to the rail rode that runs up from Utah   we could
not get any grain or flower hear only Some onions potatoes
and a few other things   we went out of town acrost a branch
and camped for diner   we tried to get Some flower of a ranch
but they had none   we went of the regular rode for few
miles   had good place to camp and went into camp about 4 o
clock   Jenie went to washing and we got considerable done

Tuesday, July 1st 1879   We started up another mountain
this morning and kept going up till 9 o clock and then turned
to go down and Soon afer we came to a ditch and a Sidling
place and while Geroge was crossing it his team turned and
his wagon went over and it went over So nice   turned up
hill   it did not take but few minues to Set it up and did not

breake eny thing but an iron on the break   after we got down
the mountain or part way we Stoped for diner in afternoon we
had very good rodes   at night we came to a very nice Stream
to camp on

Wednesday, July 2nd 1879   We Started down the Stream
this morning and came to a long Settlement along the river or
creak and Some found that we was off from our rode and
badly mixed up   we had to go down the Stream   we got
past the ford and had to turn back to the ford and acrost the
Sage brush for Sumara [Samaria, Idaho][17]   we got to Sumara
and turned west up the ditch   watered our teams   got
water to cook with and went up the mountain to find grass
we we found good grass but no water   Jennie is Sick to night

Thursday, July 3rd 1879   We had Splendid rode up the
mountain and then we came down to a ranch in a valey and we
are off from the Sublet rode[18]   now we camped clost to the
ranch and then they told us which rode to take   we had to go
acrost the Sage brush till we Struck a rode that led over to
Stone ranch where we camped   Jennie is very Sick to night
She cant eat   we got Some milk for hur at the ranch   theair
is young men living hear   Frank Frost wanted to sell him
his poney   they Said they would give him three ponies for
one of the girls   it apears theair haint meny girls

Friday 4th 1879   We Started up a rode that leads us to twin
Springs and the Sublet rode   we got Some water at the
Springs then on over the mountains and down through a
deep canion on to the head of Sublet creak we went down the
creak about one mile and camped   just before we camped we
had to cross a Small Stream and one of Mr Persells teams
came very near upsetting and we had to hold ours to keep

---

[17]This Mormon community was settled in 1868 and named for the biblical "Samaria."
Boone, *op. cit.*, p. 18.

[18]Sublett was a town located at the juncture of the Oregon Trail and the Sublett Cutoff
to California. Boone, *op. cit.*,, p. 363.

them from turning over   Jennie is no better   Frank traded his ponie from another and it throwed him and hurt his leg prety bad   this is the fourth of July   I have had so much to do I could not get time to write much for Nellie is having an awfull time with hur teath and Jennie is So Sick

Saturday, July 5th 1879   We went down Sublet creak about five miles and then out around a ranch through the meanest rode over ditches and then out over a flat about 12 miles long on to Raft creak [River] and camped for diner then on over an other flat and Struck the Kelton rode [Caldron Linn] and acrost another Stream and up on to a mountain to camp for the night   it was awfull late   most sundown   we met so many freight wagons and the Stage from Boisa [Boise]

Sunday, July 6th 1879   We passed on down the mts and through an awfull deep canion just wide enuff for our wagons and when came out we Struck a larg leavel plain and our rode Straight acrost it as far as we could See   we had dry camp for diner   Rhodes went on to Goose creak[19] and did not Stop for diner   we went on and had to turn off from the rode about one mile and when we got there who Should we find but Mr Taylors folks

Monday, July 7th 1879   We all Started out to gether   four other wagons besides and had to drive about 17 to water and fead and at night we camped clost to a Stage Station on a nice branch about one mile from rock creak   a Stage Station

Tuesday, July 8th 1879   We went down rock creak[20] about 10 miles or more   it is rock creak for Shure for it is deep cut

---

[19]Goose Creek was one of the oldest named localities in Idaho. Members of the Rocky Mountain Fur Company named it in 1832 for the vast numbers of geese that nested along its banks. A community post office was established in 1878. The town's name was later changed to Thatcher. Boone, *op. cit.*, p. 158.

[20]Rock Creek flows into the Snake River 3.5 miles northwest of present Twin Falls. The Rock Creek Station was established in 1865 by James Bascom. It was a favorite stopping place for travelers over the Oregon Trail because of its fine water. Boone, *op. cit.*, p. 319.

with rocks up each Side   we Stoped on it for diner clost to a large Station where we got water but no grass   in afternoon we went 20 miles or more   turned off from the Stage rode and down to the river then along the river down a Steap hill throught the Sand and Stoped on the river for the night   we did not get Stoped till after Sundown and then turned our horses up a canion where they got a little grass   it would of been better for us not to of turned of from the rode for we will come on to it in the morning   Jennie is some better So she Set up Some to night.

Wednesday, July 9th 1879   We drove a little ways and came on to the old rode and drove down the river to the fery which was Sevral miles   the Stage woke me just before day and we thought it was Mr Rhodes starting out for he was camped up the canion   we all crossed the fery and while we was crossing three other teams over took us   they had to wait yesterday on account of theair mules being Sick   it cost us 4½ dollars to cross Snake river   after we got acrost we went about one mile up on to the hill and camped on a nice Stream that run in to Snake river (it falls down the bluff a long ways)   we went out 11 miles more over rocks and Sands to the old diserted home Stage Station on the Malad²¹ Stream   it runs down an awfull deep rockey chasm and larg falls   we have very poor grass   we thought we was going to have good and we was going to lay over

Thursday, July 10th 1879   We are having awfull times this morning   one of our mules is Sick and the Break [brake] on our wagon is broke So we got Mr Percell to help and maid a new one   William got a piece of wood Tuesday to fit Charleys wagon   we got Started after 8 o clock   went about 10 miles

²¹There was a Malad range of mountains, a river, and later a town. The name was first applied to the river as "Riviere aux Malades" or "Sick River," because a party of trappers led by Alexander Ross became sick from eating spoiled meat. *Idaho Historical Department, 23rd Biennial Report, 1851-52*, Fritz Kramer, "Idaho Town Names," p. 81.

and came to good piece of grass and turned out for diner Percells Taylors and our family Stoped   Rhodes went on. the other four wagons did not Start out this morning   they could not find one Span of theair mules and Franks horses. our mule feels Some better to day noon   I did not cook diner to day   had plenty cooked   I must write to Mrs Leaming after diner we hitched up and went about 5 miles more and came to where Rhodes was camped   we hurried and got ready and done Some washing   it is very warm to night Frank found his Ponie and came in Soon after we Stoped for night and about Sick

Friday, July 11th 1879   We went 12 miles and camped at the foot of Kings hill[22] clost to a ranch   it is very warm   the Sun Shines so hot   I have quit cooking big diners   after diner We went up the hill and it is rightley named the kings of hills   after getting up the hill we had very good rodes crossed two Small Streams of water and went about 12 miles to an old Stage Station called cold Springs   theair is two houses   I done me Some bonets   Mrs Purcell Irond   we built a fier in the house   we all had a fine lot of young rabits   theair is a ranch clost by the name of Glen   he is acquaitned with Wm Buttler

Saturday, July 12th 1879   One of our mules came very near dying last night   he had his hind foot in the haulter   Noah Taylor found him   the mule was away ½ mile from camp William huried up theair   tried to cut the chain but could not so he cut the haulter off and it is so bad we will have to lay over till noon   I washed Some to day and after diner we drove on about ten miles   Struck the rode that came in from the middle ferrey and then on to a Stage Station and camped near a ranch that is fixed up the nicest I have Saw in

[22] King Hill was a town named for a hill that rises nearby that looks like a king's crown. Boone, *op. cit.*, p. 210.

Idaho   nice garden and flowers but the creakets is awfull bad   we camped by a Stone fort that was built to fight the Indians

[In margin:] Franks ponie got away this morning   he had to leave it and told Wm to get it if he could   he got it and is going to take it

Sunday, July 13th 1879   We had no grass last night and had to get hay for our horses at the ranch   we Started about 8 o clock and drove 10 miles to an other Station   got some more hay for our horses   ate our diner   we have not Seen eny of the other teams yet   I expect they have gon on to Boise city   we have Franks ponie   the girls ride it all the time   it is very gentell   We drove about 13 miles in after noon and Stoped on top of hill So we could get good grass in a holow   we are about ¾ from a Stage Station called Soles rest

Monday, July 14th 1879   We traviled about 16 miles to day and Stoped about noon near Black Station and layed over in afternoon for it is 16 miles more to Boise and our teams are tired and we cant get water till we get theair   it is very warm   I wrot Some cards to day and a letter to Mrs Leaming   Jennie and Nellie went down to Stage Station to See Mrs Black.   then She came out in eavening   She is quite prety girl and very good apering girl

Tuesday, July 15th 1879   We went on to Boise   we camped for diner at the mill just before we cross the river.   while we was stoped for diner William sold Frank ponie for 30 dollars and then we went on to town and got Some grain and Some mules Shod and then we went on through town and while we was Stoped theair was lady came out and talked with me   I got one letter from Hellen   this is very pretty place the pretyest I have Seen for Some time   we went out of town about two miles to where Percells was camped last night at a farm house where we could get hay and Stoped and Set our tent up in a yard under Some Shade trees   I have the Sick headache   Oscar was hear wating for us to come up and was going to get Franks ponie and go on

Wednesday, July 16th 1879   William had to go back to town this morning and get Some more mules Shod and got Some provisions   I was buisey fixing around the wagons and cooking Some   I always have So much to do when we Stop   we Started on and went about 8 miles and went down the river and camped for the night   had plenty water and wood but had to buy hay at one dollar a hundred   we are clost to Boise river   this is nice valey

Thursday, July 17th 1879   We left Boise river and went the Stage rode over the willow creak and watered at the Stage Station and went up to the Summit and camped for diner without water for our Stock   I took the bowell complaint and the newraligy to in my Stomach and was awfull sick after diner we went on over to the piett [Payette] river and down that about five miles and camped just before we came to the Store   we traviled about 28 miles to day

Friday, July 18th 1879   William is Sick this morning So we are going to Stop   I feel awfull bad   Mrs Taylor and the girls washed in fore noon   The Sun is terrible hot   theair is the most rabits hear I ever Saw   you can See a dozen or more at once   We are camped clost to the Piett river near the willows   when we are under them we can feel a mist falling all the time   I am glad to get our things fixed up once more

Saturday, July 19th 1879   We loaded up and Started on this morning but William is not able to drive or Set up eny   I have been giving him medison   I could not Sleep much last night and I am about worn out   to day at noon we camped on the Piett at the Fery   theair was three other teams came up behind us and camped   after diner we crossed the fery and went on over and Struck the Snake river and went down

that about 2 miles and came to grass and camped for the night
Snake river is very larg Stream hear   after Sun down theair
was quite wind Storm and blowed the Sand So bad I had to
put the fier out and every thing is full of Sand   I could not
cook nor fix eny thing   William is a little better

Sunday, July 20th 1879   We Started down the Snake river
Stoped to water   William not able to be up yet   9 o clock
we came to black Smith Shop and we Stoped to get Some
mule Shoes Set. Taylors went on till they find a place to camp
for noon   after we got our mules Shod we went on and over
took Taylors at a Spring   the rodes are very dusty   we went
on down the Snake past another Stage Station on the weazer
[Weiser] creek and a Store we got Some crackers at weazer
we was 70 miles from Baker City[23]   in after noon we went on
the bank of the river in a dug rode and camped for the night
clost to the river whare theair was Som dry grass and bluffs on
the other Side

Monday, July 21st 1879   We went on down to the fery on
Snake river and crossed over into Origon   theair was a
young man by the name of Rolen from Origon camped near
here last night   he took breakfast with us this morning   we
went up the mountain and then down to a Stage Station and
then Soon Struck burnt River and went up it over hills   it
Seams So Strange for we are going down hill So much and yet
we are going up Stream all the time but we dont travial on the
Stream all the time   we camped on Small Stream at night   I
feel awful discouredged to night

Tuesday 22 July 1879   We got Started by 7 o clock   traviled
few miles   came to Stage Station and Stoped to enquire and
found they had Some goose berries and currents So we got
out all of us and went in and picked 3 gal goose beries and 1 of

---

[23]What has been Baker, Oregon, for many years has just now been renamed Baker
City.

currents   got Some potatoes, turnips and beets   we then
went on and camped for diner on Burnt river clost to a quartz
mill   the children went to See it after diner   Charley Shot 2
large chickens   they are young ones and very nice   we are
having very good roads for crossing the mts   Some of the
way it is dug in the Side of mts away up   theair was Some
very high rocks   on one rock I saw the name of J.E.
Leaming   we pass ranches every little ways and Some nice
ones   we Stoped clost to one to camp and got our mules un
harnessed and he told us of a better place So we hitched up
again and went on over to it   just before night we passed the
Express ranch of W.E. Durkey[24]

Wednesday 23rd July 1879   We did not travil So very far
this fore noon   we did not Start till half past 7 o clock and
Stoped at half past 10 So as to get fead and watter for our
Stock   if we go to pleasant valey we cant get very much grass
on account of So much Stock theair   the Stage passed before
we started   we passed on in to pleasant valey   it is quite
nice valey on the head of Burnt river   as we come in to the
valey you can See mountains with Snow onthem   we Stoped
at Mr Grays ranch and got Some butter and milk   we then
left burnt river   went over a ridge for few miles and on to a
branch of powder river and camped in about 3 miles of Baker
City clost to a ranch   they had to take the mules a way up on
a hill about a mile   we had plenty milk for Supper

Thursday, July 24th 1879   We went on into Baker city and
got three Shoes Set on our mules and while theair we came up
with two other families that are going to Walla Walla   two
ladies came to the wagon and talked with me   they want to
hire a girl and came to See if theair was eny with us   we went

---

[24]The Durkee family was well known among Baker County settlers. The existing postoffice by that name was established in 1902. Lewis A. McArthur, *Oregon Geographic Names* (Portland, 1982), p. 239.

out of town five or Six miles and camped for diner   those
two familys are with us   they came from Kansas and Started
the 23 of April   we are on powder river and it is quite nice
valey and the Mountains to the South are covered with
timber and Snow on the tops   after diner we went on over to
north powder mills   we got off from the rode Some and had
to turn back which maid us Some later geting in to camp   we
went to the mill and got more feed and then went down below
the mill about one mile on to the river and camped on Some
nice grass near Sheap ranch

Friday, July 25th   We are laying over to day to let our teams
rest and we have such nice grass   it is where a man kept for a
meadow but gave it up   I washed little in after noon   I
went down to ranch little while   quite nice looking woman
theair   She is quite young and has Small baby   I am very
tired to night   plenty of mosketoes hear   we are on Powder
river   william went down to ranch   had a nice talk with Mr
Alexander V. McCarty   He tells him of good Sheep ranch
near La Grand[e]

Saturday, July 26th 1879   We Started down the river but
Soon left it and went on a little past Stage Stand and on over
and struck creak to camp on it   noon took the horses up
hill   after diner we went about 2 miles and came to a very
nice Spring   got Some water to drink and then folowed
down that hill   we Struck grand round [Grande Ronde]
valley   it is Such a Splendid valley such a growth of vegetation   We Soon came to Union city   it is quite a nice
place   we Stoped and bought Some grain and maid Some
inquiries about our road   good many came out to talk with
us and Seemed to think it strange we came all the way with
teams   we went on out of town and got Some potatoes at Mr
Beards   the woman gave me some beats   She was from
Missouri and was So glad to See me   She had notion to hug

me She Sais. We went out and camped at a mans house by
the name of Moris and took our teams around back of his
farm on the hills   I was over to house in the eavning and
helped hur do up hur dishes

Sunday, July 27th 1879   I went over to Mr Morises and got
Some milk and went down in the garden and got all the beries
I could eat   Jennie and Nellie went with me. Mrs M——
gave us a mess of fresh apples to cook   we went on acrost the
valey over to Summervill   did not stop long theair and
Started up the blue mts about 5 miles to Phillips creak and
camped in a canion for the night and took our mules up on
the hills   we have been traviling through the big pine timber
Since we came to the Mountains to day and we are right in
the timber since we came to the mountains   to day we are
right in the timber to night it Seems rather lonlay   to night
we are about 35 miles from Weston

Monday, July 28th 1879   We Started on our Journey and
Started up the mountains   theair was two teams passed us
before we Started   we have been going up hill all the fore
noon and Stoped to feed away up on the Mt among the big
pine trees   it has been a very nice Scenery to day but I could
not enjoy it much for I have the neuralgy in my face So
bad   I took cold Friday the day we stayed   We Stoped at
the tole gate all night and I had to walk the ground   I
Sufferd So much with my face and teeth

Tuesday, July 29th 1879   We Started very early this morning
we want to try and get to Leamings to night if possible   we
went down the mountain very fast for us this morning   went
down to the foot hills and bought Some hay fore noon and
camped for diner near a log church   after diner we went on
in to weston   it is a very nice Sight when you are coming
down in Sight of weston   we stoped theair and got Some feed
and Some flour   I Saw Mrs Beath theair that traviled with

us Some   from theair we went to centervill and on out to
Leamings and got theair after they had gon to bed   they was
very glad to See us   they were living in quite new country
Wednesday, July 30 1879   William went up to the mountains with Mr Leaming to See about geting house hear clost
by   I Stayed and had good visit with Mrs Leaming   theair
was another lady hear to Sew Some on machien   Mrs
McCone hear in evening awhile
Thursday, July 31st 1879   I have been terible Sick all the
fore noon with bowell complaint   William got home in
afternoon   George went to Weston and went to work on a
farm harvesting

EPILOGUE I

Notes on the "family journal" of William T. and Laura Wright

   The attached journal was written by my great-grandparents,
William T. Wright and his wife, Laura. In 1879 they and their
family went from near Carthage, Missouri, to Weston, Oregon,
about thirty miles south of Walla Walla, Washington.
   Their daughter, Jennie, who is often mentioned in the journal,
was my grandmother. I did know her. In fact, I spent three or
four days with her in her apartment in Seattle, Washington, in
1946 or 1947, when she was quite elderly, and I was a junior or
senior in high school.
   My recollection is that she said she was twelve years old at the
time of the journey, and she walked most of the way. When they
were crossing the Rocky Mountains, she caught Rocky Mountain
spotted fever and during the weeks she was sick she rode in one of
the wagons. She must have been a lively gal because she ran off
with the hired hand, a man named Berrry, and married him when
she was relatively young, 16 or 17. They went north to Lind,
Washington, which is north of Walla Walla and about 50 or 60

miles southwest of Spokane. They had five children and all except my father stayed in that area. The family farm is now run by my cousin, Jerry Branson.

So I was born with the last name of Berry, graduated from college and was married under that name and didn't change my last name to Wright until 1953, when my brother and I took my stepfather's name. It was pure coincidence that Wright was my great-grandmother's name, also.

Supposedly William Wright was prosperous for the area and the time. They only stayed in Weston, Oregon, two or three years and then moved to Freewater (now Milton-Freewater). According to family history he is the one who gave the land for the railroad depot so the trains would bring their line through the town of Freewater.

Among the comments I remember my grandmother making about the journey was that for the most part they traveled six days a week, and on Sunday they stopped to do the washing and bake bread. She said there were two major problems on the trail: The biggest was wood. There was absolutely no wood and precious little water. If it had not been for the railroad, they never could have made it because the railroad people provided wood and water. The second problem was not the Indians, as one might expect. The men had to stand guard every night against other white men trying to steal their livestock and especially the horses.

L.W. "Pat" Wright,
Phoenix, Arizona

EPILOGUE II

Obituary for William T. Wright. *Milton*, (Oregon) *Eagle*, March 13, 1903.

W.T. WRIGHT DEAD
A Well Known and Highly Respected Citizen Passes Away

Died, at his home in this city, early this (Friday) morning

W.T. Wright at the age of 73 years, 2 months and 6 days.
Death was due to pneumnoni contracted while on a recent
trip to his farm near Snake river.

W.T. Wright was an old resident of Milton, where he lived
for the past 20 years, and enjoyed the respect and esteem of
the entire community. He was successful in busines and has
been one of the most earnest workers in the upbuilding of the
city. His death will be a loss to the entire community. He
leaves a wife, son, Charles, and two daughters, Mrs. Nellie
Russell and Mrs. Ira W. [Jennie] Berry, to mourn for
husband and father.

Funeral services will be held from the Christian church at
2 o'clock p. m Saturday, March 11th, conducted by R.L.
Cartwright.

EPILOGUE III

Obituary for Laura Childers, formerly Laura Wright. *Milton*
(Oregon) *Eagle*, May 2, 1919

BODY OF MRS. CHILDERS LAID TO REST
FUNERAL SERVICES HELD MONDAY MORNING
AT CHRISTIAN CHURCH, MILTON
Crossed Plains by Mule Team in 1879 and located in
Walla Walla Valley in 1880

Funeral services for Mrs. T.I. Childers who passed away
Thursday of last week were held at the First Christian
church Monday Morning. Reverend Floyd A. Ross offici-
ating. The deceased was 75 years of age and was a member of
the Christian church for 58 years being a member of the local
church since its organization. Interment was in the local Odd
Fellows cemetery.

Mrs. Childers (nee Lattin) was born in Trumbull county Ohio, November 25, 1843, and was married to Wm Wright in 1861. To this union four children were born. Mr. and Mrs. Wright crossed the plains with mule team in 1879 and settled in the Walla Walla valley in 1880. Mr. Wright died in Milton in 1903. A few years later Mrs. Wright became the wife of T.L. Childers of Milton.

Those left to mourn the loss of a good mother and wife are T.L. Childers, the husband, Mrs. Nellie Kay of California, Mrs. Jennie Berry of Seattle, and C.A. Wright of California and a number of other relatives.

LUCY AND ALLISON ALLEN
Courtesy of Mrs. Tilly Fender, Hermosa Beach, CA

Minnesota to Montana, 1881

§ Lucy Clark Allen

INTRODUCTION

It was in the summer of 1881 that, according to Lucy Allen, she and her husband, Allison, began their long journey to Montana, after living several years in Osakis, Douglas County, in west central Minnesota. They had experienced several years of bad crops, and that brought them hard times. Lucy wrote on Monday, August 1, 1881, that the family was made up of 8 children, whom we list here:

Olive (Ollie)	age 15	Allison, Jr.	11
Asenath (Sena)	13	Lewis E.	10
Alice A. (Allie)	?	Leon (Lee)	6
Minnie E.	?	Clarke	1

Allison, Sr., was the father and husband on the journey. He and Lucy had been married on April 10, 1864. Lucy reminds her readers on October 30, 1881, that on that date she turned 37 years of age. Allison was 39, his birth date having been February 27, 1842.

One reason they were going to Helena was that Allison had a brother there who encouraged them to move to Helena.

After a year in Helena the Allen family moved on to Washington Territory. At first they settled in Spokane, then they moved to Half Moon Prairie, some fourteen miles north of that city. There they are supposed to have traded with the Indians for 160 acres of land. Allison built the first saw mill in that part of eastern Washington. He also farmed some.

Lucy Allen, our diarist, lived until August 31, 1909, when she died at age 67. The Certificate of Death of the Washington State

Board of Health declared that she died of "Diabetis—of long duration in all probability," and was in a coma for the last twenty hours.

The word about this precious diary came to us in a letter written by Mrs. Tilly Fender of Hermosa Beach, California. She told of having discovered among the papers of her late husband, Robert Fender, a diary written by his grandmother, Lucy Allen on a journey from Fargo, North Dakota, to Helena, Montana. She gladly sent us a photocopy of the diary and also a portrait of Lucy and Allison Allen and gladly gave us permission to publish the rare document.

FOREWORD TO LUCY ALLEN'S DIARY

The year of 1880 will long be remembered by myself and husband as one of the years of partial falure of the wheat crops in Minnesota—that is, the part of Minnesota in which we lived. Which was in Osakis, Douglas Co. This year of 1880, our crops (and in fact nearly all of our neighbors) hardly paid the expence of harvesting.[1]

And in fact, the two or three previous years were poor cropt and the farmers were becoming—what in western terms are called "hard up," my husband especially so, as our farm was small, and our family a large one. It was either "sell out," or become bankrupt entirely. We got the idea of going farther west. So in the fall of 1881, we sold "our little home" and in

---

[1] "The years immediately preceding and following 1880 mark a transition point in Minnesota's wheat trade. The center of wheat production shifted from the southwestern to the northwestern part of the state. The main outline of the railway system was completed. Two new primary markets, Minneapolis and Duluth, rose to prominence. The new-process milling, which developed in the state, made a change in the relative value of winter and spring wheat in favor of Minnesota, the great spring-wheat state." Henrietta M. Larson, *The Wheat Market and the Farmer in Minnesota, 1858-1900.* Columbia University Studies in History, Economics and Public Law (New York, 1926), pp. 118-120.

March, he and our oldest son, a lad 11 years old, took our two span of horses & waggons (leaving the rest of our family still in Osakis) and started for some of the big farms up west. They found work on a farm called the Richison farm, near Moorhead Minn. A very large farm, 25,000 acres. They worked there 14 days, and then sent for us. And May 25 we started, and went in the cars, to Fargo [North Dakota] where my husband met us at the depot. We staid in Fargo just nine weeks, my husband working in the meanwhile, with both teams. We made some very plesant acquaintances and a good many—as I believed—true friends. At least they were sorry to have us go. Fargo is situated on the west bank of the Red river of the north. The City of Fargo is a very pleasant busy place, and a great business center, for the surrounding states & Territory. There are in Fargo some of the largest business houses & Public buildings in the west. The surrounding country is very level, and looks beautifully covered with large fields of wheat and oats. And in places not cultivated, with grass and wild flowers, among which, is the wild rose.

Fourth of July in Fargo was one of the most pleasant we ever spent. The beautiful park, on the east side of Fargo, near the banks of the river, which was composed of noble cotton woods, made a cool shade, sheltering some thousand of people from the heat, and dust. There were parades, of the Fargo & Moorhead bands, a company of soldiers fire & hoock & ladder companys. And ever so many more. They all looked splendid, although not very joyous on account of the news of the shooting of Garfield.[2] Well I for one would like very much to live in Fargo and it was the same with the rest of the family, nothing but plesant remembrances of the place. When we started from there, all agreed to keep a diary, from the day we started, until we reach Helena the place where we

---

[2]President James A. Garfield was shot in the back on July 2, 1881, in the railway station in Washington, D.C. He died on September 19.

intended going from the time we sold out in Minn. But our
funds were not very great, though Allison always declared he
would go if he had to stop by the way and work. Allison has a
brother in Helena who he has not seen in 25 years, and
Helena is to be our destination. So here is my diary which will
not be very perfect in some parts as to wording but I tried to
keep faithful record of the principal places and the chief
events of our journey dated from Aug the first 1881.

Lucy J. and Allison Allen.

THE DIARY OF LUCY J. ALLEN

Monday, August 1, 1881.   All the fournoon we packed all
the goods we are to take with us. In the afternoon, quite a
number of our friends come to see us off, on our journey and
say goodbye, among whom were Mrs Duvall, her 3 daughters
& son, Mrs. Pray & Sister, and a number of others. At half
past 3 in the afternoon we started from fargo D.T. [Dakota
Territory] on our journey towards Helena M.T. [Montana
Territory] (hope we may have a safe and pleasant journey).
After 5 in the evening we came to Shianee [Sheyenne] River
crossed over on a long bridge and camped for the night near a
cornfield.   cooked our first meal which was supper, on the
camp fire.   looks something like a storm.   this will be our
first experience in sleeping in our canvass covered wagons.
Well they all seem to enjoy it.   there are quite a family of
us   My husband myself, 4 girls 4 boys, and a young fellow
we will call dick.   he has worked for Allison all the spring
and wanted to go with us to Montana.   he is quite handy,
drives one wagon. We go with 2 teams one carried the family
and the other luggage. There was an old bachelor who
intended going with us, but when we started he was no where
to be seen although his wagon was there.   perhaps he will
overtake us.

August 2.   Started from camp on Shianee river.   they tell
us we will cross it again at Vallie City.   last evening after
supper the bach[elor] came driving into camp   he was greatly
troubled as some one had stolen his gun & revolver.   did not
say much but wondered who could have taken them. Allison
tried to comfort him;   well this fournoon we have passed some
very nice farms and passed through a place called Mapleton,
about 10 oclock.   there saw the old Baches mules as he had
driven ahead, but did not see him. We will call him Conner
after this.   we reached a place called castleton [Casselton] at
3 oclock did not stop sooner on account of scarcety of
water.   cooked our dinner on farm No. 1 on what is called
the great Dalrymple farms   the RR passes through them.
were just breaking camp in order to go on a little further, and
if possible find a better camping ground when 2 men accosted
us, and asked to search our wagons, as Conner had had a
search warrant gotten to search us for the missing gun &
Revolver. Allison helped them to remove the things from the
wagons, but of course they did not find the missing articles.
but Dick owned a revolver looking something like the revolver
discribed in the warrant so they requested us to go on to the
village of Castletown, which was near, and wait there untill
they could telegraph back so as to be sure about it. We passed
up to the village, and waited there, about two hours, when
they came to Allison, and told him it was all right we could go
on and that they were sorry they had been obliged to bother
him, and wanted to *treat*.   but he thanked them and we went
on a little further & camped for the night on a farm run by a
man by the name of Rose, whom we had been acquainted with
in Fargo.   hope we have seen the last of Connor.

August 3.   During the night there came up a thunderstorm
and such raining I never saw before. The wagon covers were
new and therefore not properly stretched on the frames did
not shed the rain very well.   it was not long before we were

wet through, bedding and all.   it was of course impossible to sleep, and I could hear above the thunder and the torrent of rain on the cover, the voices of the girls singing to the tops of their voices, and they kept it up, they and the rain untill morning. When daylight came we drove our wagons up to the farm house and took shelter for the family. When the sun came up it stopped raining and of course we hung out our bedding and dried it so we could start in the afternoon.   here we began to meet grasshoppers, by the cloudsfull.   we traveled on and soon reached a place called wheatland. traveled 15 miles further and camped. the country is *very* beautiful around here.   slightly rolling Prerrie.

August 4.   this morning we started again over a rolling Prerrie (heretofore we have traveled over perfectly flat Prerie) in sight of the dakota Range, a succession of rolling hills.   the first villiage we passed was tower City a pleasant place with nice farms around with beautiful riponing wheat.   6 miles further we came to Carleton a station which will not amount to much. After passing through some very large farms some of whose buildings made a small villiage of their own, came to a place called Vallie City.   cming to which, about 2 or 3 miles east we went over our first real rough road.   the town is situated among the hills   it lookes like a little jem   the shinee [Sheyenne] R. running to one side and all bounded with beautiful trees and bushes. After that we had some quite high hills to climb and after those there were some more nice farms with cattle and sheep and ripening grain   the reapers at work.   then came some more level country with once in a while a knoll.   took the wrong road.   struck across the prerrie in search of the right one   camped on the railroad at 25 min. past 7 in the evening by the side of an alcholi lake the first alcholi water that we have tasted.   do not care about any more of it.   it is awfully nasty.

August 5.   This morning we broke up camp, drove through a hilly country west about three miles.   we came to a place called Sanborn then we traveled untill we went 25 miles and reached a place called Jamestown. Nothing of interest to write about. The country was verry hilly, and not good farming land (only a few places) grasshoppers very thick over the country, and doing great damage. Jamestown in situated in a high pleasant valley and very levil.   passed throught James-town, over Jim river, on a long shakey bridge.   left our bucket on the bridge, and climed a very high hill on the west side.   struck quite a smooth country   camped now, at about half past six, two miles from Jamestown today.   we heard there was an outfit ahead of us about a days drive.   we hear that they are going like us to Montana.   we are in hopes of overtaking them.

August 6.   passed this morning through large fields of flax. We started from camp at half past six in the morning.   passed over some hilly country, with occasional small valleys between, and atop the hills a long stretch of levil land but very poor & stony. We passed Eldridge station at nine minuits to eight. stopped at a nice farm near the station called the Fulton farm with 800 acres in wheat & oats, and 200 in Flax.   passed over the hilly land 8 miles to elton Station.   over took three teams belonging to a man by the name of hasett about noon.   camped for dinner.   made acquaintence with the people   they state that they are bound in the same direction and likely to join in company, and we are very glad indeed, as it seemed as if we were adrift and no other Ship in sight, and after getting in sight of covered wagons, we all set up a shout.   well here we are camped for noon, and they seem very pleasant peoole. They are Husband, wife, six children, and to men along as help, by the names of Wagoner and "Ben Burt."   so there will be quite a company of us. We are

camped tonight near a station called Midway. After being
settled for the night a young man came into camp, asking us if
we would honor them with our company for the evening.
seeing our wagons pass with ladies along, they telegraphed for
more ladies, as there was not a woman in 30 miles around
they had quite a company however. The girls went with thier
Father and they declared they never had a better time in thier
lives   had a real social dance and supper.

August 7.   today is the first Sunday out from fargo 7 days
out today, and I will spend the day or most of it in writing in
my diara.   this is a pleasant place to camp for Sunday. A
nice spring near by, and plenty of good grass for the horses. I
think we shall like our fellow travelers very much   we have
visited back and fourth and are getting well acquainted. And
now comes the most curious part of my report.   yesterday I
forgot to put in my diary Connor who had us searched for his
gun & revolver is with us.   he said he was sorry for the
trouble he put us to and so fourth.   he said he did not
think we (that is Allison) had it, but Edwards who lives in
fargo made him think Dick had it   Connor went back to
Fargo and searched around there and at last found them in
the possession of a tramp near the railroad then hurried and
overtook us, he seemed overjoyed to meet us again but we
cannot say the same of him. Today we washed some and it is
Sunday too.   but necessity etc. etc.   and I have also baked
some light bread which is quite a luxury after so nuch hot
bread called Flapjacks.   the way I bake light bread is this. I
have a large camp kettle, flat bottomed with a tight cover. I
put my dough in the kettle and set it by the fire to rise.   in
the meanwhile I have a hole dug in the ground, and build a
fire in it. When my dough is light, and the hole in the ground
is hot, I take the coals out, and put them in a pile at one side.
Then leaving a few small coals at the bottom of the pit, set the

kettle of bread on them, put the pan snugly in the top of the kettle, fill it with coals & hot ashes, then pile the rest of the hot ashes around the kettle in the pit and in an hour I can bake a large loaf. I have baked 7 or 8 such loves in a day, besides doing considerable else. I begin to enjoy this kind of life very much.

August 8.   Left Midway—it is called Midway, on account of its being midway between Fargo and Bismark—at half past six.   traveled some very hilly country.   reached Crystil [Crystal] springs about 9 oclock A.M. Crystil springs is a large boiling spring between hills—traveled on—after watering the horses, and filling the water kegs—over some levil but poor land.   and a great deal of hilly stony land.   we traveled 12 mis. and camped near 14th siding for night.

August 9.   Started from 14th siding, or (steele farm) 10 min to six. About the same lay of country as the day before, with once in several miles a large farm, with solid looking farm houses. I would not live on one of them if I could have a gift of them all.   they look so dreary & lonesome.   stopped about 10 at another station called 15th siding.   the only habitation we saw, after leaving camp this morning.   after this came the same dreary hilly country the soil very sandy in places.   saw our first cactus and sand burrs and an occasional small village of perarie dogs.   we are now camped for night near a farm and station called Clark.   it is almost desolated of every kind of vegitation by grasshoppers as are nearly all the farms this side of fargo.   this country will not amount to much as farming land on account of them.

August 10.   started from camp about 7 this evening. came to the outskirts of the town of Bismark as seen from the east side it looks like a pleasant place.   camped there until the afternoon. After dinner, came two miles to the west side of the town.   this side of the town does not look so pleasant.   we are now camped near the Missouri river.   it is the strangest stream I ever saw.   it seems composed of sand bars and a small amount of water   at night the river will be flowing next the bank near us.   and the next morning if the wind blows from shore, it will be flowing on the other shore with a sand bar between us and the river or sometimes sand bars divide it into two streams; today Allison and Hasset went to see what were the chances to cross the river   there is no bridge here   the only way of crossing is on a large transport or steamer which takes the cars on and ferries them to the other shore. And our only way to cross would be to hire cars and load our teams and waggons on them and then the boat take them over, then we would have to pay our way separate from the cars to cross over the familys which would cost us about 30 dollars.   that was 28 dollars more than we possessed.   then they went to see what the chances were to get passed to the end of the R.R. adn work out our passage when we got there.   the contractor told them if both men would work at Bismark a month they should have a pass to the end of the road. As this is our only chance they will work here of course.

August 11.   the men have fixed the camp here on the bank of the river and it is a dreary place   today they commenced work for the railroad they get $4 per day with their teams the water of the river is very riley, so we are bothered for water.   our two families make quite an encampment.

August 12.   today the men are at work, and we women try to wash a little and get the meals, but the wind blows hard and the sand flies in clouds.   no shelter but our waggon covers. it is verry difficult to do ennything and have it clean.

August 13.   got the meals as usual   try to sew and mend a little.   the men say that is hard working on account of the wind and flying sand.   the weather is verry warm, which adds much to the general discomfort

August 14.   get the meals as usual and bake bread, so uncomfortable here that we can scarcely live.

August 15.   got breakfast, and the men went to work again. we baked bread in the forenoon; they have found out that there is a negro saloon near our camp, much to our disgust. numbers of half drunken negroes and steamboat men are continually passing.   the steamboat landing is on the other side of our camp so it seems we are camped between two fires. Alice has been quite sick for a few days which makes it more unpleasant.

August 16.   today has been the first still day, and it has been verry warm.   the negroes made last night hideous with their yelling, and with firing an occational shot.   that and the barking of our dogs who do not like our surroundings enny better than ourselves, made a dismal night of it and of course we did not get much rest.

August 17.   quite a pleasant day today   cooked the meals and try to eat in the dirt and sunshine.

August 18.   Alice is much better which makes my heart much lighter. A couple of steamboats landed near today, loaded with indians and soldiers.   there are a camp of indians between us and town   today has been quite warm.

August 19.   the girls took a ride across the river to Mandan on the boat that takes the cars[1] over.   three of them went on the trip.   they had a pleasant time.

August 20.   during the night the negroes made it livlier than usual with firing at each other and yelling.   several bullets passed over the waggons.   the men will move us from this place as we are in danger here of getting killed.   they were too drunk to hit each other but were in danger of hitting some one else.   two drunken men came into our camp this

---

[1]"Taking the cars" was the language used in those days for "taking the train."

evening but were quickly marched out by our men.   our men will hunt us up a more pleasant place if possible nearer their work, ennywhere will seem better than this place.

August 21.   today we broke up our camp, by picking up and loading our effects and loading them on our waggons, and moved half a mile the other side of the saloon, and near the mens work.   think this place will be some better than the other   it is more quiet.

August 22.   got the meals and made an awning from a small tent to eat our meals under from the terrible heat of the sun.   one of Allys horses had a bad tumble down a verry steep long bank.   did not hurt him much but was shaken pretty bad.

August 23.   Allison used Connors mules   his horse is quite lame   Connors team was not in use as he had hurt his ankle.   the men joke him about the manner of his getting hurt and tell him that he undertook to carry away a plow.   the way was this: the plow was verry large, one used in gradeing on the R.R. the largest Connors ever saw it was turned bottom upwards, and as he stood looking at it it fell over, hitting him on the ankle. At first they thought his ankel broken but it is only badly bruised, and verry painful.

August 24.   Connors ankle is swolen verry badly; it has been a verry uncomfortable day here today   the wind blown hard all day and the way sand flew was awful.   no trees no grass even it is the most desolate country I ever saw

August 25.   nothing of importance occured today nothing but the same wind and dust   some of the children went up the river a way, some two or three miles and found a small grove near the river   in the grove they found some ripe grapes which after being cooked and sweetened made quite nice sauce.   we are all in a great hurry to leave here.   the work is verry wearing on our horses.

August 26.   this morning Allison tole me to bake a good lot
of bread and cook such provision as could be taken that way,
as the contractor told them he would give us passes to go on
the morrow.   we are greatly rejoiced at the news.   have
been verry busy all day.   will go tomorrow if we can secure
empty cars.

August 27.   last evening Hasset Allison ben and Wagner
went into town to see if they could get an empty car.   they
succeeded in securing two so early this morning we commenced packing our goods on our waggons and moved to
where the cars were   one car they packed the waggons in
which they had to take to pieces.   the other they have
packed the horses.   all day long until nearly night it took
them, and they all worked hard.   well after we had everything
in and ate our supper we all went to the depot to wait until
they were ready to put us across the river.   we had to wait
there three or four hours (after buying some provision Allison
has only a dollar and half to bless himself with) provisions are
verry high here.   well Allison is resolute and says he will go
through.   well here we are across the river at last in the
depot at Mandan, a village across the river from Bismark.
after coming here we found the cars would not go on until
morning. Well what are we to do   we expected to have kept
on the cars on our journey, but instead we will have to stay in
this place until morning with not money enough to stay at a
hotel, and we cannot stay at the depot. Allison and Hassett
said they would look around; (they have just come in and
said, pick up and come but I don't know where so I will have
to stop for tonight. . .

in the evening of the 28,   we boarded the train about 12
oclock noon and started toward the far famed Badlands:[2] this

[2]The badlands is an area in western Dakotas about twenty miles wide and some 200
miles long north and south. The land had been cut up by stream erosion into fantastic
buttes and canyons.

afternoon we passed over some pleasant country and also,
some verry hilly country, some verry high buttes and then
some level land.   then would come a solitary Railway station,
but we did not reach the regular badlands until night   the
conductor said he dreaded going down into them as the first
20 miles was a continual down grade, and it was raining hard
and verry dark with thunder and lightning.   the girls all
stood on the back platform of the cars all the way down so as
to see all that was to be seen. I had the little ones to sleep and
sat by the open window   the lightning lit up the scene
occasionally but I could catch a sight of nothing but buttes
and huge boulders which looked as we flew along black as ink,
and pools of watter like little lakes, which as the lightning
played over the scene looked black as the hills in places   it
seemed as if we were going through places just wide enough
for the train to pass through. The black walls toward high up
above us, so that the din and noise of the cars was perfectly
deafening. The screeching of the brakes (as they were all put
on) and clanking and roar of the wheels, on the rails; and the
rails were laid on rock all combined with the occasional
thunder claps and lightning flashes, made the scene ennything
but pleasant. Often the wheels as I looked from the window
would blaze owing to the friction. Well I cannot describe as it
ought to be, the grandeur and terror of that ride. I can never
forget it and I would not like to take it over again.   the girls
said they enjoyed it that it was grand & all that (ugh.)   to me
it seemed like descriptions I have read of the regions of uttter
darkness, only our darkness was lit occasionally by lightning.
Well here we are tonight spending the balance of the night in
the heart of the badlands.   it is about midnight, the blankets
spread on the railroad boarding house floor   it is a new
house and not yet finished, and the workmen on the road
board here: the cars are not to go on further tonight so we will

try to get a little rest before starting again in the morning.
August 29.   this morning we boarded the cars again about 7
oclock and came the rest of the way, through the badlands.
it was more pleasant by day they tell us   we came over the
worst of the road last   it was grand today, high buttes in all
shapes   some places looking like a grove of stubs of verry
large trees and lower stumps of trees.   in two or three places
we saw where the coal in the buttes were on fire probly set by
some passing enjine.   toward noon we came into quite an open
country the buttes being farther from the R.R.   sometime
we would pass by what resembled a huge castle in ruins. A
great menny of the buttes looked like verry large long hay-
stacks, several close together, and others look like round
stacks with quite a sharp peak, and others looked like the
peak had been cut smoothe off leaving a flat top—others
looked like someone had commenced a verry large square
tower and when half built half of it had slid in a slanting way,
leaving a half tower with one side higher than the other and
verry sharp. Oh well it is almost impossible to describe it all,
and how useless for me to try with my feble pen.   near noon
or perhaps it was just noon, as we cannot tell exactly, our
watches all were run down   we reached Glendive [Montana]
near the yellowstone [River]. So now we are in the yellowstone
country. When we got out of the cars at Glendive they said
we could not go on to the end of the cars or road rather until
three hours.   so we went into the depot to wait.   upon
going into the depot we found it serving to double duty of
depot and church. A couple of ministers were holding forth
and were there for the purpose of organizing a sunday school
at that place! We had no other place to stay from the hot sun
so our families bundled in babies and all.   the ministers
seemed pleased at so large an addition to their congregation.
So we sat on boards laid on boxes for seats, and joind in the

singing the gospel songs so often sung in far distant Minnesota songs such as hold the fort and several other peices eaqually as familiar and so it seemed good to be there; so now we are really in Montana and in the regeon of the yellowstone river   they tell us we will follow the Yellowstone for a great share of our journey. (oh but we are a great way from our destination yet)   Glendive is a pretty bad place at present, like all border towns full of saloons and ruffians there is not a s[h]ingled house here, all canvas roof and a great many places are entirely built of canvas.   this place is small now but they have great expectations of the future.   in about three hours we boarded the cars again for the end of the track which we reached about four in the evening.   here the cars that were loaded with our companys horses and goods, were switched off on a side track for us to unload. We could unload our waggons and other thing all but the horses who, poor beasts had been cramped up in a standing position, crowded together as tight as possible, for two days and three nights.   the only way they could devise was to lash three or [four] telegraph poles (that were lying near) together with ropes, and rest one end of them on the ground the other on the car, thus they led them one by one down to the ground   poor creatures they were verry tired   I never saw horses so glad to roll and shake themselves. After they all had been cared for the men began to unload the goods. This place is verry pleasant, quite a stretch of level perarie and would make nice farms. In the distance the buttes of the badlands look blue and hazy.   the sun is getting low and supper must be had so I must put up my writing for tonight.

August the 30th near the R R   last night we did not get our waggons together although they got the goods unloaded, so we took possession of the empty car and made our beds in it.   in the night an enjine backed the car we were in (with some flat cars attached) some 20 rods away from our camp. I did not know but they were going to run away from us at first.   it frightened Lee pretty badly. He made the night musical for awhile but I soon quieted him after awhile! Well this morning the men commenced putting together the wag-gons and loading them.   one of our horses is quite sick. think it must have hurt her rideing on the cars.   poor old Nel! hope she will soon be better; and one of Hassetts horses has cut his ankle pretty badly with his picket rope. This afternoon the girls with Ben Dick and Allison went horseback after some plumgrapes and choke cherries. Allison and two of the men are sick (Allison quick sick)   I do hope he will be better soon, so far away from civilization, it is terrible dis-couraging. Nell is no better tonight.   it is quite cold tonight and looks like a storm. I have tried to bake a lot of bread for our onward journey.   also have picked our things together so as to get them under cover at a moments notice.   it is thundering now.   our bedding is under shelter of our wagon covers.   here it comes the rain and the little ones are crowding in the waggons so as to be out of the storm. Some of Hassetts goods are out yet they will get wet, it hails quite hard.

August 31.   last night we had a terrible storm.   some of the bedding got wet, but we managed to pull through the night. two of the men who went hunting yesterday afternoon came back about dark thoroughly drenched and with no game. they had been told that game was plenty near the hills but they found none; this forenoon finished packing the waggons and about 10:00 started again on our journey toward yellow-stone valley. After going a mile and half we forded a verry swift stream called cedar creek   it was a muddy stream and and a verry rocky bottom.   from there we traveled some verry hilly country.   today we saw antelope: dick tried to shoot some but could not get near enough.   the girls gathered

some plums, near a ravine.   at the head of the ravine was a
nice spring of cold watter.   from there we climbed some very
high sandy hills.   after climbing those we passed over quite a
stretch of level land, then decended more hills and climbed
menny more until about half past six in the evening.   we are
now camped in a small valley   we found here plenty of grass
for the horses, and also water.   it is a beautiful spot where we
are now camped.   beyond us we can see the yellowstone
winding along close to the high buttes which here in places
rise in a perfectly perpendicular line from the waters edge, on
the oposite bank.   the little valley we are now camped in is
situated between high buttes, and is just large enough to
make a small farm.   twould be a pleasant place to live if one
could have neighbors, but there is no human habitation for a
great menny miles from here.

September the 1, 1881.   it is just one month today since we
left Fargo   this morning we broke camp about nine oclock,
traveled until nearly noon   came to a creek, or small river
called the Glendyve [probably O'Fallon Creek].   the watter
is so high from the recent rains that we cannot ford it.   there
are a great menny freighters waiting here for it to go down.
we will have to spend the night here.

September 2.   today has been quite plesant and warm, some
of the freighters have struggled through so we thought we
would do likewise.   cannot afford to stop long in place as
provisions will fall short. We now encamped in the Vallie of
the Yellowstone   on one side of us is the Vallie and River,
and on the other are some very high Buttes   the girls have
climbed to the top of the highest, we have formed a circle with
our waggons, at one side is the huge campfire from which we
all cook.   it looks quite cheerful, the girls have come back,
and report the view of the vallie and River from the top of the
butte as seen under the rays of the setting sun; it looked very
pretty.

September 3.   This morning we forded the powder river
the water is very muddy but we all crossed in safty only up to
the horses belleys.   passed over some beautiful country,
then climbed some very high hills, some of them we had to
double the teams.

September 4.   Today pass some more beautiful country,
climbed some tall hills. We had to pay toll, had to double the
teams, on both wagons and when we were up we *were* up, I
can tell you among the clouds. Oh! it is terrible these
hills.   have another long pull. Camped tonight near Miles
City in a dreary spot   near by on a knoll, are a couple of lonely
graves,   have seen some very large herdes of cattle today.

September 5.   This morning about nine oclock we started
on through Miles City, stopped awhile in town (Saw some
one there Allison knew) then crossed tongue river which
flows near the town.   it is a clear swift stream, its banks are
lined with large cottonwood trees. We then crossed some
beautiful level country, six miles of it.   passed Fort Kehow.[3]
here we crossed the Yellowstone on a rope ferry, or rather a
flat boat propelled by putting on ropes, stretched across.   it
cost a dollar a team to cross.   we are now on the north side
of the River.   we passed a flock of 300 sheep, waiting to be
ferried across.   here we had to climb some very steep and
high buttes, met some Indians, of whom we bought some
buffalo meat. The first we have had.   they tell us there are a
great many Indians ahead in the country we have to cross.
we came over some more levil country, then more hills.   the
scenery was very beautiful here.   came along the banks of
the yellowstone   passed over some beautiful natural meadows, where the herders had been herding their sheep. The

---

[3] Fort Keogh was located on the southeast bank of the Yellowstone River in eastern
Montana. It was built in 1876. It was designated by this name in 1878. It was named for
Captain Myles W. Keogh who had been killed in the Battle of the Little Big Horn on
June 25, 1876. Robert W. Frazer, *Forts of the West* (Norman, Oklahoma, 1965), p. 82.

meadows were as levil as though rolled with a roller.   tonight are camped in a beautiful grove of cottonwood, on the river bank.   there is abundance of grass for the horses.

September 6.   Today is a very pleasant warm day, which seems so nice after the last few cool ones. Some of the men think this will be a good chance to rest the horses; and they go hunting buffalo, as this is such a good camping ground Allison and Hassett, also Dick start out.   the first time Allie & Hasett have tried to hunt. They may be gone three or four days.   today I will bake bread as it is early morning and the girls will do some washing. Tonight is a beautiful moon-light night and the girls and boys are making the woods ring with their shouts playing hide and goseek.

September 7.   Passed a quiet night last night.   it is bright and clear this morning, will be a warm day. What a pleasant spot this is, I dont wonder the Indians loved it, I believe if it was near inhabitants *I* would like to live here, but it is so wild and uncivilized.   the girls are having a glorious time romping about.

September 8.   Last night about midnight as they were all assembled around the campfire singing and telling riddles, the men came home tired and uncessful.   the Indians have driven them so far back that it is useless to try for anything traveled untill they found it useless, then returned.   so this morning we broke camp again, do not know as we will go far as our Nell horse is sick, she seemed sick last night   is stiff all over, and can scarcely walk.

September 9.   Today we have come rather slowly on our journey   the day has been very warm and dusty.   passed over a toll road   there [are] a great many of them in this country on account of the bad hills.   some man will fix a passable road over or around a bad Butte then build himself a cabin at the foot, then charge travelers from 50 cts. to $1.00 to

pass over it.   they get rich in this way. We came to the river
about 4 oclock and camped for the night.   our horses are
tired, poor old Nell, if we should lose her it will be a great loss
to us, as we are unable to replace her,   some of the men have
gone to hunt rabbits.   they came to a ranch who had a
yearling buffalo.   the men bought him, killed him and
instead of rabbits it is buffalo, and it is handy, as all hands are
out of meat.

September 10.   Started on our journey again this morning.
during last night it commenced to rain and through the day
we have had occasional showers, it was a windy, cold and
dismal day altogether.   with the sickness of our horse, it
makes a person feel rather blue. We camp tonight in a
beautiful grove, in the centre is a clear spot, and all around are
tall cottonwood trees, and underneath is a perfect mass of rose
bushes, their red buds, or seeds, look like red berries.   they
must have been a lovely sight when in bloom   the country so
far has splendid scenery and all that, but is unfit for homes.
it looks rather dubious at present about our getting to our
journey's end on account of our horse's sickness.   there are
5800 sheep near us.   they are going to drive them eastward,
also 7000 cattle.

September 11.   We have come about 13 miles today, and
will camp here over sunday.   there is an Indian encampment
about a mile from us with 250 lodges.   we met large numbers
of them today, all mounted on nice fat poneis.   they need
not call them poor Indians   they are better provided for
than most poor white men.   we are camped near the Yellowstone. We met another drove of cattle.   another horse came
near tiring out (Old Bill, though not very old). the reason for
our camping so early. Allie spent his last penny for a box of
crackers, price 25 cts. We are 50 miles west of Miles City.
Some Indians have just come into camp, *the horrid beggers.*

Sunday 12. The day is drawing to a close, been a sunny warm day. I baked bread   had good luck. An Indian came into camp this morning quite early.   the men thought they would play a trick on him to get rid of him. The Indians are terribly afraid of sickness, and especially small pox, which is sure death to them. Ben hadent got up yet.   he pretended to be sick and the rest stood around pretending great sympathy and giving him water from a cup. The Indian kept at a distance, and leaned over on his horse and looked at him a while then said *ugh* small pox and left a streak of dust behind him. The buffalo gnats are terrible thick, I shall have to close and get ready for night   the sun is sinking behind castle butte. Today one of the men killed a rattlesnake, gathered lots of Buffalo Berries today. they are very nice. They are quite plenty in this country. Nelly horse no better.

Monday 13. Another days journey nearer the setting sun. Oh! what a lonely drear feeling comes over a person when they think how far they have drifted away from familiar scenes and loved ones, and are all alone in a strang new country. Traveled today about 18 miles, went slow on account of Nell, hate to leave her as she is much a favorite.   we hope she will get better. We traveled a hard hilly road today. About 3 oclock we struck the river.   we do not travel on it all the time but the road generally strikes it about noon and night there there were 30 lodges where we came near it today, with about one thousand ponies grazing near on the hillsides, and in the small valleys. We are camped tonight in a small valley and trying to cook some supper over a sage brush fire; one of the men of our company shot some sage hens.   they are larger than perarie chickens. Oh for some vegetables. They are hard to find in this regeon.   the night is setting in quite cool.

September 14th. We spent last night quite comfortably in

the valley, although the Indian dogs and kyotes made considerable noise during the latter part of the night.   last night
there was a fine display of northern lights. Owing to the
scarcity of water in the valley, we commenced our journey
verry early in the morning, the first thing we climbed a verry
long and tedious rainge of hills and just as we made the top of
the last long hill the sun came over the tops of the distant
buttes and valleys, and making a grand and beautiful scene.
We rested the horses and enjoyed the view quite a spell.
about 10 in the forenoon, we came to the river in a valley
called Peas Bottom.[4]   distance from our last nights camp
about 12 miles. We came down to the valley down the
awfullest steep hill I ever went down   the horses in places
slid down on their haunches.   here we found the largest belt
of timber along the river we have seen on our journey. This
valley is from a mile and half to 3 miles wide. We are camped
tonight one mile from terrys landing. We are on a small Island
surrounded by a broad shallow creek which we forded to get
here. Allison traded poor Nelly horse today, to a ranchman,
for a stout kyuse horse, he is small but tough and well and old
Nell can travel no farther.   the ranch man thinks if he turns
her loose in a good pasture she will get well. Well good dear
old Nell we hated to part with you for you have been a faithful
friend in pleasant and likewise in stormy weather and we shed
a tear at parting. Allison priced the grain here   oats are 60
cts per bushel   they pay 7 cts per bushel for threshing.
Onions are 10 per pound, verry small ones at that.   potatoes
are 5 cts per pound.   wheat 7 cts.
September 15.   today being sunday we concluded to rest on

[4]Fort Peas was a trading post for furs of all kinds established near the mouth of the
Bighorn. The trade was mainly with the Crow Indians. The post was named for Major
F.D. Pease. Mark H. Brown, *The Plainsmen of the Yellowstone* (Lincoln, Nebraska,
1961), pp. 220-221.

this Island, until tomorrow   two of the men went hunting
today about dark one of them came into camp with a fine
black tail deer which he had shot   the other man has not in
yet. I baked bread today and the girls did some washing and
this afternoon they gathered some wild grapes which grow
near in great plenty.   tonight they are invited to a social
gathering at a familys by name of Green   the people around
here are anxious for us to settle here but there are too menny
Indians for me   I dont think I would like them as neighbors.
September 16.   well this morning we commenced climbing
the everlasting hills again   we left the valley about 9 in the
morning   passed today several cattle ranches.   the houses
are low dirt covered structures with floors to match   it is
owing to the scarcity of lumber and shingles that makes them
build their houses so. Some of the people are verry wealthy in
cattle & horses. The road has been a hard one today owing to
the deep sharp pitches in them caused by the action of storms
and water at some distant time. We crossed the ferry at Terrys
landing a little before noon, to the south side again.   they
charged 2 dols a team   on this side of the river it has been some
pleasanter, but before comeing to the river we passed some
beautiful sandstone cliffs that looked as if hewn smoothe.
they were in places near 5000 feet perpendicular.   at the
ferry we met ready to cross about 6 or 8000 indians oh what
an immense herd of moving living men women papooses,
dogs, ponies and filth   oh! ugh! augh! terrible, awful,   we
are now on the indian reservation.
September 17.   We have come over some verry hard road up
hill and downhill, until afternoon and then we reached the
river again   we have come over some terrible steep high hills
today   they tell us there is worse ahead of us. This afternoon
we have come over a better country. We are camped tonight
(that is Allison and I dick and my children) in a beautiful

grove near the river   the other teams that [were] with us are gone further on   they think of going up the Judith Basin near by us is an immense rock about five acres square.   it is a great natural curiosity.   it is called Pompeys pillar.[5]   it is perfectly square and quite perpendicular on all sides and is 500 feet high, stands about 50 feet from the river bank.   there it stands all alone in its glory no other rock or hill near.   it is formed of hard sandstone. We have camped early on account of our hard days drive.

September 18.   this morning we were all quite well rested have spent a quiet night   the horses seem well rested too they had good pasturage   we drove 25 miles today over verry good roads. Then we came to another ferry, and here we overtook Hasset again. We crossed the Yellow Stone river, and are now off the reservation, and I am very glad of it too, as I dont fancy the Indians.   there are so many bad looking scamps among them.

September 19.   Today is sunday again.   we are resting, not far from the river, plenty of wood water, & grass.   last night we ate the last bread we had and the men have to go for more.   they rode to a ranchman, and hired out to him for a few days, thrashing.   he let Allison have some flour & potatoes.   as we have some venison left, we are getting along nicely. We will move our camp this afternoon, near his house which is 3 miles from here. We are to move so as to be near the work.   the place is called Huntly where we crossed the river.

September 20.   Well here we are near the Ranchman's house.   this place is the battlefield of General Baker, where

[5]Pompey's Pillar is an isolated mount 200 feet high, located on the south bank of the Yellowstone River. It was named by William Clark of the Lewis and Clark expedition on July 25, 1806. He gave it this name in honor of little Pomp, the child of Sacajawea and Charbonneau. Clark carved his own name on the rock. *American Guide Series, Montana* (New York, 1949), p. 193.

he fought the Indians in 74.[6] Today has been a nice warm day, lovely Indian summer, large numbers of Indians have visited the ranche today.

September 21.   The thrashing machine hasent come yet. Today has been equally as beautiful as yesterday. have spent the day in sewing and getting the meals. I hope the weather will continue to be as pleasant as it has been lately. The Yellow Stone people are kind hospitable people. The thrashing machine will be here in the morning

September 22.   Another beautiful day. The thrashing machine came at noon, and they have thrashed some. Every man has to pack his own bed. The family's name is Reed and consists of Mr. Mrs. 2 daughters and some young men.

September 23.   Still continue to have pleasant weather. The thrashing is nearly done, and if nothing happens we will be able to start on our journey again tomorrow.

September 24.   Today about 2 oclock we started from the rancho and traveled over a very steep hilly road.   passed a small villiage called Coulson.   came to the River about 5 oclock, and are camped now, in a beautiful cottonwood grove, where there is plenty of forage for our horses. We have come today about 10 miles   the place or rather valley we are camped is called Clarks fork.[7]   this is the largest valley we have traveled on the yellowstone   the widest part of the valley is 15 miles to forty long.   it is a pleasant looking valley with some nice looking ranches.   spent a pleasant evening and night at this place.

September 25.   Today we have come through a pleasant

_____

[6]Major E.M. Baker was in command at Fort Ellis, a minor post in the Yellowstone Valley. There was an attack by Sioux and Cheyennes on his post, and the men were playing poker, so it was dubbed the "Battle of Poker Flat." The major, himself, is said to have been drunk during the battle. This affair is well described by Mark H. Brown, *op. cit.*, pp. 196-201.

[7]Of the Yellowstone River.

country.   passed some nice ranches and climbed some steep
hills. Have come in sight of the snow capped moutnains.   the
wind has blown rather hard and the dust has flew in our faces
all the forenoon. About noon we stopped at a bachelors hut
and cooked our dinner   tonight we are stopping in an empty
hut near the river.   it is quite cold and we have built a huge
fire in the stone fire place which is quite pleasant.

September 26.   today has been quite cold and windy with
occasional showers of rain and sleet   we have climbed more
[hills?] and came down another about a mile long.   and in
places very steep then we came to the yellowstone again and
another valley. Along this place there [are] occasional small
islands in the river covered to the waters edge with cotton-
woods. We are camped in a natural meadow near the base of
the long hill that we came down.   it is verry cold and frosty,
rather a disagreeable night for camping.

September 27.   Started from camp on the meadow this
morning, verry cold and windy. I thought we had climbed
high hills and went down them but oh when you got among
the clouds then a person can call that high and the poor
horses show it too. They cannot hold out at this rate long. In
the forenoon it was nice roads, but directly after dinner we
commenced to climb the buttes. Oh the sharp pitches, now
up then down had to lock all the wheels in places going down
then all hand walk going up to lighten the load, with one
behind each waggon with a good sized stone to block the
wheels, when we had to let the horses stop to rest,   poor
horses they had to pull terrible. Altogether it has been hard
for man and beast. One redeeming quality the roads had this
afternoon was there were no ruts in the road.   they were
smooth but long and steep both up and down. Montana is
rightly continual mount and valleys between.   these hills
have nice pine timber on them   there is splended views in

this territory. When you have climbed some high butte the view well repays the labor of climbing.   well tonight we are camped in a small vale among the everlasting hills. the poor horses they are nearly done out. We are near a stage station on a creek called white beaver.

September 28.   started from white beaver creek quite late on account of the horses straying so far during the night.   it froze quite hard during the night   ice formed on the stillest part of the creek.   forded the creek at two other places during the forenoon and afterward climbed hills the rest of the day   we are camped now late in the afternoon near clear spring station 80 miles from Bozeman.   the horses are nearly played out and ourselves too. We have a good view here of the snow covered mountains and before we get to bozeman we have to cross a renge of the mountains.

September 29.   today we started early in the morning to a place called sweet grass a small valley through runs a creek full of nice trout   here they (our men folks) met a man at a small store, whose name is Harrison who told them that himself and brother wanted to hire an irrigating ditch cut wider and that he and brother would pay well to get the work done and likewise he had a large pasture and abundance of grass in it.   we could let our horses run in it a few weeks and as the horses are of the first consideration (being almost used up) and we are also entirely out of funds and provisions the men conclude to stop awhile.   so here we are camped in a pleasant grove near Mr. Harrison's house.

September 30.   Today Allison has taken Harrisons horses and gone to Bozeman to get provisions before commencing work. Bozeman is 75 miles from here.   it is quite cold with every sign of storm.

October 1.   last night snowed some but long before noon the snow was melted away.   the distant mountains are white

though and look cold in the afternoon sun   rather disagreeable and sloppy.

October 2.   rained last night.   about 10 Allison came back.
One of the horses he took came home during the night from
where he had camped for night.   he took another horse and
started back again to where he had left the other horse and
waggon and will now continue his journey to bozeman if
nothing further prevents.

October 3.   Today was quite pleasant and the girls did some
washing. Harrison Ron and dick have gone hunting near
some mountains called the Crazys.   there is plenty of game
so Harrison tells us.   we are alone in camp and waiting
anxiously for Allison to come back from Bozeman.   it is
verry lonely here in a strange place without him.

October 4.   The hunters have returned from their hunt
brought home a fine bear of a specie called silver tip, also
Allison came back from his trip   made quick time

October 5.   rained again last night.   the men commenced
work on the ditch.   the horses have good pastureage, and
they hope they will gain some strength by the rest, also flesh
as they are verry poor. They have need of it to climb over the
bozeman range when we start on again. I baked bread in Mrs.
Hs stove which seemed nicer than baking by the camp fire.

October 6.   today has been verry pleasant   Alice with Mr
& Mrs Harrison went trout fishing.   they brought home
some of the largest and best trout I ever ate.   they are
different than our brook trout in Wis. & Minn. having black
spots. Olive got the meals for the men.

October 7.   last night it stormed and rained all night   toward morning, a messinger came to Mr. H. with a note from a
man who lives two miles from here, telling him that some 17
head of his horses (Harison has a good number of them) was
in a pasture belonging to John Webb. Harrison thought that

verry strange as he and brother had been down to the pasture
a day or two before and found them all right also our horses
were with them. Harrison brothers farms join, and their stock
run together also a neighbors four head of horses, named
Laroche. There were some 2000 worth of horses altogether
(after receiving this news he posted down to his brothers and
they went together to the big pasture.   they found only four
head of horses left in the pasture, that had come back or
rather escaped in the storm and darkness of the previous
night, for they found the further bars to the pasture let down
and the horses gone.   they say it is the work of indians.
Harrison brothers, and a neighbor started on the trail of the
redskins and horses, breathing vengance dire upon the mar-
auders if they should come up with them: we heard in a day or
two that they the Hs. were joined by several of cowboys who
are a tough set of men to deal with, and All. H. is an indian
scout used to their ways.   they will show the thieves no
mercy if they find them.   this morning another of our horses
and three of Hs came back to the ranch.   got away during
the night from their captors, and near noon a man came
leading back another of Allisons horses.   he had dropped
behind during the previous night being unable to keep up
with the rest, so we have ours all back but one.

October 8.   Today is a warm pleasant day.   four more of H.
horses came home during last night broke from Hoffs pasture
where the 17 head were when H. got the news.   there is
great excitement about this afair as they are quite sure it is the
work of indians and they fear a raid on the flocks in other
parts   it seems the indians have stolen Horses in this section
and the adjoining country a year or two before, and some of
them have been heard to boast that they would set the whole
country afoot yet they (the people) think they have commenced to try it.   in the raids they have made previously

they have stolen and drove off every head of horses some of the settlers possessed.   they think it the work of the crow indians and half breeds backed by the squaw men, a vile set of men who are living with squaws.   if caught they will have a hard time as there is only one law in this country for horse theives.

October 9.   cook sew and work   all quiet around here nothing heard today about the men after the indians. We are all very anxious.   heard from our other horse she was seen by some of the cowboys grazeing alone near a creek some 10 miles away   dick will go after her in the morning.   hope he will get her as it would be impossible for us to get on without her.

October 10.   the excitement continues about the horses. every day some one rides over to talk about the one topic of the day   the news came today that two others have lost horses.   further down the valley and on the same night that they did the stealing here it seems a preconcerted affair, a regular band of theives.   dick came in toward night with our last horse   I am afraid they will not be much rested.

October 11.   well the days go slowly by   cook sew and work. Alice & Mrs. H. went fishing   got a large string of trout verry fine ones.

October 12.   Ollie has gone today toward bozeman to a Mrs. Hoppers who sent for her. Mrs. Harrison and I took her over to the stage station.   she will take the stage tonight and will stay until we come along and it will be pleasanter for her than camp life.

October 13.   the men continue working on the ditch   it is quite cold nights and mornings   looks like a storm tonight
October 14.   havent heard from absent men for a day or two   it has been snowin so much the last day or two that the

men had to stop work.   it looks like clearing up tonight.
the snow in the valley is about a foot deep   makes it dissa-
greeable in the camp.   it will soon off we are in hopes, then it
will be much better.

October 15.   Mrs. H. has received a note today from one of
the cowboys that he brought from her husband stating that
they were on the track of the robbers.   he was quite a
distance from home   would follow them into the british
possessions if they did not overtake them before.   he said
the robbers were rushing along fast that the indians were
driving the horses over all the stony ground they could in
order to leave no trail if possible but H. is used to their ways
and can track them easy enought.   the snow is melting off
fast. Mrs. H. kindly allows me the use of her sewing machine.
she verry restless about her husband, and takes long rides
every day or two to learn if possible enny news from the absent
ones.   she is a splended horsewoman.

October 16.   the days are about the same   cool nights
pleasant days though damp under foot.   the men are pro-
gressing with the ditch.

October 17.   Alice and Mrs. H. went horseback riding
today   they had a pleasant ride. There came today a large
band of indians on the opposite side of the yellowstone from
us   they are friendly indians so Mrs. H. says: they are called
Bannocks   we can see them plainly from here.   they have
their tents up tonight and we can hear them yelling and their
dogs barking and they are beating their buffalo hide drums.
one neighbor who lives a half mile from here feels uneasy
about them   think they will be killed. I stop nights in the
house instead of covered waggon   it is so cold for the little
ones.

October 18.   today Mrs. H. and myself visited a sick woman
who has been bedfast several months   it doesnt seem much

to be the matter with her   I think she is more discouraged than enny thing else   she needs cheerful company the most of ennything

October 19.   nothing of interest has happened   nothing but busy moments sewing cooking working on the ditch.   the indians are gone from the other side   they are going on a grand hunt. I visited today the other Mrs. Harrison   she is sister to the Mrs. H. we are camped near.   they do not live far apart   they own a large number of cows and have made a great deal of cheese and butter during the summer.   sena stays with her while her husband is away

October 20.   today was very cool.   we took another visit to the sick woman then came back by the dutchmans house a dutch bachelor   he has killed a beef, and he gave each of us some, which was verry nice, also some rutabagas, and Mrs. H. a squash, which she says she will make some pies with then came home and got supper.

October 21.   Today has been bright pleasant   Alice & Allie took the mens dinner to them as they have been doing every noon now for a long time on account of their working such a distance from camp. Allie has been helping a man dig his potatoes.   ben went away yesterday to help a man dig his potatoes   will be back soon. Allison and Dick keep on with the ditch   they think they will soon be through now this place.

October 22.   Ben came back last night   they have allmost completed the ditch   Ben and dick each shot a goose   game is verry plenty—ducks geese trout and in the hills bear and elk are plenty.

October 23.   last night we were sitting around the light reading when we heard some one calling over towards Wabe Hs. Mrs. A Harrison went over   Alice went with her when they came over their they found Wabe and Warren

Larouche come back from the chase. When they had got a long distance from home they found they should not overtake the thieves, and they thought as All H. was the best shot and rider that he and one other should keep on, and Wabe should go back to the ranches and look after the familys and what was left and the other men to about their own work as it would not require so menny to go after the horses. Wabe reports that after they had been out two days they came one morning upon the body of one off All. H.s best yearling colts   it was so large of its age that they had undertaken to ride it and it wouldnt go so they in anger had killed it. Wabe said all had thought so much of that especial colt as it was a great pet, that he actually shed tears of grief and rage. Mrs. H. cried like a child when she heard of it.

October 24.   Well the time is passing and we will soon be on the road again. Got a letter and wrote one to Ollie.   she reports a pleasant trip.   the people are very kind to her. The people in this country are very kind and hospitable.   they are anxious we should settle in this country but Allison has set out to meet his brother in Helena, who he has not met in 25 yr and so we will go on. I [like] this vallie very much.

October 25.   Still the days come and go.   the weather continues fine.   if it were not that they have too many Indians for neighbors, I should like to live in this place

October 26.   My sewing is all done, and I have commenced getting my things in shape to start on again. Alice and I have washed up our clothes, so as to be clean once more. This camp life is a dirty one. Cooking over a camp fire is plesant when one gets used to it, and know how.   we get along verry well.

October 27.   Today I have baked a large quantity of bread to take along to eat on our journey   the men think they will be through about noon tomorrow. Ally has put the boxes on our waggons. We had set the box cover and all off under the trees   it was handier so much easyer to climb into while in camp   have everything packed away. Mrs. H. has received another letter from her husband today   said they had tracked the wily reds to the line and beyond and had secured the services of the sheriff to take them and the horses too   it is now after supper and we are sitting by the camp fire   the Mr & Mrs Wabe H. are here and the girls, with the exception of Ollie, are singing, seeming to enjoy themselves hugely.

October 28.   We started this afternoon on our journey toward Helena. Ben and dick have concluded to stay in this valley a while longer. Mr. H has not returned yet.   we have come this afternoon 7 miles   the wind has blown cold and in our faces all the way.   we are stopping tonight in a mans house by the name of Coe, verry pleasant people.

October 29.   Traveled today over some very rough hilly road.   the wind has blown cold in our faces all day.   are stopping tonight at Hunters hot springs[8]   took a bath in the bath house   it is verry warm and warmed us through, which seemed pleasant after our cold ride.   the steam is rising in the frosty air in clouds verry curious.   these springs a hot spring by the side of a cold one and the stream from each flows together into and through the bath house making the water in the bath room just warm enough.   there are a great menny of these springs in Montana.

October 30.   Today was sunday, but as the days are growing colder we concluded to move on   we have climbed and decended high hills all day; this afternoon it rained all the afternoon and it was after dark before we reached our present stopping place, at a private house.   their name is Bowers.

---

[8]Dr. Andrew Jackson Hunter settled at this locale in 1864. He had come to Montana seeking gold. He named the hot springs for himself. He was from Missouri. Brown, *op. cit.*, p. 336.

Ugh such a night dismal and cold and muddy.   today I am
37 years old.

October 31.   Last night during the night the rain turned to
snow, and the ground is white and it has snowed more today
which made it unpleasant and cold riding. We are stopping at
Hoppers station[9] tonight where Ollie is.   she was verry glad
to see us as we were her.   they would like to keep her here
but we cannot think of leaving her behind. Oh we are to cross
the range tomorrow a part of the rocky mountain   I fear we
will have a hard time   it is snowing yet and will be hard
traveling in the snow and mud.

November 1.   Another weary day has come to a close, and
how can I describe the weary misery of this day   at early
morning we started with our family   two teams and waggons
to cross the range   at the foot of the range was a house where
two men lived.   they told us of a road around the end of the
range that was 6 miles further traveling but would be easier
traveling for our horses as we would escape some verry high
climbing, and as the road was verry slippery and muddy
would be better for us to go around.   so we started around
and the girls said they would walk over the range   they and
Lewis, Allie and father drove the teams and I and the little
ones rode; well they walked over the highest range and met us
about midway; where there was a station kept by a german
and where we got us some dinner.   they (the girls) had
waded a creek, and as the snow was melting and it was slushy
and muddy they were wet to the waist   their shoes were wet
and it was cold.   well all this afternoon we have climbed and
slipped several times stuck fast in the mud, and had a hard
time starting again. Allison would get his team up a long
muddy hill then wade back to the other team and urge that
up, while the girls and boys plodded on foot sometimes nearly

---

[9]Hugo Hoppe was an Indian trader, accused of selling liquor to the Crow Indians.
Brown, *op. cit.*, pp. 337, 434.

to the waist in snow; all this dreary day it was the same climb and climb, urging the tired horses up one terrible hill slipping and toiling along, then gaudeing [goading] them down another untill as night began to fall we began the long desent. we came at the foot after dark, to a ranch, where we asked to stay all night (it was about nine in the evening) the woman only was at home. she said the family could get housed, but there was no place in the stable for the horses.   so the poor beasts had to stand out in the snow all night.   gracious here we were huddled all in one little low log hut the snow watter drip driping down all night through the mud covered roof, and down the sides of the house   it was dismal indeed   the horses I think had the best of it, the girls are wet and their father too, but we managed to find some dry undergarments and I made a little tea over a smoky stove with green pine wood, which revived us a little as we huddled down on our blankets all that miserable night with the music of the dripping water to lull us to sleep but verry little sleep we got except what tired nature compelled us to.

November 2.   well with the first streak of day we were up and folding our damp blankets   I made another kettle of lukewarm tea and with a little bread and meat we managed to still the cravings of hunger, then loaded our effects harnessed the poor horses to the waggons again and started toward Bozeman which we could see from where we stayed last night   the road to B. was pleasant verrry pleasant compared to the journey over the range, though we climbed two pretty long high hills before reaching Bozeman, which we did about noon   here we did some tradeing getting some shoes for some nearly naked feet and laid in a supply of provisions of which we were greatly in need.   we are now in the gatletin [Gallatin] valley a verry nice looking country compared to what we have passed.

November 3. passed a quiet night last night and rested good so today we all felt quite well. forded the Gatletin river twice and came over some pleasant country passed a nice country church, and some good hay ranches, beside other ranches, good for farming. Are stopping tonight at ranchmans by the name of Nicols. there is a large hog ranch joining this. they grow large fields of peas to feed their hogs upon. this is a beautiful place. we have come over some curious looking country since mounting the range, high abrupt hills, deep pitches then a stretch of smooth valley then some rough pitchey road again with abrupt jogs in the road that look as if they were the bed of some mountain torrent as doubtful they were. there are a great menny patches of alkali dust through this valley which I do not much like the looks of.

November 4. we have traveled some verry rough country again today, and likewise smoothe country or that we came to after climbing some high hills came toward night to raders-burg a small Burg, among the hills, which will be a large place at no distant day. we are stopping tonight in an empty log house, near a ranchmans and on the ranchmans place.

November 5. have come today over crow creek range the ground all the way over was red, but the most curious part of the road was the harness and the covers on the waggons looked green caused by copperas[10] in the soil while travelling over it we are stopping tonight at a place called bedford, in another empty house it is quite cold tonight.

November 6. this has been a verry cold windy day all day it seemed as if we would freeze the wind blowing cold and in our faces, making it hard pulling as it made it uncomfortable for us. we are stopping tonight at what is called the half way

---

[10] Ferrous sulfate.

house, about 13 miles from Helena, so one more day will close
our weary wandering at least for awhile. I really hope.

November 7. This morning we started verry early. we
came over some hilly and some rough rocky road, about
eleven we came in sight of Helena. As seen at a distance it is a
pleasant sight, but after reaching the city (except for some
verry fine and even some splendid mansions and business
houses) it did not look so pleasant as at a distance. the
ground is very rough and gulleyed as it is built over an old
mineing place. we reached our brothers house about one
oclock. they received us verry kindly which made us feel
very pleased as our wandering has been a long hard one and to
be welcomed so pleasantly, especially as we were in not good
trim. after our rough travel by waggons and by camp fires
we were dusty weary and tanned and it seemed like getting
home   will stay in Helena all winter and Allison will look us
out a home, a home!   how welcome a resting place will be   I
like the looks of Allisons brother & family. I never have seen
them before, nor has Allison ever seen his brothers wife
before   she seems a verry pleasant person   I hope we will be
great friends

my journal of our wanderings over the plains of Minn,
Dakota and the yellowstone valley in Montana is at an
end.   it is very imperfect but oweing to our mode of traveling
and my chance for writing I have done the best I could

Lucy J. Allen
Helena
Lewis & Clarke Co
Montana

November 7, 1881

Kansas to Wyoming, 1881

§ Virginia Belle Benton

INTRODUCTION

Virginia Belle Benton was 18 years old when the family left northern Kansas for Wyoming. The diary that is published below was written by her day-by-day. Their wagons were pulled by mules.

The writer of the diary was the daughter of the Rev. and Mrs. George Washington Benton. The father was not only a minister but also a medical doctor. Other family members who traveled with the wagon train were:

Gazelle Benton—Virginia's sister.

John and Martha Benton—Virginia's brother and his wife. These two had been married on December 4, 1878. They spent the rest of their lives in Wyoming.[1]

An unnamed and undated newspaper clipping told of the marriage of 22-year-old Virginia and a prominent Wyoming rancher as follows:[2]

> Married—Nov. 18, '85, in the mountain town of Benton, at the new residence of and by Elder Benton, Mr. Willis M. Spear and Miss Blue Belle Benton. A large party of relatives were assembled for the occasion, all bent-on making the affair one of much pleasure. In response to the Minister's injunction, made in flowery terms the sturdy Spear vowed to shield the modest Blue Belle from the world's chilling blasts, as together they tread the winding pathway through Life's meadow.

[1] Martha Charlotte Benton's obituary was poublished in the *Sheridan Press* on Nov. 12, 1945, p. 1. She died on Nov. 10, 1945.

[2] The Willis and Virginia Spear papers in the Wyoming State Archives, Museums & Historical Department, Cheyenne. MSS. 450. Typescript of the papers of Ellis Spear, presented by Jessamine Spear Johnson, March 1942.

The diary that follows was published in *Annals of Wyoming*[3] in its issue of April 1942, and it is with permission of the present editor of that publication, Rick Ewig that it is here published once more.

We usually feel that we should publish something of the life of the diary writer; however, her biography was published in a book, *Women of Wyoming* by Cora M. Beach,[4] and we have added that biography as an Epilogue to the diary.

VIRGINIA BENTON'S DIARY, 1881

Wed., June 15, 1881:   We left home about eleven o'clock and after eating dinner with one of our neighbors we traveled about ten miles to our nearest [?] of Riverton, Nebraska,[1] when we camped on the banks of the Republican river until the 18th. Several of our friends came to see us there and to see how we liked camping. Saturday was a very busy day but we finally finished the business that kept us there and left sometime in the afternoon and camped near a sod house which was built on the prairie miles away from every other home and when the men went to the house to see about milk and water they found notice on the door, saying the well had gone dry and the drought had taken the corn and vegetables and they were going back where there was more rain. So we had to take our water keg some distance away to a small stream and also take the teams there to be watered. We had no intention of traveling on Sunday but with such a scarcity of water and no milk we decided to move on, which we did and

---

[3]"The Spears of Sheridan County," XIV, No. 2, pp. 99-127. The diary is on pages 108 to 120.

[4](Casper, Wyoming, 1927), pp. 493-94.

[1]The starting point of the Benton journey was Smith County, central Kansas, immediately south of the Nebraska border.

as it rained we only went far enough to be able to procure milk, water and wood.

Mon., June 20:   We traveled all day and camped at night just as a heavy rain storm came on and continued half the night.

June 21:   We reached Kearney and camped on the west side of the city.

June 23:   We camped west of Elm Creek Station.

June 24:   We reached Plum Creek Station and as it rained again we were sheltered by a merchant in rooms above his store.

June 25:   We crossed to the south side of the Platte river and camped that night in the sand near the home of a minister, with whom Father was acquainted. Another severe rain, hail, and wind storm came up and tore our tent and blew it over but luckily we could sleep inside the wagons as the fleas were intolerably thick here and would have eaten us alive if given half a chance.

June 27:   We stayed there over Sunday and Mon. We only traveled about 20 miles as the rains had made the roads too muddy and where there was no mud it was sandy and the thermometer stood at 92 in the shade.

June 28:   We traveled another 20 miles and reached the abandoned Ft. McPherson[2] and as a terrible wind storm came up we were given permission to camp in one of the vacant buildings which we were very glad to do as we could not have stretched our tent. That day our dogs saw a band of sheep for the first time and killed one before we could reach them so we bought the one they killed and enjoyed eating fresh mutton.

---

[2]This military post was established 2 miles west of Cottonwood Springs, Nebraska, on September 27, 1863. It was abandoned on March 19, 1880. Robert W. Frazer, *Forts of the West* (Norman, OK, 1965) pp. 85-88. See also Louis A. Holmes, *Fort McPherson, Nebraska* (Lincoln, 1963).

June 29:   We took the opportunity of washing and afterwards we went to visit the National Cemetery[3] (which was taken care of by an old Irish gentleman and his son) which looked so very pretty and green that we thought of an oasis in the desert. We were invited to spend that evening with a family living there, and enjoyed the music which we unitedly produced without stopping to consider whether our voices were cultivated or not.

June 30:   We stopped at noon near the home of a Swede who presented us with new potatoes and some fresh mutton and we entertained two guests at dinner that evening. We camped near North Platte city and Mr. Nickham and his daughter (who were our guests at noon) gave out an appointment for religious services in the Baptist church there and Father preached to the few who could be notified in such a short time.

July 1:   We stopped on our way through North Platte and ate ice cream. (A great luxury)

July 3:   We traveled about 25 or 30 miles and camped near the river again over Sunday, which proved to be a hot windy day. Two cowboys, Black and John Meyers, and a Doctor camped there also.

July 4:   Was very cool and chilly in the morning, scorching hot afternoon. We traveled as far as Brule Station and camped.

July 5:   We only came about five miles this side of Big Springs [Nebraska] as we had another storm from every direction. a little boy wanted to come with us to Cheyenne. He had come from Chicago.

---

[3] Frazer, *op. cit.*, p. 185. As Fort Mc Pherson National Cemetery, Maxwell, Nebraska, it has continued to the present. Here are buried those who have been killed in all the wars since.

July 6:   A "Dr. Powell" came along with a blanket, one that someone had given him, and as we thought him queer we were glad he was not going our way. We ate dinner at Denver Junction and passed thru Julesburg [Colorado] and camped on Lodgepole Creek [Nebraska]. We ate dinner at Lodgepole station and camped for the night about two miles from Colton Station, where several families were camped who were on their way from Texas to Oregon.

July 8:   We reached Sidney [Nebraska] in time to see the soldiers on drill with their horses. We received several letters here, had our teams shod, and traveled nine miles farther before camping for the night.

July 9:   We traveled 17 miles and camped beside a spring where thistle roses, rock lilies, primroses and other flowers were growing.

July 10: Sunday again—we wrote letters.

July 11:   Traveled 25 miles and camped near Bushnell station [Nebraska]. Showers again. Dr. Powell reappeared and ate supper and breakfast with us.

July 12:   We ate dinner near Pine Bluffs, Wyoming Territory. Passed Egbert Station and Widow Brown's sheep ranch and camped where the swallows had built their nests in the cliffs.

July 13:   We came five miles up on the prairie and could see the mountains like a great bank of clouds in the distance. We traveled 26 miles and camped near Cheyenne—east of town near the lake. Cheyenne is 13 years old and the houses are low on account of the wind. We all received letters here. Prayer meeting night so Father and sister went to church and met the Whipples.

July 14:   Mrs. Whipple came to visit us in camp today and took me home with her for awhile. This afternoon we passed

through Cheyenne and our road led us out past the Fair
Grounds and Ft. Russell.[4] We camped near Whitcomb's
sheep ranch and Father and sister drove down to get milk for
the children. The housekeeper told them the romantic history
of Whitcomb's marriage to a descendant of a Sioux Indian
princess, and showed them the oil paintings of the daughters
who were away at boarding school.

July 15:   Traveled about 21 miles—stopping at the foot of
the mountains for dinner and camping in an open park on top
of the mountains, which we were told were the Laramie Mts.

July 16:   Our first morning in the mountains, so far from
every human being but ourselves and such a silence and hush
over everything. Not even a bird call could be heard. Delight-
fully cool and fresh after the rain. I wanted to walk and
examine every boulder and every plant by the way. We saw a
mountain looking like a fortress, and another place like a
graveyard with headstones, a pulpit, seats, a bar and a platform. We ate our dinner where we could see the Tower of
Babel in the distance. It rained in the afternoon and we
passed a rock that looked like a square tombstone with two
rosebushes beside it. We had a very, very steep hill to ascend,
where there were three springs and then a gradual descent of
12 miles thru the Cheyenne Pass where the road was just wide
enough for one wagon at a time. One place was so slanting
that my left hind wheel was moving in space for one breathless
second, but luckily the wagon did not tip over, and we
reached the valley safely. Camped about one mile east of
Laramie City. We had another downpour of rain which made
us sad and sloppy.

July 17:   Father, John and Gazelle went to the Baptist

---

[4]Fort Russell had been established on July 21, 1867, three miles west of Cheyenne,
Wyoming, on the north bank of Crow Creek. It is now the Francis E. Warren Air Force
Base.

Church to Sunday School (Pastor away) and were invited to dinner by one of the Deacons, so accepted the invitation. Another storm. John and Gazelle came back to camp but Pa stayed and held services in the evening and stayed all night.

July 18:   Rained again and we were invited to move into the vestry of the church, which we were glad to do and have a dry spot to sleep in.

July 19:   Mr. and Mrs. Blackburn called on us. Father and John went to Cummins about 30 miles away in the Rocky Mts. to see if it would be a good place to camp while we were waiting word from Frank, who had gone on to Oregon and Washington. Gazelle and I attended Young Peoples' meeting in the evening. Rainy again.

July 20:   Mother returned Mrs. Blackburn's call and I stayed all night with Mrs. B. as Mr. B. was away, and she was nervous about staying alone.

July 21:   I read "Bitter Sweet"[5] from Mrs. Blackburn's library. Pa and John returned. I stayed with Mrs. B. again and read part of "Stepping Heavenward,"[6]

July 22:   Finished reading and went back to church. We packed up and started for Cummins in the afternoon—camped about 7 miles from town.

July 23:   We traveled about 23 miles and passed thru the little mining town of Cummins[7]—camped about 2 miles beyond, beside a spring on the mountainside. Father bought

---

[5]Josiah Gilbert Holland, *Bittersweet* (New York, 1858).

[6]Elizabeth Prentiss, *Stepping Heavenward* (N.Y., 1869). One early commentator wrote of her as "a writer of religious and juvenile fiction."

[7]Now known as Cummins City. Mae Urbanek, in her book, *Wyoming Place Names* (Missoula, Montana, 1988), p. 47, tells of the founding of the town by John Cummins, a miner. He salted the region with copper ore samples and sold it for a huge price to an eastern company; then he absconded with the money to Texas. Nothing exists there now. The Bentons camped in the Cummins City area from July 23 to August 16.

some wild respberries from some small boys and we had a feast.

July 24:   Father, John and I went to Sunday School in Cummins at 3 o'clock, 24 persons present. In the evening Pa, Mat and I went to church service; Mr. Nixon preached.

July 26:   Gazelle and I picked some raspberries and made jam.

July 28:   I went berry picking with some ladies from Cummins—when I came back to camp found Mr. and Mrs. Blackburn, daughter and niece, Mrs. Wyman and Mrs. Kelly, calling on Mother. They all went to gather berries afterwards. Yesterday was Mother's 58th birthday.

July 29:   John and Mat began hauling lumber to Laramie. Pa and I went to the Betsy Jane Mine and called on Mrs. Blackburn. Mrs. Wyman, Mrs. Kelly and Dr. Watson with his sister Mary went with us to the Quartz mill.

July 31:   Wrote letters in the A.M. After noon, Father, Mother, John and I went to Sunday School. Father preached in the evening. Mrs. Bacon, Mrs. Watkins, Miss Watkins and I were the only ladies there.

August 1:   Mat took a load of lumber to Laramie. Pa and John went down to Cummins to help him and came across Mat Derley of Hennepin, Ill. He is a relative of Martha's (John's wife). The men went hunting—started for Tie Park—came back before dark.

August 2:   Sue (the mule) was sick so Mat did not return till after dark. Pa and John engaged to get 10 cords of wood—8 ft. long for $25.00.

August 3:   John and Mat chopped and hauled two loads of wood to the quartz mill and Father hauled a load of lumber to Cummins for Beard & Thomas.

August 4: John and Mat hauled three loads of wood and Pa hauled one load of lumber. A balloon passed over about sunset.

August 6: They took the wood to Cummins and broke a reach so did not get back until noon. Pa went down town on horseback and took supper at the Betsy Jane. Mr. Wyman and his little girl came for medicine for the baby. The people in Cummins had a fracas with Milo Kendall—the Constable —and drove him away.

August 7: Father and I went to meeting in the morning and heard Mr. Sanders read his sermon. Six of us went to Sunday School in the afternoon and Mr. Derley came home with us and stayed all night. He and [John] went hunting up to Tie Park[8] on the 8th and John and Mat took two loads of lumber to Cummins. I read "The Fishers of Derby Haven."[9] Rained very hard.

August 9: J. and M[atha] went to Laramie with lumber. It rained in sheets and comforters in the afternoon and we sat in the tent and listened to Mr. Derley telling how he found thieves on the Kankakee River—where he was acting as a detective a good many years ago.

August 11: John's team strayed away Tuesday night and the boys had to hunt for them. Pa was so worried that he started to Laramie to look for the boys. Mrs. Gage, Mrs. Edmunds and several boys passed on their way to the berry patch. It stormed. I started down to Hardings and met Bacon, Mr. Derley and Gazelle coming up—rode back with them.

August 12: Very foggy. No man in camp so G. and I had to hunt up Kitty and Kizer, the little mules—which we suc-

---

[8]This was a place where they stored and processed railroad ties.

[9]This was a book by Hesba Stratton (1832-1911), (London, Religious Tract Society, 1866).

ceeded in doing after a great deal of tramping. The men came back and brought letters.

August 13: Mrs. Harding and I went berrying. John hunted for Kitty and Kizer and found them helping themselves to pie in Mrs. Watkins' kitchen window.

August 14: Father, John and I went to the school house and Father preached. About 50 people present. It rained. Mr. Peabody and Mr. Banks addressed the S.S. A Bible reading was given in the evening.

August 15: Mr. Linn came to our camp and told us about the route up to the northern part of Wyoming and about the fish, game, lovely water and tillable lands on Goose Creek—as he had seen it in passing thru. Mr. Banks and Miss Forbes came and borrowed my side saddle. Mrs. Gage and Mrs. Watkins came for a few minutes. John and Mat put their wagon boxes back on the running gears.

August 16: We packed the wagons. Mr. Peabody, wife and two boys, Mr. Banks, Mr. Sales, Elder Watson (of Laramie), Mrs. Cook and Mr. Blackburn came to maek us a farewell call. We started while it was raining and passed thru Cummins. Camped that night about eight miles from there beside an irrigating ditch.

August 17: We stopped at Sodogreen's to get some good water to drink and stopped near Hutton's ranche to get our dinner. It stormed but we finished our journey to Laramie and camped on the West side of the river. Father and mother went to stay all night at Blackburn's.

August 18: We went shopping at Wagner's and I bought a pair of shoes $2.50, a porte monnai[e] 50c, gloves $1.00, 3 hdkfs, 50c, and then went to Mrs. Blackburn's and she gave me 4 chromos. We went to the ticket office to see a huge stuffed bear and in the evening went to prayer meeting at the Baptist Church. Mrs. Andrews, Mrs. Barron, Mrs. Bannon,

Mrs. Wilmot, Mrs. Riggs, Elva Bunker and some other ladies were there.

August 19: We left Laramie and traveled thru red earth and sand for 18 miles and camped by the Lewis Ranch all night. Came down the Laramie River.

August 20: The mules had strayed, so while the men were hunting them, Mrs. Lewis and her sister came and visited with us and then we went to the house and visited them. We started as soon as the mules were found and crossed the river at Little's ranche and came up Cooper Lake station, past the steam construction for forcing the water to the R.R. tank, then thru green brush and swamps to a road on the north side of the R.R. and to the head of a lake near a snowshed, where we camped for the night

Sunday, August 21: The mules were all gone to the Laramie River so the men had to go after them. Pa shot an antelope, 2 miles from camp and Gazelle helped him bring it up before breakfast. Mr. Clark and wife from Cedarville, Kansas, passed us and went to Lookout station to camp. As it was a better camp and they were going to northern Wyoming too, we moved camp to Lookout station for the night.

August 22: We traveled thru sand and cobblestones to Rock Creek station and camped there. Father found that the Mr. Thayer who owned the store there was a cousin of his first wife (Maria Morse). Mr. Thayer's two fine sons came to camp to call on us and Mr. John Thayer came and spent the evening. He has been a U.S. Senator from Nebraska, and Governor of Wyoming. J.W. Austin and family were camped at this place also with some young people of their party and we enjoyed hearing them sing in the evening. "Tenting on the Old Camp Ground" and "My Pretty Quardoon [Quadroon]" were especially sweet to hear in the open air.

August 23: We came nine miles up into the hills and

stopped for dinner. There was neither wood, water or grass but rocks all around and sand and red earth. In the afternoon we reached the 22 mile ranche and camped—no wood, poor grass but very good water, Mrs. Evans who lived there invited us in to have some music in the evening.

August 24:   We traveled over a rocky sandy road to Yankee's ranche—camped for dinner and found to our surprise that they had a piano there. Afternoon we passed Mountain Home ranche[10]—entered La Bonte Canyon and camped beside the stream in a beautiful spot with the wooded cliffs towering above us. The ruins of an old stage station were there and the grave of a murdered man (Ed Hewitt—July 15, 1878) himself a murderer. A lonely place but with the Clark and Austin party and some soldiers who were camped there we became a little village of white tents.

August 25:   We passed Hall's ranche and stopped at Point of Rocks Station at noon, then at Point of Rocks filled our keg with water and came over the mountains. Camped beside the LaParele [LaPrele] creek in the canyon. Found Mr. Austin's kitten.

August 26:   We passed Slaymaker's ranche and got some water at Mason's cut off, came within 15 miles of Ft. Fetterman[11] and stopped for dinner, where there was a ranche. Came 12 miles to Spring Canyon ranche and a half mile farther we camped beside the LaParele again.

August 27:   We passed Ft. Fetterman and crossed the North Platte bridge thru sand 15 miles to Sage Creek station

---

[10]Also known as Camp Marshall, a telegraph station about 66 miles west of Fort Laramie. Grace R. Hebard and E.A. Brininstool, *The Bozeman Trail*, (Glendale, CA, 1960), Vol. 1, p. 81.

[11]Fort Fetterman was established on the south bank of the North Platte River, near the mouth of La Prele Creek. It was here that the Bozeman Trail forsook the river and turned north. Although it is a ghost now, some buildings still remain. Frazer, *op. cit.*, p. 181.

and camped. We went to the Clark and Austin camp and had a good time singing again.

Sunday, August 28:   The Clarks and Austins went on to Brown's Springs. A Texas Ranger got his breakfast with us and told us stories of his adventures. A Dutchman, Winters, came after dark and got a cup of tea. [29th] Mr. Winters and Mrs. Fifield ate breakfast with us. We came 12 miles to Brown's Springs and stopped for dinner. In the afternoon we passed Dry Cheyenne station. 9 miles from there we reached Stinking Water creek and 4 miles farther to Sand Creek where we camped for the night. We first saw sage hens this afternoon and killed several.

August 30:   We found the water tasted of sage and our sage hens tasted of sage and when Mother sent me after whole pepper and told me to grind it in the coffee mill, I got cuble [cubeb] berries instead—so our breakfast was very spicy. Five miles from there we passed Antelope ranche and when Father went to the door to make inquiries there were 8 men, one Mr. Fifield, gambling, which so horrified him that we hurried away and drove two miles farther thru sandbeds and stopped for dinner in a dry creek bed. After dinner we came about 14 miles and struck a roundup. They gave us some meat. It was dark but we kept on until we reached Hathaway's old ranche or 17 Mile R. and camped beside Mr. Clark's outfit.

August 31:   We traveled 17 miles to Hathaway's new ranche, crossed Powder R. and camped near old Ft. Reno.[12] Pa saw two Englishmen who were going to the "Big Horn." Some of the cowboys and Mr. Fifield came down and Pa preached to

[12]The Federal Government built three small forts in 1866 and garrisoned them to protect travelers along the Bozeman Trail. They were Fort Reno and Fort Phil Kearny in northwestern Wyoming, and Fort C.F. Smith in Montana. Fort Reno was abandoned in 1868. T.A. Larson, *Wyoming* (New York, 1977), pp. 68ff, and Robert A. Murray, *Military Posts in the Powder River Country of Wyoming, 1865-1894.*

them. John was sick. Mr. Clark was very much excited as he considers all cowboys' desperate characters. He drew all his canvas down tight around his wagon, crawled inside and kept his hand on his gun until they all left camp.

September 1:   We left old Fort McKinney depot—stopped at Steve Farwell's store for some supplies and came on to the Nine Mile Hole where we camped for dinner. It was so warm and windy we could scarcely keep our eyes open to drive so we decided to stay here until tomorrow as there is a prospect of getting some antelope. Pa and a ranchman went hunting but they failed to find any antelope. An old man who looks as if he and beer were boon companions camped beside us this evening and he informed us that he is Colonel McConihe.

September 2:   Mr. Lambert and McConihe ate breakfast with us. We came 18 miles to Crazy Woman's Fork and Harris's ranche, and ate dinner—then six miles farther and camped for the night. Weather very cold. Mr. McConihe ate supper with us.

September 3:   McC. ate breakfast with us and the English-man with Mr. Serithers came along just as we started. We came by the Nine and Six Mile ranches and stopped on Clear Creek near Ft. McKinney.[13] Father went over to the fort and made an appointment to preach in the Company quarters at 3 o'clock on Sunday. Mr. Lenney came back with him.

September 4:   Father and I went to meeting in one of the buildings used for the telegraph office. Mr. Lang was usher, and the house was crowded. As we were returning to camp it began to blow and storm—exceedingly cold to us for this time of year. Emily Fordice came to camp and visited a long time. Rained tonight.

---

[13] Fort McKinney was established in 1877 on Clear Creek, a branch of the Powder River. It was abandoned in 1894. In 1903 it was made into the "State Soldiers' and Sailors' Home." Frazer, *op. cit.,* p. 183.

September 5:   Pa got some fresh vegetables—3 cabbages, 5 cucumbers, 2 beets and some turnips and onions—which taste good to us. The Clear Creek water is so delicious that we can hardly get enough of it after all the alkali and sage flavored water we have been forced to drink on our way up here. This evening Mr. Sparks, Co. A. cornet player, and Mr. Ackerman, the trumpeter of Co. G. 9th Cav., came over and spent the evening.

September 6:   We woke up to find the ground covered with snow. Got our letters and papers so read them.

September 7:   We started out again—came thru Buffalo and about 4 miles from Snyder's to Rock Creek—stopped for dinner. Mr. Fifield went by on horseback. We came on past Lake DeSmet to Sturgis ranche (Buttermilk Sturgis) on Shell Creek and camped. While we were spending the evening with the Sturgis family, Miss Lida Davis, Miss Burgess and Mr. Babcock came to ask Miss Sturgis to go to a dance at Sonnesbergers.

September 8:   Mr. Sturgis, Father and John went to Big Piney to look for a ranche. I read "Milbank." [Millbank][14]

September 9:   It rained. Pa and John went to Piney again but came back without finding one.

September 10:   Miss Davis, Miss Burgess, Mr. Snider and another man rode past, on their way to Big Horn. Pa and John went to Goose Creek. I read "Marian Grey" (consider it slush—Kept the mules from straying and killed a rattle-snake.

---

[14]*Millbank* was a novel written in 1871 by Mary Jane Holmes, a most prolific writer. The books Virginia Benton tells of reading during the remainder of her journey were also written by Holmes. One early biographer of this writer describes her works as "pure in tone and free from sensational incidents." Most would say today they were over-sentimental in tone. She wrote 28 novels and collected stories. Virginia Benton wrote off another of Holmes' novels, *Marian Grey*, "Consider it slush." See entry for September 10 below.

September 11, Sunday: I read "Work or Christie's Experience" over again. Sid Sturgis, prospective Sheriff James, Mr. Fifield, and Oliver Hanna called at Sturgis. Mr. Hersey and Mr. Carns came by. A theatre troupe went by, going to Ft. McKinney.

September 12:   Miss Wright and her brother stopped here on their way home from Sonnesbergers. Mr. Canning and some other folks, from the fort, went by a fishing. Mr. C. stopped to buy some sugar.

September 13:   Father and John came back and Mr. Wolfe came with them to see the harness, wagon, and the white mules "Sam and Sue" which father is trading for 160 acres on Little Goose Creek,[15] 1½ miles above Big Horn.

September 14:   We left Shell Creek and ate our dinner near Mr. Terrill's ranche, where Mr. Wright is living. Came by way of Meade's cut-off to Little Goose Creek and saw our new home in all the glory of autumn tints in the leaves of the wild plum and choke cherries, cottonwood, quaking asp, birch and willow. We are content with the two room cabin for a haven of rest after three months of camping, although doorways and window openings have to be covered with blankets and sheets. Doors and windows cannot be gotten short of Cheyenne or Laramie.

---

[15]Little Goose Creek and Big Goose Creek have their confluence in the city of Sheridan, which received its name and first postoffice in 1881, the same year the Bentons arrived. Urbanek, *op. cit.*, p. 179.

EPILOGUE

MRS. WILLIS M. SPEAR[16]
State Regent Daughters of the American Revolution

"As the twig is bent the tree inclines" is a trite saying that applies to Mrs. Willis M. Spear, the daughter of Reverend and Mrs. George W. Benton. She was born December 6, 1863 in Berlin, Wisconsin, and her early childhood memories are of the return of the family to Illinois and the migrations to Kansas and later to Wyoming. Reared in the home of a Medical Missionary who was at the service and call of all who might need him over a radius of sixty or seventy miles, she early learned the meaning of the word "service," and the fact that a life spent in the poursuit of selfish pleasure was barren indeed.

It was at the age of eight years that she recalls the first winter they spent in Iowa at a small place called Tyson's Mills, where her father preached and ministered to the sick, and later the residence in Kansas and eventually the final migration to Wyoming. She was educated in the public schools of the localities in which the family lived and for a time she attended private schools, and later study classes helped her to acquire information on subjects in which she was much interested. She says "the school of experience" has been her greatest teacher, however, and that her special interests, music and art, have been pushed aside for the practical part of living.

The greater part of Mrs. Spear's life in Wyoming has been spent on the ranch which was the original holding of her father, for just prior to her marriage to Willis M. Spear, November 18, 1885, he purchased the ranch from Mr. Benton, and this continues to be the Spear home during the summer months and as much of the time during the winter months as they can manage. The Spear family lived continuously on the ranch until the winter of 1902-1903 when they found it necessary to establish a residence in Sheridan where their children could have the advantages in school

---

[16]Cora M. Beach, *Women of Wyoming* (Casper, WY, 1927), pp. 493-94.

work offered by the higher grades, and here too, they built a home. The change in ownership of the ranch saw no diminution in its social life for it continued to be the center of social activities for the young people of the community as well as those older. Mrs. Spear was president of the Woman's Christian Temperance Union, and as a member of the First Baptist Church in Sheridan, taught in its Sunday School, was a member of the choir, a church trustee and treasurer of the building fund for the church. She was secretary of the Old Settlers' Club of Sheridan for fifteen years and is still a member. In 1911 she affiliated with the Sheridan Chapter, Daughters of the American Revolution, and served it as treasurer, historian and regent. She was elected State Registrar of the organization in 1918, re-elected in 1920. In 1922 she was elected State Treasurer and two years later, Vice Regent, succeeding to the office of State Regent early in 1925, upon the resignation of Mrs Bacon (the then State Regent), and was elected to succeed herself at the Conference in 1926. She is also a member of the Sheridan Woman's Club, the Book Review Club and the Sheridan Music Club.

During the World War she was a Captain of a group in selling Liberty Bonds and had charge of seven counties in raising funds for an ambulance to be sent to France from Wyoming "Daughters" for the use of the soldier boys.

Mrs. Spear is a woman of high ideals, a worthy daughter of worthy parents, kindly and charitable in her dealings with her fellowmen. Her home is one where hospitality reigns and the door has "the latch-string on the outside." She is a warm and loyal friend, a true and much-beloved wife and mother.

Mr. Spear, too, is of a family of early Wyoming pioneers and is one of the highly respected men of his community, and has been honored in many ways, at present he is the Senior Senator from Sheridan County, which office he has held for six years. He is one of the large stockmen of his locality. Mr. and Mrs. Spear have had the following children:

Jessamine, born in 1886, married in June, 1906. William V.

Johnson, and they have the following children: Annabelle Johnson, born 1907, married December 10, 1925, Jackson Moody; Phyllis Vie Johnson, born 1908; William Spear Johnson, born 1912; Elsie Eileen, born 1915; Torrey Benton, born 1916; Victor Elarth, born 1922; Homer Bradford, born 1925. Living in Kirby, Montana.

Willis Benton, born 1888, married in February, 1914, Ruth Henderson, of Washington, D.C.

Philip Torrey, born 1892, married in October, 1915, Jessie Mather of Fremont, Nebraska.

Elsie H., born in 1896, married in June, 1916 to Harold C. Edwards. Theri home is in Sheridan and they have the following children: Virginia Maye Edwards, born December 22, 1917; Elsie, born August 15, 1919; Charlene Howard, born October 5, 1920; Lois Adeline, born June 26, 1925.

Missouri to Idaho, 1881

⸜ Emily Towell

INTRODUCTION

It was the fertile Weiser River Valley in southwestern Idaho that attracted settlers to make their homes in that area. The little town of Middle Valley, known now as Midvale, became the locale of settlement in the late 1860's.

The first white family to settle there were members of the John Reed family, who arrived in 1868. They built a one-room cabin on the bank of the Weiser River. John Reed constructed a sawmill on Pine Creek. The Reeds raised a family of eight children.

Other settlers came in the years following, but the most noteworthy boost came when there arrived in 1881 when a train of forty covered wagons came from Mercer County at the extreme north of central Missouri, and settled along the banks of the Weiser River at or near Middle Valley. The diary that follows is that of Mrs. Emily Towell, who traveled with the Mercer wagon train from Missouri to Idaho. Emily and her husband, Alexander, were not the usual young married persons we might expect to travel the Oregon Trail. Emily was born in October 1829, so was 52 years old at the time of their long venture. Her husband, Alexander Towell, was 66 years of age.

The Idaho State Historical Society in Boise has been most cooperative in helping with our research about the Mercer Wagon Train and has provided us with a list of the members of the wagon train that some of the travelers made after the long journey. We have poublished this list as an epilogue to Mrs. Towell's diary.

The diary itself is now the property of the Idaho State Historical Society, and that organization has been most gracious in letting us have it for publication. One thing to notice is that the Towell family was made up of seven children: William, Thomas, Richard, Otho, Frank, Martha and Effie. Every day of their journey was filled with much activity.

EMILY TOWELL'S DIARY

On May 11, 1881, a small company of people gathered in Mercer County, Mo. This was the beginning of a long and eventful journey westward to the much-talked of Oregon Territory. The group numbered 47. There was much excitement that day. Every imagination was fired with dreams and visions of new homes and fortunes to be made in the fertile West. Tilford Lindsay was made leader of the wagon train for he had made this journey some time before and was more familiar with the routes and roads to be traveled. The parting from our relatives and dear ones was very sad and heartrending. There were many tears shed as those last fond farewells and goodbyes were said. Our hearts were heavey and leaden for we little knew when we would see those dear faces again. Alexander Towell's brother, Baron Towell, and nephew, Rufus Clampit, met us at Princeton, county seat of Mercer county,[1] in Missouri and accompanied us on our journey the first day. We drove fifteen miles and camped at the Moss School house.

It was raining on the morning of May 12. We passed through Goshen City and drove on to Grand River Botton where James, Mahala and Frank McCloud joined us. The night was spent here.

---

[1]The most noteworthy of Princeton's daughters was Martha Canary (1850-1903), better known as "Calamity Jane," who spent most of her grownup life in Montana and South Dakota. She took great pride in being able to out-chew, out-smoke, out-swear, and out-drink most of her male friends. *Missouri, A Guide to the "Show Me" State* (New York, 1941), p. 474.

May 13, we left Grand River Bottom and crossed the river, driving onward to Cainsville. On this day we were struck by a bit of ill luck. John Michael's wagon broke down and had to be taken back to town for repairs. We made our camp beside a little church house near Rush Creek.

A hearty breakfast was enjoyed on the morning of May 14. A pleasant and refreshing breeze was stirring and all were in excellent spirits. We drove through a small town, known as Blythedale, and on to Big Creek where we stopped for dinner. After eating we resumed our journey, and drove through Eagleville [Missouri]. When darkness was upon us we stopped beside a small stream.

May 15 was Sunday, therefore, deemed it wise to rest, but the present camp to our way of thinking wasn't a very desirable place to spent the day. For that very reason the horses were hitched up and we drove upon a hill. This was a country of gentle rolling prairies and was delightful to the eye. This was in Ringold and Taylor counties in Iowa.

May 17 found us in a very attractive portion of our great country. There were nice groves of trees, and very fertile farms, also, an abundance of good pure water.

Our camp was made beside a little prairie school house on the evening of May 18. We found the roads very muddy here as it had been raining most of the day.

May 20. We passed over some vary fertile land which was worth from ten to twenty dollars per acre. Here the stock law[2] was in force. The "Caravan" wended its way along the banks of the West Nodaway River, and passed two wagons, each drawn by six yoke of oxen. Camp was made about one mile east of Red Oak.

---

[2]Usually referred to as "herd law," concerned the ranging and grazing of cattle. Ramon Adams, *Western Words* (Norman, OK, 1944), p. 146.

We entered Red Oak on May 21. It is located on the [East] Nisna Botna [sic] River. We passed through Emerson just as the sun was casting his last golden rays over the land, and dusky wings of night were slowly spreading great shadows over the land. This delighted eyes of the travellers. Green trees bordered the river which reflected the quickly changing hues and shades of the twilight. In Mills County, Iowa, there were farms where the corn had not yet been gathered. We had never before seen as much corn as there was here.

May 22. We drove until we reached the [West] Nishna Botna River which was extremely high and we were forced to cross at Massadona [Macedonia]. There were lovely fields of wheat, and the farmers were busily engaged in the planting of corn. This land produced approximately seventy-five bushels per acre. That was easily believed after seeing some great corncribs and great stacks of corn, piled all over the ground. The horses were watered at springs and wells all along the way. So far all the water was very good, and we were duly thankful for this. There were very few cattle to be seen here. The land owners here are a very clever and industrious people, judging by the appearance of their farms. The Nisna Botna river was crossed by ferry about 26 miles south [east] of Council Bluffs, Iowa. From this point we drove to Silver Creek and camped.

We arrived at Potawatamy [sic] County, Iowa, on May 23. We drove up a long hill and then descended, wound around between two hills and there lay the great Missouri river. On one side were lowlands and on the other side of the river great bluffs rose and towered over us. At the base of the bluffs were many dwelling houses. Every night in preparation for camp, the wagons were drawn into a circle and staked down. The horses were tied at the back of the wagons. The men took turns acting as sentinals. Two men would stand guard until midnight and then two more men took their places to stand guard until dawn. This was done to safe-guard against horse thieves and other pilferers who might menace the camp. Another reason for staking the wagons was to guard against possible wind storms. While in camp at Council Bluffs, a man entered camp and met the guard. The guard asked him why he was there and he in turn said he was trying to find a place to spend the night. The guard informed him that we were not keeping "tavern," but he might find an empty box-car to sleep in. It was believed that the man was planning to take some of the horses if he had not been seen by the guard. Even though we were not in our homes, a great many of the home tasks and duties of the housewife must be performed as usual. Chief among these tasks was the weekly family washing. The wives and mothers busied themselves with this task while the men went to town to seek information regarding the next river crossing. In town James McCloud's horses became frighted of the trains and the wagon upset. Luckily, however, there was no serious damage.

May 25. We left Council Bluffs and drove through the lower portion of the twn, which had been under water previous to our arrival. There were many skiffs (boat-like contrivances) scattered about the town. The river was very high and swollen and we could not reach the ferry. This necessitated another means of crossing. This crossing was made by means of the "cars."[3] Seven teams and wagons could be carried across at once. This was a three-mile ride, and when the journey ended we found ourselves in Omaha, Nebraska. Omaha had many beautiful structures and was quite a large city. We ate our dinner a short distance out of Omaha, near a little stream, and then drove a distance of ten miles before nightfall.

---

[3] In those days folks often spoke of traveling in "the cars." This meant going by rail.

May 26.   We drove through some country that did not make a very good impression on us, as it was poor and barren. There were no beautiful trees or grass here. The land was not fenced and was very meagerly populated. The Elkhorn river was crossed next. The water had been very high, also and the bottom land was very wet and muddy. The bridge was safe, however, and a man with a horse and buggy, piloted us over the bad places. His horse mired and all of the men assisted him out of his predicament. The Rawhide river was crossed near Elkhorn. From this point we drove onward until we were overtaken by darkness.

May 27.   The roads at Schuyler were quite muddy as it had been raining. The next town was Richland. This section of land was very thinly settled. We travelled close to the railroad for some distance and camped about four miles east of Columbus [Nebraska].

May 28.   We drove through Columbus and stopped at the edge of town, near the Loup river and ate dinner. We had to ford one prong of the river and cross the other prong on the ferry. The Loup river is similer to a fork. The wagons jolted and rattled over the quicksand and sounded very much like it was rock we were crossing. The Lindsay team took the lead. The cost for ferrying was two dollars per team. After driving for a short distance, camp was made on the sand.

On Sunday, May 29,   everyone remained in camp until after dinner. The horses were hitched up and we drove upward to higher ground. Everyone was in good spirits and the boys were enjoying themselves immensely. A pretty grove of trees near a dwelling provided a very delightful camp ground.

May 30.   The "Caravan" reached Jackson near the river Platte. The Platte river is a large stream and has no timber on its banks. It is nearly level with the earth and for that reason it presents a strange picture. We viewed our first sod houses[4]

between Holt and Hall counties in Nebraska. As the rainfall
had been very heavy the streams and rivers were all over-
flowing their banks, and the roads were in very poor condition,
making progress impossible. Silver creek was high so the
women and children crossed on the railroad while the men
took the wagons and forded the stream. The water was swift
and dangerous, and ran into the wagon beds. Once across the
creek, we hesitated just long enough to eat a cold lunch and
feed the horses. At night camp was made about three miles
east of Clarksville.

Meric [Merrick] County, Nebraska, May 31.   We passed
through Central[5] and on June 1, we drove into Grand Island.
Grand Island is a railroad town and was very attractive.
Camp was made on Wood river which has a scattering of
timber along its banks—a mill was also situated here.

June 2.   We passed through the town of Wood River. The
night was spent at Beauty [Butte?].

June 3.   The women folks did the washing and we remained
in Beauty until noon. The water at this point was very poor.
At noon the wagon train was moving onward. This part of the
state appealed to us a wee bit more than what we saw of it
when we first entered. However, it did not appeal to us
strongly enough to make us desire to build our homes here.
In Kearney City there were many wagons camped on the
outskirts of the town. We paused long enough to exchange
conversation with some of the travelers. The cars on the
railroad were speeding past every few minutes. The passengers had a great deal of fun waving to the occupants of the
wagons on the road. They motioned with their hands, pointing

---

[4]Because of lack of wood, people who settled on the Great Plains built themselves
houses of slabs of prairie sod. Cass G. Barns, *The Sod House* (Lincoln, NE, 1970), *passim.*

[5]Later Central City. *Nebraska, A Guide to the Cornhusker State* (New York, 1949), pp.
331-32.

westward to show how much faster they could travel than we. The wagons were just plodding snails in comparison with the speeding cars. Again we drove beside the Platte river. There were hills on one side, and many sod houses also.

June 4. We camped at Elman [Elm] creek. It rained during the night. Nearly all dwellings were built from sod. We passed near enough to one to one to see it. The walls were plastered and were just as clean and white as those of any frame building.

At Plum creek, Nebraska, we camped in a low wet place. This was on Sunday, June 5. One of the horses was so lame that it was impossible to go further. Willie Caseldine went in search of a better camp site. The water was very poor and we were anxious to move on. The day was intenseley hot and there seemed to be a storm brewing. There was much discomfort among the members of our little band. At dusk, little Frank McCloud, son of James and Mahala McCloud, became very ill and went into a violent spasm. Someone was dispatched for a doctor immediately. The doctor said that Frank's would soon be improved. Later Frank had two more spasms and once more the doctor came, but could do nothing for him. Another physician was summoned. This one said that it was conjestion of the brain which was caused by the intense heat. During the night, the storm which had been threatening all through the day broke in all its fury. Lightening danced across the heavens in bold streaks of fire; the thunder rolled and crashed; the wind howled and shrieked like wild and fearful demons. Then came the rain; it rained as it has never rained before. Would the night never end? Yes, even the longest night must draw to a close. Day dawned finding nearly everyone wretched and ill. The physician's advice was for all of us to leave this camp immediately and find good water.

The following day, June 6,   William Evans traded the lame horse for a good one, and we were on our way. Just out of Plum Creek little Frank went into another spasm. The doctor came to the wagon. When Frank was a little better we drove four miles further where the rest of the group were in camp. The little boy was carried to a section house where he could be properly cared for. Someone watched over him all during the night. Apparently the litle fellow was much improved during the day of June 7. He continued to feel better until evening, then began to grow steadily worse. The physician was called before the break of day, and stated that it was a hopeless case but he would do everything within his power to save him.

June 8.   Victory Evans, Otho Towell and Billy Pickett's baby were also ill. The entire camp was in a very poor frame of mind. Frank appeared to be some better, but was yet unable to travel. The remainder of the company favored moving on before they too were ill. The water was poor as it contained alkali, which made unceasing downpour, and the day was gloomy and dismal.

June 10.   George Tod and James Rhea remained with the McCloud family to help care for Frank. The rest of the group went in search of a better place to stay. Everyone was reluctant to leave part of our number behind with sickness, and possible death as their grim host. After driving 16 miles, we were overtaken by James Rhea at Willow Island, who was bringing us word that Frank had passed away. Dudley Evans and Elvin Hague went back to assist with the last and final rites. It was a very sad mother and father who saw their baby, their most treasured possession, taken away from them. The child's sweet baby prattle was sorely missed. There were many mounds at the side of the road, giving mute evidence of suffering and sorrow. In trials and desolation the Savior said,

"Father, not my will but Thine be done." So it be with us,
not our will but Thine be done, Father.

> Abide with me; fast falls the eventide;
> The darkness deepens—Lord with me abide;
> When helpers fail, and other comforts flee,
> Help of the helpless, O abide with me!
> Heaven's morning breaks, and earth's vain shadows flee;
> In life, in death, O Lord, abide with me! —Amen.

[The following words are written in another hand: Emily
Towell became very ill at Willow Island, and her son, Otho,
required anxious and vigilant care during the night. William
Evans and Bill Pickett were sent back to Plum Creek for
medicine. Dudley Evans and Elvin Hague rode into camp
about midnight, weary and spent from a 40-mile ride. They
had been with the McCloud family.]

June 13.   We stopped a short time at Brady Station, in
Lincoln county, Nebraska. The invalids were feeling better.
We passed through Brady and drove beside great bluffs.
There were great herds of cattle and sheep in the Platte valley.
We liked it here even if it wasn't a farming district. We
crossed the North Platte river on the railroad bridge and
entered Platte city. There was evidence of a bitter cold winter
all around. There were stacks of carcasses all over the ground.
Great herds of cattle had perished in the cold. Many thousand
carcasses had already been hauled to the river. The night was
spent at O'Fallons. We saw a herd of two hundred bulls.
There were few flowers to be seen, only withered poppies,
prickly pears and sunflowers. Now and then we glimpsed a
few spears of green grass. There were a great many wagons
going by also. Three miles east of Ogalala, [Ogallala], near
the bluffs, we stopped to camp. Everyone who was able to
climb, went exploring on the bluffs. There were mountain

gooseberries, wild currents, and gorgeous wild flowers growing in profusion.

We reached Big Springs [Big Spring, Nebraska] on June 17. We arrived at Denver Junction on the following day, where we paused to eat lunch, then drove on to Julesburg [Colorado].

June 18.   We arrived at Sydney [Sidney, Nebraska] and ate dinner. Here we were joined by James and Mahala McCloud. The camp was made six miles west of Sydney.

We remained in camp on June 19,   as it was Sunday.

June 20.   During breakfast a bit of excitement occured. A mare, belonging to William Evans, ran into a barb-wire[6] fence and was injured. She was frightened by the railroad cars which were constantly passing by. We stopped at Potter Station for dinner. We were surprised when we met a mule train returning to Sydney. We had become acquainted with the people in this caravan as they had passed us on the road. We could tell by the expression of their faces that something dreadful had occured. A gun, which was in the wagon bows, discharged, accidently killing two children in the wagon directly behind. The mother and another child were wounded, and the same shot went through the ear of a horse. They were returning to Sydney to bury the children. A desirable camp was found on the banks of Lodgepole creek. A storm threatened to break soon, and it was necessary to be prepared for it. Cora Linsay and Thomas Towell became very sick while we were there.

June 21.   We passed through Antelopeville and stayed at Bushnell [Nebraska] that night.

[6]On the Great Plains was early used for fencing due to the lack of wood. It's invention is usually attributed to Joseph Glidden of De Kalb, IL. Amos Crouch, *Antique Wire Illustrated*, (Chandler, OK, 1978), *passim*.

June 22. The morning was extremely cool and called for warmer clothes. The road followed Lodgepole creek for some distance. Everything in this vicinity was exceedingly dry. There were only stations along the railroad and no settlements. Here and there a ranch could be seen. There were great herds of cattle grazing along the creek and antelope were plentiful. At Pine Bluffs [Wyoming] we saw the largest herd of sheep ever seen hereto fore. Our resting place was beside Pole creek.

June 24 found us in a section of country where there had been a fierce hail storm recently, judging by the damage done. We were traveling on a high sandy plain, and the sharp thin cold air stung and nipped our faces. Warm coats and shawls were very necessary. Dinner was prepared near Atkins Station. The beautiful Colorado mountains and Black Hills[7] could be discerned, rising and towering far above the earth in majestic serinity. We entered a valley and drove until we came to a lake west of Cheyenne. Here we spent the night.

June 25. We drove into Cheyenne. Cheyenne was an attractive and pleasant little town. The soldiers were stationed here, and our beloved "Stars and Stripes" floated peacefully and serenely above the hospital. The wrong road was taken out of Cheyenne, and we were forced to strike across the country, following a dim trail to reach the Cheyenne Pass. The outlines of the distant snow-capped mountains became clear and concise as we drove onward. The wagons were drawn into their usual circle for camp at Lodgepole creek. On the following morning we left camp by way of a small valley and drove up into the hills. Here the earth was a colorful shade of red. The road stretched ahead of us like an unending scarlet ribbon. The hills were covered with sage, and pine trees increased in number as we ascended higher and higher.

---

[7]Now called the Laramie Range.

No brush could paint the glories that met our eyes; no pen could write all the wonders we beheld, and no tongue could ever find adequate phrases to describe this startling beauty. There were awesome rocky cliffs towering skyward, hills covered with everygreen trees and carpets of soft green grass. A gorgeous array of wild flowers vivid splashes of cover in the wilderness, called forth explanations of surprise and pleasure. Trembling, quaking aspin trees bordered beautiful streams, flashing clear and irridescent in the golden sunlight. As we beheld these awe-inspiring wonders, our hearts arose to Him, our great Creator, in prayer and adoration. Truly, we were viewing the fingerprints of God! The caravan drew out of the hills into a valley near Larmie [Laramie] City. This made a delightful camp site. Beautiful snow-capped mountains could be seen to the south and west.

June 26.   We entered Larmie City. The country around Larmie was sandy and desert-like. A little mountain stream provided a pleasant camp site.

June 27,   Amanda Evans was ill. After driving all day over hills and rocks, we were glad to rest in a little spot near a pretty little stream.

June 28.   Mrs. Evans was still unable to travel and we stayed in camp for another day. The men went hunting and returned with two antelope.

June 29.   We crossed Rock Creek and stopped beside the creek to eat lunch. Three men took pails and went to the creek for water. They found the stream full of trout which could easily be dipped out if some of the water could be diverted from its course. They promptly set about to do this, and when they returned to camp their pails were filled with fish. A mad scramble ensued, for everyone snatched pails or vessels of some description and rushed to the creek. In a short time the very delicious aroma of frying mountain trout assailed the nostrils of a hungry and expectant group, causing their mouths to water. There was plenty of fish left over for further meals. It was a rare and unexpected treat that none of us will ever forget. Objects, which are a great many miles distant, often times seem very near in high altitude. Such was the case in the mountains of Wyoming. Alexander and Richard Towell started walking to the snow line after a pail of snow. It looked like it might be about one half a mile from camp. After they had walked several times this distance, they decided to turn back as it was growing quite late, and darkness would soon be upon them. Back in camp everyone was growing anxious about these two. It was getting quite late and they should of been back long before. Dark—still they didnt come! We all feared for their safety. We were afraid that some wild and savage animal had run across them, or worse than that, that they had become confused and were wandering around in the forest. At last we decided it was time to do something. The men mounted horses, took their guns and rode forth in search of Richard and his father. They rode for some distance and fired several shots. Richard and Alexander were close by and Alexander called to them. We left Rock Creek and drove to Medicine Bow and Mass Creek.[8] Our camp was close to a ranch and not far from a soldier's cemetery. They had all been moved to another burial ground and only the head boards and roughly hewn coffins were left behind. There were other graves too, possible graves of emigrants.

June 30.   We were still in the Rocky Mountains. The weather was a great deal warmer than it was even though we were near the snow line. When we reached the North Platte River it was time to stop and prepare for the night. Our camp was near a cemetery, close to a ford where the river is divided

---

[8]This was Nash Creek, Albany County, (WY). Urbanek, *op. cit.*, p. 142.

by a small island. There is an interesting story in connection with this place. It was related to us while we were in camp here. It seemed that a small band of emigrants camped at this selfsame spot some years before we stopped here. They were attacked by the wily redskins and massacred. This accouned for a cemetery being located in such an out of the way place.

We left the cemetery camp on July 1, and crossed the North Platte river. Some excitement happened while we were making this crossing. The stream had to be forded as there was no other means of crossing. When the wagons were in the middle of the stream, Emily Towell called her husband's attention to the current. He became confused, thinking they were floating up stream instead of going straight across. He turned the team down stream. William Evans, seeing the danger, leaped into the swift current and swam to the horses. He turned their heads and prevented a tragedy. The Lindsay team became unhitched in the river and some quick thinking saved them. At this point the land is very barren. The water is poor. The only growing thing here was sage brush. The road wound around the base of a high mountain. A little further in the distance snow could be seen. In the evening we camped beside a spring on the side of the mountain.

July 2. We ate dinner in Rawlin[s], Wyo. We also laid in supplies. Here we left the railroad and drove 12 miles to the Sweet Water route.

July 3. There was not much activity in camp until noon for it was Sunday. We moved on to Bell Springs in the afternoon and camped. Bell Springs has its formation under a mountain of rock. The horses were turned loose to graze on the grass around the springs, and one of them mired down.

July 4. We crossed a sandy desert about 25 miles across. During the night it rained and made the air considerably cooler and traveling was much more comfortable.

July 5.   John Evans became sick. We were still plodding over a sandy stretch of desert. There were mountains and green trees in the distance. The women-folk washed clothing at the Sweet Water river. This is a very swift stream.

July 6.   The wind was cold and piercing. Gravel and sand were being blown constantly in our faces. We were traveling up grade most of the time and it was very difficult to make much progress.

[July 7]   Again we camped at Rock creek,[9] a lovely thick carpet of green grass, near a huge bank of snow, provided a lovely camp site. We were surrounded on all sides by bluffs. The night was bitterly cold and all the pails of water froze over during the night.

July 8.   The morning was very cold but not as cold as the day before. Soft fleecy clouds hung in the sky and the wind seemed a little more tolerant. The children explored everything within their reach. They found delicious wild strawberries and brought them back to camp. A great part of the day was spent driving on the sumit of the mountains. The roads were in good condition. The night was spent three miles south of Pacific Springs.[10]

July 9.   The road was downgrade and about one hundred feet in width. On either side of the road were banks of snow. We met a band of cattle from Idaho, about seventeen hundred head. We stopped on the Little Sandy river.

Sunday, July 10.   Provisions were getting very short. The

---

[9]Site of Old Rock Creek Crossing on the Overland Trail. Later there was a railroad station on the Union Pacific with section house, pump house, and water tank. It became the center of a great deal of activity by horseback and wagon loads. There was also a general merchandise store. During the early 1880's 175 freighting teams operated out of Rock Creek. *Wyoming, A Guide to Its History, Highways, and People* (New York, 1952, 4th printing), pp. 234-35.

[10]A pleasant stopping place about three miles west of the Continental Divide whose waters flow toward the Pacific. *Ibid.*, p. 151.

weather was a trifle warmer, but there was a great deal of snow on the ground. A few spears of grass and sage brush seemed to be the only vegetation here. Miles and miles of prairie land lay before us. As we were driving along we encountered a band of ponies going westward.

July 11. We emerged from some strange appearing hills and crossed the green river on the ferry and drew into camp beside the river. An Indian buck and his squaw came to camp. Their little papoose died and they were on their way to bury it, they told us. Nearly everyone had caught colds up in the mountains and Willie Towell was quite sick.

July 12. The day was clear and pleasant for travelling. A distance of twenty-eight miles was covered. Mr. Lindsay had a sick horse to contend with and this slowed us down considerably. Dinner was eaten beside the river, on a nice grassy spot. A small grove of trees provided adequate shade. Night found us at Slate creek.

July 13. We saw a band of cattle from Oregon and Idaho. This made us feel much nearer to our destination. At Rock Springs there were hundreds of names and dates carved in the rocks above the springs, names of emigrants who had gone on before us. Some of our crowd cut their names beside those of their predecessors.

July 14, found us driving a mountainous country. There were steep slopes which we ascended and descended. Much grass and timber were growing here. On one side were huge mountains of rock, and on the other side were beautiful timbered slopes. There were flashing mountain streams and springs here and there. At night we camped near a little store. Alexander Towell was feeling a bit ill.

July 15. Some of the boys went on ahead to see about securing provisions. We crossed mountains all day, higher than those we crossed some time before. Descending a very steep mountain slope, we entered a valley where there were a number of houses and stores. The residents of this valley were busily engaged in railroad building. We rested that night at Smiths Fork,[11] on Bear River.

July 16. The river was crossed on a toll bridge. We then drove up the valley where the railroad was under construction.

July 17. We had only gone a short distance when one of the horses became lame and we were forced to stop. This was in a small valley where grass was very plentiful. A nice clear spring was situated here which made it quite convenient for us.

July 18. We drove through a narrow canyon and entered a beautiful and well cared for valley, known as Bear Lake valley.[12] It was fenced and irrigated and the residents were all very busy as it was haying season in the valley. We camped on Bear river.

July 19. We reached Soda Springs, Idaho, and camped. Soda Springs was a very interesting place. Wherever we stepped on the rock formation around the springs, hollow echoes resounded. Mr. Lindsay was impressed with a little town near Soda Springs which was settled by Mormons. The railroad was soon to make its debut here, therefore, it looked very promising. Accordingly, Mr. Lindsay selected a claim. Mrs. Lindsay did not wish to stay here unless some of the others would stay too. Ten miles further up the valley we stopped at Hubles Springs.[13] A ranch was located here, and some of the best appearing cattle and gardens we had seen.

---

[11] Named for Jedediah Smtih, one of the most noteworthy of the mountain men. *Ibid.*, p. 186.

[12] The northern half of Bear Lake is in Idaho; the southern half is in Utah. The valley is about 20 miles north and south and 7 miles east and west. Lalia Boone, *Idaho Place Names*, (Moscow, ID, 1988), p. 22. William B. Smart, *Old Utah Trails* (Salt Lake City, UT), p. 72. Number 5 in Series.

[13] This was undoubtedly Hooper Spring, part of the Soda Springs complex. Aubry L. Haines, *Historic Sites Along the Oregon Trail* (Gerald, MO, 1981), pp. 280-81.

July 22.   We were still discussing the future possibilities of
this lovely valley. It would not do for farming because of its
location. As it was too near the mountains it would be subject
to early frost which would make the production season very
short. However, it was an excellent locality for the cattle
raising industry. Mr. Lindsay talked with many of the residents and became thoroughly convinced that this was the
place for him to stop. He could see no reason for going any
farther when this valley suited his tastes perfectly. We were
very sorry, indeed, to part with our good friends, the Lindsay
family. We stopped long enough to wish them success and bid
them farewell. In the evening we were overtaken by Leander
Lindsay as we were preparing to camp. He said that his folks
were hurrying to join us. There was much happiness and
rejoicing when we heard this news.

July 23.   Our caravan passed through Fort Hall, driving
steadily toward Blackfoot, Idaho. When darkness closed in
we were five miles from Blackfoot camped beside the Blackfoot river.

Sunday, July 24,   we remained in camp until noon, and then
drove to Blackfoot. Some Indians came to our camp at
Blackfoot and asked for bread. The first bread we offered
them was a trifle burned and they refused to take it. We
stocked up in the supplies and provisions necessary while we
were in Blackfoot. The ferry carried us across the Snake river
which is a curving and winding stream. The night was spent
close to the river.

July 25.   A sixty-mile stretch of desert lay before us, and at
noon we had covered twenty-three miles of the distance. The
day was warm and uncomfortable for us. We stopped at a
house for water. It cost fifty cents a span.[14] Water had to be

---

[14] A span is a liquid measure when it is used as the distance between two sides of the
top of a bucket. That would be nine inches.

hauled sixteen miles to this place and that accounted for the high price. A cold lunch was prepared and soon we were on the way and covered a distance of sixteen miles and went into camp after dark in a dry dusty place. The place did not appeal to us very much but we were tired after riding so far and were glad to rest.

July 26.   We followed a road that left the main traveled route and led to Lost[15] river, which was eight miles from the place we camped. It was much further this way but we preferred this to so much dust from other wagons, and the long drives without water. We hesitated just long enough to eat a light lunch and water the horses. We then drove twelve miles over dusty roads. The wind was blowing and raising great clouds of dust. Travelling here was very disagreeable. John Evans became quite ill. Camp was soon made on Lost Soldier river,[16] near a little store. There was plenty of grass for the horses to feed upon.

July 27.   The women did the washing, and the rest of the day was spent in resting for a long drive on the morrow.

July 28.   We drove out into the desert for fifteen miles without water. We saw great bands of cattle, sheep and ponies. The road led over the mountains, through lava beds formed by extinct volcanoes, and over land which was formed chiefly from volcanic ash.

July 29.   After driving the short distance of one mile, we came to a stream where there was a great deal of grass and we stopped here to allow the horses to feed. Wood River made an excellent camp site as there was an abundance of good

---

[15] Big Lost River, Idaho, is so named because it flows into the Big Lost River Sinks adn completely disappears. It was also called Godin Valley, a name given to it by the trapper, Antoine Godin, in memory of himself. Boone, *op. cit.*, pp. 30, 156.

[16] The first settlers came to this locale in 1880. The name was later changed from Soldier to Fairfield, a name which they thought described the country's beauty. Boone, *op. cit.*, p. 131.

water and fire wood. Wild currrants, red and yellow and black, were growing on the banks of the river.

July 30.   We drove over Camas Prairie. The wind was blowing cold and disagreeable.

July 31.   The day was exceedingly cold. A thin sheet of ice froze over the water in the water pails. Ice and snow could be seen on the mountains. We stopped to make camp at the end of the valley. We learned that the stage had been robbed here a few days before, and some horses had also been stolen. It was even more interesting to learn that the thieves had been captured and properly handled for their misdeeds.

August 1.   We traveled over hills and through canyons a greater part of the day. At Castle Rock we ate a lunch. We camped about one and a half miles from the Dixie Post Office.[17]

August 2.   This portion of the country was very hilly and rolling. Driving over hills and through interesting canyons we reached the little Boise Valley, and spent the night. This was near the mines consequently, every space where there was room enough for a hut and a little garden spot was occupied.

August 3.   We entered Boise Valley and camped near a ranch near the river. We crossed the river.

August 4.   The valley is a very rich looking place. Wheat, oats, barley and all kinds of vegetables. There were orchards, and the trees were all full of fruit. The branches hung low with their delicious burden, and seemed to be almost staggering under thir heavy load. There were apples, pears, peaches, plums and apricots. Many varieties of berries and grapes were also growing here. Boise City was a lovely town. It seemed to be concealing itself in foliage and beautiful green trees. The Caseldine and McCloud families, Elvin Hague,

[17]There were several settlements named "Dixie" in early Idaho. The founders were southerners who came west during and immediately after the Civil War.

George Todd and James Rhea turned back to the Boise
Valley. They wished to find work and stay there for a time.
The rest of us moved on toward the Payette river and
camped. The children wished to have a barbacue while we
were camping on the Payette river. A great many rabbits were
killed and dressed for the occasion. Everyone was busy
making preparation for the barbecue in the evening. The
children scurried here and there, gathering wood for the
bonfires and had them all ready to light. In the evening the
older folks joined the group and everyone joined in the
merriment and fun.

August 6.   We remained in camp while some of the men
went to search for Crane Creek Valley. This was about thirty
miles from the Payette Valley.

August 7.   The men returned. They could not find the
Crane Creek Valley. A council was held to determine the
number in favor of going on to a valley where the choice of
land could be obtained. Everyone was in favor of going at
once.

August 8.   We crossed the Payette river. An old man
accompanied us as our guide to the Crane Creek Valley.

Little progress was made on August 9,   as the roads were
very rough. The night was spent in a small valley. When
morning came we looked about us to see what the place was
like. There wasn't sufficient water for irrigation, therefore we
could not stay here.

August 11.   Driving over hill and dale we reached Dixie
Valley, and from there we drove on to Middle Valley.[18]
Middle Valley was a very fertile little valley, nestling down
among sage covered hills. The Weiser River wended its way,
peacefully through the little valley. Great promises were held

---

[18]The town of Middle Valley's name was later changed to Midvale. Cort Conley,
Idaho for the Curious (Cambridge, ID, 1944), pp. 564-65.

forth to the weary travelers. Nearly all of the little band
decided to stay in Middle Valley. Others took land in Sal-
ubria, Indian and other valleys. There were new hopes,
aspirations and ambitions as there was much work to be
done. Homes must be made. At last the long journey with its
hardships and heartaches was over!

EPILOGUE

Migration of 1881: Mercer Co., Mo., to Midvale, Idaho

Persons	Surname	Given Name	Persons	Surname	Given Names
9	Towell	Alexander	7	Lindsay	Tilford
		Emily			America
		William			Leander
		Thomas			Kelsey
		Richard			Flora
		Otho			Susie
		Frank			Cora
		Martha	3	McCloud	James
		Effie			Mahala
3	Caseldine	William			Frank
		Martha	4	Michael	John
		Lawrence			Vashtie
3	Evans	John			Plinn
		Amanda			Florence
		Dudley	1	Oatneal	Chester
5	Evans	William	4	Pickett	Bertha
		Victoria			William
		Seppie			Joseph
		Walter			Lucinda
		Emma	1	Rhea	James
1	Hague	Elvin	1	Todd	George
5	Holt	James			
		Mary			
		Dan			
		Addie			
		Mattie			

Total: 47 persons

Kansas to Oregon, 1883

❧ Sarah J. Collins

INTRODUCTION

The diary of Sarah J. Collins is an enjoyable one. Mrs. Collins had an eye for detail and the ability to express herself naturally and clearly. She also had a good sense of humor, waxing mildly sarcastic in regard to small town pretensions and minor human failings. Her record of travel is of particular interest to this writer because it precedes completion of the Oregon Short Line-Oregon Railway and Navigation Company link with Union Pacific by a year, thus nearly marking the end of enforced wagon traffic into the Pacific Northwest over the Oregon Trail route. Much of the land described by Sarah seems empty to her, but it is definitely no longer a wilderness. The roads are generally good; feed, provisions and services are available along the way; the railroad is under construction.

In Idaho the Collins party followed an early alternative route to the Oregon Trail, the Goodale Cutoff, across southern Idaho. It was a shorter route than the main trail along the Snake River and traversed some very grim country between Arco and the Boise Valley, following a narrow space between the mountains and the lava beds. The country made a strong impression on Sarah. Even here the conditions were far better than in the 1850's and '60's.

John C. Collins was born March 1, 1844. According to the 1900 Census, his birthplace was Illinois; his father was born in Ohio and his mother in North Carolina. This information may be incorrect. The 1860 Territorial Census of Kansas lists a John C. Collins, age 15, born Ohio, living with the James A. Lock family— as was Mathias Collins, age 8, also born Ohio. These people were living in Bourbon County. Crawford County, in which John and Sarah Collins lived, was created from Bourbon County in 1867 in southeast Kansas.

Sarah J. Casey was born April 6, 1845 and her birthplace, according to the 1900 Census, was Iowa; her parents were both born in Kentucky.

John and Sarah were married about 1870; their home was in or near McCune, Crawford County, Kansas. John was a farmer. There is nothing in Sarah's diary to indicate the reasons why they came west, why they chose North Powder, Oregon, as their destination, or whether they already had relatives in the area. In 1893, ten years after their arrival, the tax list amount for J.C. Collins (in Polk's Eastern Oregon Directory No. 1) was $1,220.00, indicating that he was a substantial landholder. John and Sarah were childless; the 1900 Census states that Sarah had never had children. In 1900 her mother, Susan K. Casey (born Kentucky February 1826) was living with them. Susan indicated to the census taker that she was the mother of ten children, seven of whom were still living. C.K. Casey, one of the seven adults in the Collins party, may have been Sarah's brother and was probably the "Charlie" referred to in the diary. He apparently did not settle in Oregon. Sarah also had a sister living in Baker but when she arrived there is not known at this point.

By 1903 the amount given in the tax list section of the directory, under John Collins, had dropped to $550.00, indicating that he had reduced his holdings. In 1905 the amount was $665.00 and, in the same year, Sarah J. Collins paid taxes ($20.00) on property in Haines—perhaps the home of her mother. Haines had been started in 1883, the year the Collins party arrived in the area, and their farm may have been as close to it as to North Powder, although the latter was given as their address. The directory for 1908-09 lists only S.J. Collins, $175, Haines, in the tax list section. This may refer to the homes of both Sarah and her mother.

John C. Collins died January 23, 1909. Sarah J. Collins died of a stroke March 14, 1913 at the depot at Haines; a sister, Mrs. I.J. Herrmann of Baker, was with her when she died. The funeral was held from the home of her mother, Susan Casey, of Haines. Susan lived until 1917. All three are buried in the Haines Cemetery and have handsome monuments carved in granite that was hewn from the Haines quarry.

Sarah's diary has been edited with a minimum of changes. Her spelling is at times inventive, but not enough so as to cause much confusion. I have inserted letters or words in a few places where clarification seemed necessary, and have omitted any punctuation that did not seem to fit. Her thoughts have been separated by providing an extra space between words, wherever this seemed appropriate in order to clarify her meaning.

The diary is a typical pocket memorandum book of the period, leatherbound, with two flaps that fold over; the pages are rag paper, ruled with blue lines. The diary is written in ink.[1] A tintype group photograph in a pocket may depict some of the people mentioned in Sarah's diary.

OVERLAND DIARY OF SARAH J. COLLINS

Items from McCune, Crawford Co. Kansas to Baker Co. Oregon.

May 1, 1883   our party of 7: J.C. Collins and Wife, C.K. Casey, L. Carnes, W. Jackson, J. Edmiston and Wife, bid a dieu to Parents Brothers Sisters and Friends   eat dinner at Osage Mission, Camped in 3 miles of Era [Erie] the Co Seat of Neosho   a dull place   a Family Camped here from Barry Co Mo. who had a sick horse

May 2.   Our Neighbors Horse is better this morning, but

[1]Sarah's diary has been in my possession since November 1987. On March 17, 1988, I purchased it from its owner, Glen Nantz, auctioneer, formerly of North Powder and now of Pendleton. Nantz acquired it from Ernest J. Rostock, antique dealer and retired educator, Pendleton; Rostock acquired it from a man who said he was a woodcutter and that he had found the diary in an old cabin in the Blue Mountains. Sometime during 1988 I will place the original diary in the manuscript collection of the Oregon Historical Society.

not able to travel. Eat dinner at big Creek and Camped on Cole Creek 2 miles from Humbolt [Humboldt] a Lovely Place to Camp   a spring on the bank of the Creek.

May 3   Fish for breakfast   Humbolt a Nice Town   went 3 or 4 miles saw a sign Cats for Sale   Came to a new Town Houses all new name Pickaway [Piqua] where Will saw the Train giveing a Cow the Bumping degree.   next Town Neosho Falls was disapointed heare   expected to see the grandest sight of our Trip   saw two finly dressed Indian Ladies on the streets   theire was an arch over the gateway of the Fair Grounds with the words in Blue and gilt letter, Welcom. I supose in honor of President Hayes and Governor St John   I think McCune has grounds for feeling slited Cool adn misting all day

May 4.   LeRoy the first Town in Coffe[y] Co is a nice one. Burlington the County Seat is a Beautiful place situated on the west side of the Neosho River.   from the appearence of the Place I think they Enforce the Temperance Law.   we traveled a bout five miles from Burlington Camped in a lane   the Boyes made a Big Camp Fire and three men visited our Camp   they was very much opposed to St John and Temperance and of Cours every other good Law, and said Preachers and theire Families was the worst people in the Neighborhood   John saide we wasent a fraide to Campe theire   then they went home in a worse humor than the[y] Come.

May 5.   went through two little Towns to day Strawn and Hartford   Coffe[y] is the best County we have traveled through yet   Some splendid Farmes. Lyon County is pretty Country thi[n]ley settled   I stood up in the Waggon twice to day while on high ground and Counted thirteen Houses each time

May 6.   Camping to day on Cotton wood three miles from

Emporia   the Boyes saw some Black Squirrels today. Six
other Waggons Come into Camp   nice looking jermans   the
women had a dutch roundup.

May 7.   Emporia is a Large Town.   they drink Beear hear
and Sprinkle the Watter on theire streets   had the Pleasure
hear of shaking hand with Elder Kelley of the M E Church
next town Americus   next one Dunnlap in Morris Co.
have seen Considerable Rock.   only seen two Fields of good
Wheat   plenty of good Watter

May 8.   Camped on Big John Creek   Fish for Breakfast.
J. Edmiston's Cousin visited our Camp this morning
Council Grove the Co. Seat of Morris   the pri[n]ciple part
of Town is on the west side of Neosho River.   some good
Land near Town   they put theire Corn in with Listers
Claime to raise 80 Bushel to the Acre.   after leaveing the
Grove we saw Some young Mountains   the Boyes went on
one to take a last look at McCune   eat dinner on Large
Creek   a Spring in the Bank. Parkerville and White Citty
are small Towns   we see a great deal of Wild Land   I think
it will remain so for some time.   High winds to day   they
all have Winde mills   they get some good of the winds that
goes to waist   have seen some KS Plaines this Afternoon
Counted houses twisce 8 or 10 once and some of them looked
to be 10 miles a way   drove late to get wood and watter.

May 9.   Saw some verry nice Country and some very rough
Crossed Republican River at Junction Citty   saw some
young Rocky Mountains   the Vallies look nice   eat dinner
on Smokey Creek one mile from Junction Citty the Co Seat of
Davis [Geary] a poor Country sand Valleys Rockey hills
Camped on four mile Creek.

May 10.   a little better Country to day   more Settlements
dinner on Timber Creek.   saw several good Fields of Wheat
they say they raise Corn to Burn but sell it for 35 ct. a bushel.

May 11. Camped on dry Creek last knight   Clay Center County Seat of Clay is a nice Place and has a good Country arounde it.   good many large Cribes of Corn, Wheat looks well   they fence with Cotton wood Trees   seem to be large Landowners

May 12. Camped on Parson Creek. Clifton a nice town Part in Clay and a part in Washington Counties   next Town Clyde in Cloude Co a pretty Country arounde it.   the Country near the Republican River is very Sandy

May 13. washed yesterday afternoon on Elm   a rain last knight   the wind so high had to take down the tent until knight   a visit from Scotchman

May 14. Cool   Clouded up and the Coldest day we have had   Concordia the Co. Seat of Cloude is a thriveing Town

May 15. Camped in a Lane   good watter   picked up limbes a long the lanes   a good deal of range   not much Stock on it   Scandia a nice little Town in Republic Co. Shade Trees in Town and on Farmes. Republic Citty 2 years olde   nearly all sod Houses to day

May 16. Camped near as little Town   Hardy   just across the line in Nebraskey   next Town Superior.   very nice lookeing Country   hauld our Wood   high winds   Counted Houses   seven and a Schoolhouse

May 17. harde rain this morning   lay up untill noon   a hilley roade and windy   seen 178 Box Cars Standing at a small Station

May 18. Camped at Red Cloude   we see they have no Temperance Law heare   It is the County Seat and only Town in County.   very windy   the people live in the Pockets or under the hills   Sod Houses plastered and lookes very nice inside   some nice house plants   very nice people the[y] had two Violins   J. Edmiston and a Son of theirs

favored us with some music   saw our first Dog Town to day
and a Wolf, and Camped on Blue Creek.

May 19.   some good Country to day   high winds and
misting   three other waggons Come up with us   plenty
watter   no wood   use Cornstalkes and Buffalow Chips.

May 20.   our Company went on and we are keeping Sabbath.   windy to day   we are in sight of one house

May 21.   heard Ho[r]sethieves had been heare lately   Sat
up last knight and watched our Teams   Cool and Clear   the
people are gathering corn   Plowing and planting Corn   a
nice looking Country but nothing to burn but stalks of
Corn.   sod houses   Minden a very nice little Town.   very
rough Country   Plat River up   a bridge 1 mile long   met
5 or 6 Teams on it   wasent very safe. Camped at Kearney a
very stirring Place   saw some movers with Cattle in Harness.
no settlements in Platt Valley   they are digging a large ditch
I suppose for Irigating the Valley   good roades   no windes
traveling along the U P.R. Roade   Hay 20 cents a bunch

May 23.   a level road   some mud holes. Plum Creek[1] a
very nice Town   next Town Cozad a station named for a man
from Sincinnatti who ownes land   build a Brick hotel and
School house   potatoes 28 cents a bushel.   lookes like a
Chain of Sande hills along south of us.   next Town Gothens
Burg [Gothenburg].   a little Better Country   we can see
three covered waggons on the south side of Platt   we see a
great many Sheep on the Range   as the tra[i]ns pass us the
Passengers waive theire handerkerchief at us.

May 25.   Camped last knight near the River   Rail Roade
and Sandhills   only House a Section House   the Ladies
visited our Camp. Cool to day   a fiew muddy places   rain

[1]Plum Creek was, in earlier years, the first important campsite west of Fort Kearney.
On August 4, 1864 a small wagon train was massacred near there. Mrs. Collins may be
referring to Elm Creek, a town located a few miles east of the Plum Creek site.

this afternoon   Camped at North Platt Citty this eavening
the Bridge across the River is over a half mile long. Traines
and Waggons Cross on the same one   this is the finest Town
we have seen   William Coady [Cody], Buffalow Bill, lives
heare.

May 26.   it raines every [day] heare   plenty Coal, wood
and watter along the Rail Roade

May 27.   Camped at OFallons [O'Fallon's Bluff][2] to day
five other Teams Come up with us heare. we Saw our first
Antilope heare   a drove of one thousand head of Cattle
passed us to day and theire is 2200 on behind   a good many
Cattle and Sheep one the range   they dont raise enything
heare just let theire stock live or die on the range   a good
many die   10 Waggons in Camp to knight   theire was one
hundred Camped heare last Sundy.   theire is small gnats
that nearley eat our Teames and us too up.

May 28.   saw a Dog Town of 30 or 40 Acres. Camped near
the River and Rail Roade   not a House in sight

May 29.   5 Families of us now 29 persons   a Family laying
over with a sick Horse   good roades   Cool and misty
grass very Poor   we hearde that two mules and two Horses
was Stole in North Platt last knight

May 30.   Frost last knight   Ice this morning in the
Buckett   some sand hills this morning   good roades this
afternoon

May 31.   Camped 4 [?] miles in Colerado[3] last knight   we
leave the Platt to day and go up Pole Creek.   we had more
visitors last knight   our Tent was Full   had Violin harp
and Vocal music.

June 1st.   pleasant this morning   good roades   we are in

---

[2] O'Fallon's Bluff, located on the Platte just east of Sutherland, was an important
campsite for Oregon Trail emigrants. It is a rest area on I-80 today.

[3] At Julesburg.

Pole Creek Valley   saw Cattle Men having a rounde up.
went into Camp early   a shower was coming

June 2.   pleasant to day   saw a garden and a little Patch of
Oats in Sidney [Nebraska] to day head quarters for the
Armey our first soldiers.   450 heare

June 4.   one of our Company killed a Antilope   harde rain
yesterday   Cool to day   another Antilope to day

June 5.   high winds to day   saw a man planting something
a Garden I suppose

June 6.   Camped two miles in Wyoming last knight   about
noon to day w[e] got a Sight of the Rockey Mountains Longs
Peak   they look like Blue and white Cloudes only more
pointed.   we saw 7 Antilopes in a drove running over the
hills.   we saw five thousand Sheep in a drove. Camped near
a Tank and an Irish Woman wouldent let them have Watter
for theire Horses   dident want us to Camp in a half mile of
the Station   threatened to have them arrested.

June 7.   dinner at Cheynne [Cheyenne]   it is situated in a
very nice Valley with hilles all arounde   saw our first Snow
Shed today   the Trees in the Citty are just putting out
leaves.

June 8.   laide over all day   it rained and Snowed   froze at
knight

June 9.   Clear this morning and Cool.   they have two
Engins to the Train hear   they had a Collision of two
Freight Traines a short time a go 6 miles west of Chyenne   no
one hurt   roades good   Cool.   roades hilley this afternoon.   some fine sights among the Wyoming Canions

June 10.   Clear to day   a Cool mountain Breeze   the
Rockey hills has a peculier Beauty   a fiew Pine Trees
scattered a long the hills. Sharmen [Sherman] is the highest
Rail Raode Station in the Union on the Summit of the
Rockey mountains.   there is a Stone monument theire 160

feet square   260 feet high 60 feet across the Top   it was built in Honor of Oaks and Oliver Ames Brothers   theire likeness is on [it] one the east and one on the west side   they was 10 feet long and 6 feet across the chest, the nose 18 inches on [?] Eye 12 inches   the forehead 26 inches   they worked on it three years   60 thousand dollers the cost   60 car loades of Sement   roades good and Sollid a fiew hills

June 11.   traveling in Laramie Plaines very Pleasant   snow on each Side of us   the Best part of Wyoming we have seen yet.   a good road this forenoon   good grass for noon and a harde Shower Come up, with some haile   Charley very sick   have to go on to Laramie to get a Docktor   has the Mountain Feaver

June 12.   rain all knight   snow this forenoon melts as fast as it Falles   the men are at work   Ladies on the Streets in Oilcloth Raps   no wind   a Lady tolde me they had just sutch weat[h]er for two mont[h]s.

June 13.   a nice Prarie to day and Snow on the Mountains dont look to be more than two miles a away.   some mudy places in Laramie Bottom   double Team for the First time roades rockey all the afternoon   we left the Railroade at Laramie   wond see it for one hundred miles. Teames look well.

June 14.   rock from the size of a pe[a] to that of a nigerhead all over the roades and hills a like all day   a good many mud holes, the sun shines a part of the time and raines a part.   the mountains look very nice   not much grass so many Sheep heare in the Valleys. Corn $1.60 cts per one hundred pounds nice Flowers at our Tent door grow in the sand and rocks

June 15.   fine and Cleare   better Roades today   a tole Bridge across Rock Creek. 50 cts a Team. John killed an Antilope to day   steap hills at the Creek.   another Tole Bridge on Medicin Bow Creek, 50 cts a Team.   a Store and several Houses along the Bank are some tall Trees Camped in 5 or 6 miles of Elk Mountains   snow on them

June 16.   Cleare and pleasant this morning.   our Teames and all that is in sight make 17 and 43 persons all going to Oregon or Washington.

June 18.   Cleare and fine to day   one [of] our Company killed a Beaver   Camped over Sundy in a narrow Canion on Rattle Snake Creek   one of our Company had a fine Hors[e] drowne.   went out of our way to a Bridge in a pasture   tole 30 cts a Team

June 19.   going south to day to Warm Springs on North Platt river   a spring the watter warm enough for dish watter theire is Invalides theire useing the watter   they think it helpes them   Corn $2.73 a hundred.

June 20.   fine roades   we met Famlies saturday and to day from Oregon   they say some harde things about it, no work theire.   dinner at Sulpher Springs   a store one Family theire   they wanted a man and Wife at $65 dollars a month warm and dry   some hills to day   a sage hen for dinner. some Snow watter for supper.

June 22.   Charley able to walke a rounde.   have seen some harde looking Country to day   at Barrel Springs   poor watter and no wood but sage Brush.   it burns very well

June 23.   a very good roade to day   a harde looking Country fine weather hot and dry   we drove thirty miles to day to get to watter at Antilope springes.   good watter.

June 25.   very hot through the day and watter froze at knight out in a buckett.   diner at Pine Butte   the worst hill to do down of our trip.   very good roades this afternoon. Camped at Muddy Springs   very poor watter

June 26.   Cleare and hot   better Country this afternoon some fiew Trees   a spring House built over a spring   Stone Floor plastered walls and was very nice

June 27. a hard looking Country, most of the day Crossed Green River at Green River Citty $2.00 for Ferrieng to the Team. went a mile out of our way to get to Camp at the Poorest place we have had a spring of Poor watter most every one out of sorts

June 28. hot and dusty nice level Country Poor land. a nice place to Camp in to knight

June 29. one of our Party Caught a fish last knight in hams Fork of Green River. weighed 8½ pounds dinner at Granger to day traveling a long the Oregon Short Line good watter and grass plenty mosquetoes.

June 30. good roades some fiew hills hot and dusty

July 1st. Camped on a Stream of good watter plenty of Brush to Burn and more than plenty of mosquetoes.

July 2. roades hilley to day a Town Irvin Creek, a Coal mine and seems to be quite a buissness place. had more grass along the Short line than any where on our Trip. this is a little better part of the Country. now five or six miles of rough roade fifteen miles of a Canion.

July 3. Cool this morning good watter grass and Brush to burn at Coake Ville [Cokeville] a Tole Bridge 50 cts to the Team saw two Indians with theire red blankets on Saw a fine large ranch this morning fine improvements a large fielde of Alfalfa Clover. they irigate a good roade to day only when Crossing the Rail Raode Track theire was no Crossing made and it was hard on our Waggons.

July 4. Cool this morning narrow Canions some places only wide enough for the road and a nice spring that runns by the side of it the hill three or four hundred feet high Eate our 4 of July dinner on a little Flatt with hills all a round us and wondering how our Folkes at Home was spending theire fourth we had Canned Strawberries and Cake made without Eggs. we saw a nice ranch this morning a nice Garden some

small Trees set out in the yard   a Log House   Some nice
Lace Curtains to theire Windows and from Appearance was
going off to selebrate the Fourth.   a Tole Bridge. 25 cts to
Team   Montpelier Ten miles in Idaho, a very nice Place
growing grain all arounde it   watter running all through
it   they are selebrating the Fourth heare to day   when we
see the Stars and Stripes we think we are in the United States
yet. This Valley is thickley Settled   nineteen out of twenty
are Mormons.   we see Peppement growing wilde and some
very pretty Flours.

July 5.   dinner in a Canion.   six hundred Head of Horses
passed us going to North Platt, Neb.   at Soda Springs to
day   the Spring has a peculiar taste   they are boileing up
all the Time. Watter cool we couldent drink it.   they are
improveing some heare

July 6.   some harde looking Country to day   another drove
of Horses to day   good roades

July 7.   a good Camping place last knight   good watter
grass, and Brush to Burn   some fine Cattle heare.   a very
hilley and dusty roade today   passed a Government Post
now owened by Indians   they had a garden growing.   a
bout eight miles of sand between heare and Blackfoot station.
was very heavy pulling, the first we have had.

July 8.   traveled five or six miles this morning to get grass.
and then rest. Blackfoot is a very nice Town   heare we saw
our first Freighters, three large waggons hitched to gather
with six span of mules to them   one driver   a twenty gallon
barrel for watter on each side   they have just come in over
the Desert   some more Indians heare, a nice Iron Bridge a
cross Snake River, $1.50 Tole to the Team.

July 9.   start a cross a 50 mile Desert this morning   40
miles without watter only as we buy it.   we payed one doller
for watter one place   they hall it 16 miles   the next place it
is brought with pipes from the mountains two miles.

July 10.   good roades but very dusty.   a half mile of Lava Bed that shook us up a little.   the rock are burnt Black and melted runn to gather like burnt glass.   and in some places greate openings in the Rock.   a sand storm this evening drove us in to Camp at a store at Arcove [Arco] on Lost River]   they say it is full of watter some knights and in the morning is gone

July 11.   very pleasent to day.   not so much dust   a ranch they were making Hay   had a nice Garden   some nice Flowers in Bloome.

July 12.   we are traveling between Lava Bed of a bo[u]t 60 miles and Salmon river mountains   a narrow place but splendid roades.   the winds blowes the dust some today

July 13.   good roades to day   not so much dust   Bellview [Bellevue] a mining Town on Wood River a little strip of Timber.   Every thing is very high   flour $4.00 per hundred Oates three cents a pound.   good grass to knight   hall our watter and burn sage brush

July 14.   Clear and Still   good roades

July 15.   Camping to day in a nice place on Soldier Creek in Camas Prairie.   good watter and grass and a nice looking Country. Snowes four feet deep in winter   some small fields of nice grain and Gardens   fiew settlements.

July 16.   Splendid roades   a fiew hills   fine cenery greate piles of Rock   a fiew pine trees on the sidehills   a good many names Cut on the Rock   we start on a Tole roade today of 25 miles $1.50 to Team   hot and dusty and some harde looking Country   we see greate heards of Horses and Sheep from Oregon going to Montana, and they keep the grass eat off   good many hills

July 17.   not so hot today   some fine ranches   a great many fruit trees some of them loaded with Apples & pairs

July 18.   a good many hills and then small Valleys

July 19.   Camping to knight in Boyes[4] Valley a pretty place
fine large shade trees and fine Orchards loaded down with
Fruite   some fine Buildings   Boise Citty the Capital of Idaho
is a very nice Place   Boise River runns a long the Valley and
furnishes the watter for Irigating purposes.

July 20.   roades dusty and hilley   had to drive until 10
Oclock last knight to get to watter   Pay for Timothey hay
1½ cts a pound   a good valley roade

July 21.   Hay 2½ cts a pound [they are] working on the Rail
roade   we see a good many Saloones a long the roade in
Tents   it never raines heare so they say

July 22.   Sabeth   traveled until noon to day to get grass
Camped at fine ranch near Huntington [Baker Co., Oregon]
the fi[n]est Peach Trees I ever saw.   this year the first failure
in haveing grass a mile from the roade

July 23.   hot and dusty.   hills high Valleys narrow, with
fine ranches and Orchards   a Tole roade $1.00 to Team

July 24.   Baker City the County seat of Baker Co is a fine
Town nice shade Trees.   this is a very nice Valley   near it is
Some Large Timber the First we have seen and theire is
plenty of it on the Blue mountains but scarse west of them
they are building two new milles heare a Flour and a Saw mill
in the foot hilles   theire [are] a good many men and Teams
now in this Valley gradeing for the Oregon Navigation Company's Rail Roade   it seems to me a Cooper woulde do well
heare   they use Tin Churnes Zinc Tubes[5] and buckets   no
unclaimed Land in the Valley.

S.J. Collins
North Powder, Oregon
Union Co.

---

[4] Boise
[5] Tubs.

MARY MATILDA PARK SURFUS
From the typescript of her *Composite Diary*

Kansas to Oregon, 1883

℈ Mary Matilda Surfus

INTRODUCTION

The letter came from Seattle, and it was signed by Kathleen Sidwell. She told of the diary of her great-grandmother, Mary Matilda ("Till") Surfus, who traveled with her family from Vallonia, Kansas, to Oregon in 1883. We telephoned Mrs. Sidwell and told her of our great interest in the Surfus document. She sent us a copy of the diary and gave us her blessing in publishing the precious document, which is in her possession. She told how she and her grandmother (called "Ona" in the diary), had transcribed as carefully as they could. Ona's full name at the time of the making of the typescript was Wynona Eliza (Stahlnecker) Gordon.

Kathleen Sidwell also informed us that "Aunt Till" had written a second document recording the journey. This was an account written in diary form, but it was not a day-to-day record of their journey but an extended reminiscence written soon after the family's arrival in Oregon City. Normally we would not have included such a document in our publication, but it is an apt commentary on the original diary. This record was so immediate that, despite some repetition, we publish it herein as the indented paragraphs following the original diary entries.

The family has published in typescript form both of these precious records as the *Composite Diary of Mary Matilda Park Surfus.* Those who participated in the publication were Kathleen L. Sidwell and Clarice O. Hargiss, Seattle, and Peggy E. Price, Renton, WA.

They also published a roster of the overland party, and we have published it as a postscript following her overland records.

WAGON TRACKS: THE COMPOSITE DIARY OF
MARY MATILDA PARK SURFUS

May the 21th 1883   Left Vallonia at 1 oclock
The following company left [northwest] Kansas Decatur Co
Vallonia at one oclock P.M. on overland trip for Oregon.
their names were, A F Surfus & family 10 in No. Isaac D
Surfus and family No 5.   T W Henderson & family No
5   Thomas Martin & family No 4.   Mr Tingley & family
No 6.   30 persons, 9 horses 4 mules.   3 dogs 5 waggons.
Campt on the Bever North 12 mi
traveled 12 miles and camped and ———. May 22 camped on
beaver creek.
23th   Campt 4 miles north of Indinola [Indianola, Nebraska]
(rained at night Virta had the phthisic[1] 2 dayes)
Went thru Indinola the 23rd of May & camped 4 miles north
of Indinola   It rained at night   We were all tired Vertie
was sick with asthma
24   Campt in spring Creek 24 miles from Indinola   had
the niceest place to camp (bought a stove at Indinola)
May 24.   camped on Spring Creek   Vert Better.   had the
nicest camping place.   bought a stove at Indinola camp
stove cost $2.50
25th   cold & horse bothered   took dinner on the Medicine
crost a shackley bridge, unhitch from waggons (took them by
hand)   rained most of day
May 25th   We took dinner on medicine creek   camped at
medicine Bow.   tis cold and windy   AFS. [A.F. Surfus]
horse went off   had to hunt half day for him and then he
came back to camp himselfe.
May 26   Campt in Wells Canion in Frounteir co. Neb very
rough   plenty watter & timber   Broke 3 waggon 3 bowes in
tree, rained again

---

[1] In those days "phthisis" meant any wasting away of the body, especially consumption.

May 26 camped in Wells canion in Frontier Co Neb   crost a
shackley bridge   unhitched from waggons   men took them
over by hand.   country vary rough   plenty grass wood
water   I broke 3 waggon bows   the mules went under a
tree   limbs caut bows   I yelkled who [whoa] but no stopping mules if the teams ahead are going.   our waggon bows
were higher than the others   the mules are hard to manage
I dont like them but Isaac does.

May 27   took dinner near North Platte,[2] the knats here beat
any incect I ever saw to bite & bother   the Platte river is
sandy,   to day Monday the rest washed & baked   I made
tent   twas vary warm   knats bite dreadful   alkilie here
disagreeable place   got $1. worth beans   1 pound pieplant
half box crackers   100.lbs corn   5 cts gum & candy

May 27 took dinner by north platte River.   camped on
same river.   there is a gnat here that bite worse than mosketoes   the platte river runs over sand and the river changes
its bed continually   tis raining and there is alkalie here   it
hurts the childrens feet. We camped to day   I made tent
and baked   here we got our first eatables $1. Beans   100
lbs corn $1/lb   pie plant 8 cts   half box crackers 50 cts   5
cts candy 5 cts gum.

This the 28 of May   Mr Aldridg & Co 14 in number
came   whole Co 48   Cloudy & cold today,

May the 28th Mr Aldridge & company come to us   Mr
Aldridge his two /4/ sons John and frank /Dube Will/ and
his wife 4 /6/ in No.   Lawn Aldridge & family 4 in No.
Jonah Boylan wife and baby 3 in No.   & Mr Griffith wife &
child 3 in No.   and Mr and Mrs Chute makes 16 more
added to our company   52 persons 11 waggons 14 horses 4
mules. /Oh mr Renards two families 6 in No/ Made rules
and regulations   put A F. Surfus in as captain.   are to
start in mornings at half past 6 oclock stop at 12.   Start at 1.
and go in camp at 5.P.M.

---

[2]It was at this point that they joined the overland trail route along the Platte River.

May 29   rained most all day   campt part of the time campt
at night 15 miles west of Platte City,

    May 29 camped most of the day.   it rained all day camped
    at night 15 miles west of platte city.

May the 30   high wind   campt at Alkalie Station[3] 14
waggons, made regulation first to start at half past six oclock
stop at 11   Start at one   go to camp at 5 in evening

    May 30 camped at Alkalie station   Wind blowes vary hard.

June the first   stoped half day   Some went hunting   some
washed and baked   I was sick   Wind high   rained   campt
at Spring Station 2nd

    June the 1st camped at little creek   plenty grass water &
    wood   June 2nd camped at spring station   camped half
    day   I was sick.   men went hunting   we baked washed
    ect.   came to south platte river   tis like the north platte
    sandy   here we had quite an excitement   the men led thier
    horses in the river to drink and most of them turned around
    and walked out but our horse charley drank and sank so deep
    in the quick sand that he could not get out and had to be
    pulled out with ropes and horses.

June the 3   campt near pole creek   no timber   plenty
wood on railroad all way   left South platte June 3th   traveled in Colrada 4 miles in sand hills 3 dayes   roads good
most time   June 3th AFS dog sick   also Mrs Aldridge
sick   Mr Aldridge well again   Mattie Henderson got
thresh[4]

June Sunday 3th.   Campt all day on pole creek   rained &
blowed hard   AFS dog died from drinking alkilie water

---

    [3] Alkali Station was about 40 miles west of North Platte. Charles Edgar Ames,
Pioneering the Union Pacific (New York, 1969), p. 217. Ames also has a detailed map of
the U.P. stations. It is a reprint of an 1871 map, and appears in two parts on the inside
covers at front and back of the book.

    [4] Here she refers to the disease, "thrush," an affliction that attacks the mouths of
children.

alkalie all long platte   no farming done   frequent heards of cattle & sheep,   road near railroad

    Mary M. Surfus memmerandam book sent 3 postal cards home & one letter and I saw plum trees in Bloom and some of the pritiest flowers in Wyoming Territory

    June the 3th wrote to CVS & N & SE Demos all in one

June 3rd camped near pole creek   came in Colorado have been traveling in sand hills for 3 dayes

    June 2 camped all day   Mrs Aldredge sick   also Mattie Henderson   water bad   AFS. dog sick drank alkilie water he is a large New Founland dog and they think so much of him.

4 teams stayed behind June 4th   took dinner on pole creek Campt on pole creek

    June 4 took dinner on pole creek   also camped on pole creek   the sick dog died   4 teams stayed behind

June 5th   Campt on antilope station

    June 5 camped at Antelope station   stoped half day   took dinner at Potter station   saw 3 deer   We meet fraiters almost every day   they tell us how the roads ahead of us are. My they can spin yarns.

June 6   took dinner at potter station   Saw 3 deer June 5   stopt half day to wash   June the 6th Campt at bushnell station   Ona sick & Mattie H sick

    June 6th camped at bushnell station   Ona sick and Della still sick

June the 7th   campt at pine bluffs station [Wyoming] Nice scenery   One still sick

    June 7 camped at pine bluffs   fine sceanery here.

June 8th   saw mountains in the distance   Sandy here Campt at atcheken Station   Ona quite sick   Mattie better rained again

    June the 8 company got butter 20 cts lb   potatoes 1 ct lb

June 8 camped at Atchenson station   Ona and Della well.
how glad we are when all are well   tis so hard to take care of
sick foalks on the road.   here we have our first veiw of the
m.t.s. in the distance   we thout them clouds all day. June 4
camped at little stream   see m.t.s. plainly to night.

June 10th   Campt at russels station   See mountains planily
came to Sheeanne   Learge town 8000 inhabitants in it   nice
lake near it   Wind blowes cold & it rains to day the 11th

June 10 Coame to Cheyenne Wyoming ter   tis a nice big
town 8000 inhabitants.   there is a butifull Lake near it.
and the mountains are great but not like I suposed theyd
be   not so pointed and are almost bare solid rock they are
rightly named the rockies.   the wind blowes cold and it
rained today June 11   camped at otter creek station rained
all night but we keep comfortable in tent.   June 12 camped
at station   all well and wether plesant   June 13 camped at
Arrow station.   we do not see any timber but get all the
wood we need of the R R old ties   sometimes the people
living along the R R try to sell the old ties to the men but
weve been imposed on so much that we dont believe all they
tell us.

12   campt at Otter Station   rained all night   is still raining
We keep comfortable in tent   Ona & Mattie better

June the 13th   Campt at Burord [Buford] Station   A F S
baby took very sick   heavy frost   June the 13th   Ona well
again.

June the 13th   passed granite canion   Burford Station &
Sherman Station   have campt in a vally with mountains all
around us   Crost the highest point at Marshal a small
village   had bad slough to cross   Sades baby better   Climed
up & got some snow   5 more teams joined us today   13
teams now & 5 load horses   June 13th campt on Learmie
plains

frosted heavy last night and tis June 13. Roy Surfus sick

14th   Came to Learmie City   tis nice city   Mountains all around city, rained

> June the 14 spent $2.20 cts at Chainne bought indelable
> pencil paper at Indnola

> June 14 camped in a vally with m.t.s. all around us   passed
> granate canion bashford station and sherman station

> June 14   We crost the highest point of mts on Marshall a
> small village   we climed up and got some snow. We went up
> the mts so gradually that we did not know when we were on
> top   I asked the station agent how far it was to the summit
> he laughft and said you are on it now   aint you high enough
> yet   I ans-. no Id like to go up in the clouds.

June 15th   Campt at Learmie City   went and seen Catholic Cemetry   Came through bad mud lane and alkilie   Crost one fork of Learmie river & river also several streams, are at Campt at foot of Mountains   One of mules sick

> June 15th camped on Larmie plains and came thru Larmie
> city.   tis a nice city surrounded by mountains. We camped
> part of day   went and saw catholect cematery.   came thru
> bad mud lane   had to double teams   crost one fork of
> Larmie river and the main river also

June 16th   Mule well again   Stayed all day 16th to rest wash & bake   it rained afternoon   Clouds looked beautiful over and below mountains   Learmie plains in places bare and sandy in places very rockey in places   good grass and beautiful moss and flowers   on mountains pine trees and quaken aspen   We campt on little creek   it was very swift so does all the streams   saw nice springs

> June 16 camped at foot of mts   one mule sick   stayed all
> day to rest bake and wash.   oh tis just grate here   the
> plains are so changeable   in places tis vary rocky and in
> others tis sandy level and in places there is grass and beautifull
> moss and flowers   my if I could only paint them.   on the
> mts are trees shrubby cedars and tall quaken aspens

June the 17, 1883   Came through 8 or 10 mountains streams
& several slough in the plains   the plains are betweene the
mountains are from 2 to 6 miles wide   Learmie plains are 22
miles across   the snow is melting of mountains   the streams
are terable swift but not very deep   rained & hailed Sat
evening 16th had to double teams to crost slough & today
tied ropes to waggons and 14 men helped horses pull, are
campt to night by a stream at foot of mountains   thay have
tall pine trees Very tall and strate   Make pastures of them
No farming since we left platte city   learge herds of horses
cattle & sheep   Twas very rockey to day   AFS traded for
large tent

> June 17 we camped by a mountain brook   came thru 8 or 10
> mountain streams   they are clear cold and sparkling   run
> vary swift. We came thru several sloughs in the plains   the
> plains are from 2 to 6 miles wide   Larmie plains are 22 miles
> acrost   it rained and hailed just showed us how it could
> do.   fine storm sure. We had to double teams to cross
> slough.   came to such sharp steep pitches in crossing streams
> that they tied ropes to waggons and helped horses pull   14
> men helped pull

June the 18   Crost rock creek & 6 mountain brooks   roads
rockey and in places shady   nice sceanery   Saw sage hen &
nest of eggs   paid toll at too bridges one $1 at rock creek &
50¢ at Medicine bow

> June 18 crost rock creek   camped at medicine bow,   AFS
> traded for a large tent   we saw large herds of cattle and
> sheep.   crost 6 or 8 mountain streams and saw sage brush
> and sage hens and nest of eggs   paid toll at rock creek $1.
> they told us there was no ford at all near but one of our co
> went up the stream and crost easy at a ford and yelled at us
> just as we were acrost the tole bridge   we paid tole at Indian
> creek 50 cts and at medicine bow 30 cts.

June the 19th   campt at Medicine bow   bad roads Sun
Mon & tues   mountainous & mudy,   fine scene to day

June 19 camped at small stream.   the roads have been bad
for 3 dayes   mountaineous and mudy.   but the sceanery is
just grand.

June the 20th   campt on pass creek night & half day   Creek
up   Went Southeast to bridge   paid tole 30 cts   paid $1
the 18 at rock creek & one half dollar at Indian Creek   37½¢
at a creek

June 20 camped on pass creek   roads terable

June the 21   Came to warm springs   the springs are in the
edge of platte river   they boil up higher than the river & are
warm   thare is a little town thare   thare is a bath room   I
went in & saw the Bath tub or box & the rooms   Taylors
mare sick   Alkalie all along the Vallies   We dont use any
standing watter   that which runs does not hurt anything
Most of the water we get is poor   took dinner at a large
Creek   came over bridge June the 21   June 21 sent a letter
home

June 21 came to warm springs   they are in the edge of platte
river   they seem to boil up higher than the river   the water
is hot enough to cook eggs.   Taylors horse is sick   alkilie
water did it,   is a little town here springville   we camped
here (June 21st sent a letter home)

Camt on prairie June the 22   no grass all day   Campt at
pine grove   Store thare

June 22 camped on prairie   the water is all bad   no grass
here   is killed by alkalie.   took dinner by a large creek &
came over bridge   Taylors horse all right again

June 23   stoped half day   Isaac & Tom Martin killed deer
down in Mountains by stream   Some men caut mountain
trout   AFS sick   men were afraid some of them are thieves

23th spent $8 in Indinola[5] got 5 cts pieplant   got 90 cts tea
& soap   Sydnie got $1.00 golden M discovery cts caned
peaches   40 cts pickles   Sidney largest   ever   we seen

---

[5]This is evidently a summary of things purchased along the way.

yet   nice place nice scenery   spent $1.30 cts at Chyanne
Larmie City large place   also bought single tree $1.00 1
pound onions   10 cts nuts   50 cts apples   lbs sugar 50
cts   2 lbs rice 25 cts   12 lemons 50 cts   at Evenston got
beaf 7 cts lb   onions 5 cts lb   best onion ever saw   got
blackberries 5 lbs to dollar
June 23rd stoped half day   Tom Martin and Isaac killed a
deer. Saw some rough fellows near. Some of the co was afraid
they were thieves   kept a watch that night.

June 24   We are at Sulphur Springs   Stoped to fill up kegs
(O dear my lungs hurts me so)   took dinner at Mudcreek
Camp on prairie to night   has been warm since June the
17th   June the 25th came by too forts or parts of forts &
through a plain a barren lonly place   came to whare the
ground is white with alkilie or salt some say   came to barrel
springs   tis black looking watter   6 miles to the next water
and 17 east /alkalie all along/ to Mud Creek   no wood
here   4 miles to another fort and spring and twelve miles to
bitter creek   Abe is better   frank Aldridge sick and Mr
Chute   saw too graves near springs roads   the forts are
covered with reading   Saw another old fort   the forts are
remnents of forts   10 miles from bitter creek springs to
antelope spring   tis the niceest spring I ever saw   Water
good but barrel spring and the one next to it & bitter creek
spring are salty not good at all   June the 24th came over
rough roads   came to Hell Creek this morning and 2 springs
thought we would find water in snow creek but it was
dry   had to drive till 4 oclock to find water

June 24 camped on prairie   oh my I feel bad   We came to
Sulpher Springs   stoped to fill up keegs   such water tis
horrid.   has been hot for several days.

June 25 camped by old forts   Came through a barren lonely
plain where the ground is white with Alkilie,   came to
barrel springs and oh some of the co rushed ahead   led thier
horses right in the springs [4 little shallow springs with barrel

hoops around them hence thier names] and when the rest of the co came to them the water was black and mudy. Well there was some pretty plain talk I was afraid there would be blows. We met Fraiters they tell us tis 6 miles to another spring 17 to Mud Creek

June 26th camped by another old Fort and lakes the water bad. the old forts are only remnants they are covered with names & dates. Isaac found a good bake oven in one and Sade found an old song title I Wandered to the Hills Maggie. how they did sing that the Aldredge family are fine singers are professional ones thats thier main buisness or was east. AFS is sick so is Mr Aldredge and Frank We past 4 more old forts and Bitter Creek the water in bitter creek is poison it looks alright and clear the Fraiters told us of it Before we came to it. Said dont use or let your horses drink of the water of Bitter Creek. We asked Why and he said When you go on the hill thats this side of it look over on the other hill and you can see a good reason why. and We saw lying on the hill they refered to a large horse dead. and another lying there with a man and family around it. June 27 camped at Antelope Springs and the water was cool and good and plenty What a blessing is good water. it had been a week since we had a good drink injoyed it hugely.

camp to night the 28 day Mudy Springs came 8 Miles to pritty creek 14 miles farther is Mount Brandy AFS still sick chute better I am most sick June the 28 We camp at Millers ranch nice place in canion, good spring in spring house plenty wood crost big hills today I am so tired my lungs hurts me

June 28 camped by Muddy Springs came over vary rough roads came to hell creek and two other springs But thot We'd find water in Snow Creek at noon but found it dry had to drive till 4 oclock to find water. Hell creek is a bright running stream tis awfull deep down to it and rough hard pitches to get to it that accounts for its name.

Its cold tonight the 29th of June took dinner the 29 on

pretty creek and camped at Millers ranch   had a fine
camping place in canioin. We came over vary rough roads
crost big hills   We walk up many of them I am so tired and
feverish. AFS and the Aldredges still sick. Isaac has to tend
Abes team and put up his tent   get them wood

June the 30   came over bitter creek 4 times to day   thay say
animals or man that drinks of its water will die   to night we
pitched our tents in green river city   AFS is still sick   frank
Aldridge sick   We crost green river on flat boat   paid
$2.00   they ford it in August

 June 30 camped at green River city   crost river on Boat
 cost $2. per wagon   25 cts per head for loose horses. Green
 river city is quite a pretty city   Nola Boylan is vary sick
 June 31st camped at Black creek   I am sick with mountain
 fever   so is Mr Aldredge and Frank and AFS   June 31st
 camped. By black creek   the children feel bad   there is
 scarcely a well person in the co.

July the 1th   We campt by black creek   I was real sick with
mountain fever   am still sick

 July 1st We camped by ham fork   the mosketoes are thick
 and saucy   it rained several showers   we were thankfull for
 them. · it has been extreamly hot for several dayes.

July the second   We are campt by ham fork   the moscetoes
bad   it rained a shower it has been extreamly hot for 6 or 8
days   Whole company feeling bad   past through granges
[Granger] today 2nd

 July 2nd camped at grange   to many in Co for comfort
 cannot get suplies for so many at the little stores at the
 stations.

July the 3th   Campt all day at ham fork   Lawn [Alonzo]
Aldridge waggon broke   he traded it for another but still
they stay   We stop to much   the rest wash & bake   I cant
do anything   I am still sick   tis awful hot & moscetoes bite

 July 3rd camped at Ham fork a little stream all day & also all

night. Lawn Aldredges waggon Broke and he traded it for
another. Some of Co are grumbling because we stop so long.

July the 4th we traveled took dinner at Mud Creek thay
call most of the creeks & thay are well named it rained
several showers We stayed July the 4th at Carter Station I
had hives in stomach was vary sick took dinner at fork of
bear river

> July 4th camped on Mud Creek past several creeks to day
> and inquire thier names tis oh mud creek and some of
> them are surely mudy enough.

July the 5th stayed at night at same spring Water sweet
not good at all I feel some better to day

> July 5th camped at carter station there is some springs here
> that has yellow looking water that looks and tastes like it had
> molasses in it tis no good only makes us thirstier after
> drinking

Mr. Aldredge got mountain fever We take dinner to day
the 6th at another poor spring Waschee [Wasatch] Mountains South of us dont cross them tis nice & cool has
been since July the 2nd We are in mountainous regions
again July the 6 We came to evenston. it has chinnie[6]
quarters oh my how dirty provesian cheaper here new
fruit from Oregon

> July 6th camped by spring its water tasted so strong of copper
> as we cannot drink it we can see the waschee [Wasatch] Mts
> south of us we wont cross them tho. tis nice and cool we
> feel better we came to evenstown [Evanston, Wyoming] it
> has Chinese quarters oh my how dirty and how funny they
> look and dress.

July 7th seen some nice country for the first in along
time came to utaw this morning came to Washington

[6]Chinese. A settlement of Chinese laborers was formed north of the tracks in
Evanston. There were many Chinese workers brought in by the railroad. Mae Urbanek,
Wyoming Place Names (Missoula, Montana, 1988) p. 38.

Station[7] got good water at Evenston first for 8 days   the
water is most all poor   what a blessing is good water   poor
water & hot weather is what made us sick   I am most well
now   Mr Aldridge is better   Will Aldridge is sick
 July 7th camped at Washington station   Saw some nice
 country   the first in along time and got good water all feel
 better   Will Aldredge got mountain fever
July the 7th campt in echo canion   Saw 18 Indians on
ponies   Some of company was afraid   July the 8th came all
forenoon in canion   came to echo mill   passed some of the
finest sceanry we ever saw   saw castle rock   it is the collor
of brick   so is most of the roks along the canion   a stream
runs through the canion & the RR does to   thare is dwelling
houses in the beginning of the canion with herds of cheep
Some cows & gees   some gardens eragated   farther on
thare is the nicest trees tall bushes quakenasp boxelder elder
berry goosberries currents cherries black haws thorn haws
sarves [service] berries and a number of bushes & berries I do
not know & thay are just loaded with fruit   the roses are in
bloom & some of the pretiest flowers   our road is sometimes
way up on the sides of the bluffs then way to the bottom
crosses the stream then the RR road   the bluffs and hills on
either side of the canion is half mile high   some of them red
rock   steep up with edifices domes spires steaples & arches
all naturel   July 8 campt still in canion Weber canion
passed echo town vary pritty town   also Weber town & a
little town did not learn name of it   tis Mormon town
Weber river runs through canion   thay eregate from it
 July 8th came in Utah   camped in echo canion.   Saw 18
 indians in paint   some of co were afraid of them. We came
 all forenoon in the canion   July 8th came to echo town
 /Echo mills/ and castle rock   the rock is about the color of
 brick   a creek or River runs thru the canion   so does the R

---

[7]Wasatch Station.

.

R oregon short line   in the 1st part of canion are small farms
as vegatable gardens and sheep cows geese ect.   then the
canion gets narrow and has the nicest trees of wild goose
berries currents choke cherries black haws hawthorns all
filled with delicious fruit   We were camped and got all we
wanted and wild roses and other beautifull flowers. Why it
was a feast to of good things after dreary wastes and bad
water.   the road sometimes runs way up on the side of the
bluffs and then way down to the bottom.   crossed the river
then the R.R.   the bluffs on each side of the canion here is
half mile up to the top.   the rocks in shape of castles domes
spires steeples and Arches all natural but almost perfect

July the 9th   Came through some of the fineest sceanery
saw the devils slide & saw tunnel for cars to run through   saw
most curious rocks & hills or mountains   the gap was so
narrow but one team could pass   Weber river runs through
it   on edge bushes & trees   trees loaded with fruit   our
road run on high bluffs in places   tis all together the pritiest
& grandest sight I ever saw   tis imposible to give any idea of
how the canion looked   the canion is mostly erigated
houses all long   Mormons mostly

July 9 camped in canion but here called Weber   tis a
continuation of same canion. Widens here and we passed
Weber town   Weber River runs thru canion   they eregate
from it and raise the finest vegatables & small fruit. We
passed another small town did not learn the name   tis a
mormon town.   and now we come to some of the finest
sceanery we have yet seen   the Devils slide his eye glass and
tunnell and gap   the slide is white rock   looks like marble.
our waggons were on opisite side of slide   it looked to be as
wide as waggon bed had sides like one and at top was seat
rounded off like a big rocking chair.   the slide begin at the
top of this and ran as smooth as marble clear to Bottom 60
feet long.   here and at edge of river it was rounded off in
shape of seat the same as at top. & just opisite it was the eye

glass   it was a round hole through a huge rock   July the
9th   the tunnel was made thru the solid rock for cars to run
through.   and the gap is a fearfull looking place   high
mountains of rock on each side and the canion here is so
narrow we can only see a streak of light and so deep deep
down and quite a falls and the river plunges down over rock
and forms a white spray that is fethery and flies on you and on
sides of canion and makes a roar louder than thunder. the
cars run thru the tunnel here. and the river and waggon road
so near only just room for them thru the gap.   the waggon
road just cut out of the rock up above the roaring river   the
men had us all walk for fear the teams would get unmanageble
but they were as afraid as some of the people were and
crowded as near the side of the bluffs as they could.   tis a
mile thru from one end of gap to the other. but not so narrow
all the way. it widens out in places then becomes narrow in
other places   tis grand beond description to me & most of
the co.   others could not see any thing but fearfullness in
it.   tis 20 miles thru echo canion and 30 through Weber

July the 10   came through devils gap   tis a fearful looking
place   high mountains of rock on each side & the river
running over rock makes it foam white & such a roar louder
than cars   the river & road is near just room for them
through the gap   tis a mile through from one end to the
other but not so narrow all way as in first end   echo canion is
20 miles   Weber 30 miles   campt at Ogden   large town
are Mormans settlements   they look like towns   We came
to another hot spring   it was walled up   it looks vary
curious   boils up from botom   is about 4 ft deep   thay
have bath rooms here   also a thick yellow scum rises on top
water

July 11th camped at ogdan[8] a large mormon town   we came

---

[8]One wonders that Salt Lake City was not visited by the Surfus wagon train. The story
is that the original railroad by-passed the Mormon capital taking a route farther north
which saved 76 miles. Ames, *op. cit.*, p. 267.

to another hot spring   it was walled up   it boils up from
bottom about 4 feet acrost   they have bath rooms here.

June the 12th   took dinner at a settelment of Mormans
under the shade trees by an eregating ditch   thay have nice
yards & houses 2 or 3 on one place & good orchards   We can
see Salt Lake half mile west of us—still in Utah—tis a nice
sheet of water—the largest I ever saw   the sea gulls are all
along the lake   thay are white & black   the town is named
Brigam   campt at another gentile town did not learn the
name   the Mormans tell us thay dont have anything to do
with the gentiles   thay have a tabernicle in Brigham   Salt
Lake Valley is about 20 miles wide & thay eregate it   por-
tions of it they can   thare is Mulberries   trees are planted
on the streets have berries on them   splendid orcherds in
yards full of apples,   the country is dried up intirley except
where they eregate   have to buy hay

> July 12 camped in Mormon Settlement under thier shade
> trees by an erigating ditch   they have nice gardens and
> several houses on every place.   good orchards to

July 13   campt in prairie   halled water with us   get sage
bush for fuel   past over bear river through Corinne town
[Utah]   found no water but salty stuff   came to a nice little
lake & spring this afternoon but they was salty   Mr Aldridge
is vary sick a stroke of palsy   tis hot & vary dusty   the
roads must be 4 or 5 inches deep in dust

> July 13 camped near brigam   Salt lake is the nicest Lake I
> ever saw   it glistens like glass and there is a crust of salt all
> around it   the seagulls are all along the lake they are white
> and purple.   they have a tabernackle in Brigham [City] that
> is a great building   the most wonderfull one as the 7th
> wonder of the world

> July 14th camped in Prairie   hauled water with us   get
> sage brush for fuel   passed thru mormon town and a gentile
> town   the mormons tell us to have nothing to do with the

gentiles and the gentiles tell us the same of the mormons.   we
came to a little lake but the water is salty. Mr Aldridge is
vary sick   had stroke of palsy.   tis hot and vary dusty I
think the road is 4 or 5 inches deep in dust

June [July] the 15th   came to another warm spring   campt
to night near a ranch   found good spring water   the wind
blew the dust so we could scarcley see   twas afful   twas
rocky to part way   we left the RR at Corinne   July 13th
staid & washed & baked   a family campt near us had worked
with marvin this summer he turned back with us   sent home
2nd letter   July 13 AFS traded old doll for a pony mare
July the 14 came in Idaho   we came through a cedar grove
saw more timber than we seen at all   campt on a little stream
near a range of mountains   the wind blowed the dust fearful
tis cool   July the 15th campt near raft river   We camp to
night in a pretty place   like Idaho better than Wy ter or
utah   it was cold this morning but hot at noon   We came
over a sandy plane   nothing grew atall   came to raft river
thar was a family living thare had a pasture told us we find no
grass for 18 miles but we drove a mile   found plenty grass
the people will tell the bigest falshoods to get to sell thir hay
June [July] the 15 came to kizer creek   tis a nice creek   We
seen some nice country but they have to erigate   We saw
some curious stones mountains   one looked like rusty stove
pipes standing up right & one like pleats standing up   Idaho
is altogether nicer than W.T. [Wyoming Ter.] or utah   the
streams are plenty   water good   no alkalie here not much
in utah but salt in utah. We are in Albion [Idaho] town
today   tis the dearest place we come to since we left warm
springs.

   July 15 came to another warm spring   it was in a slough with
   tall grass all around   We did not learn any thing about it
   But camped near it the 15th and some of the co took a bath in
   it.   found a good cold spring too.   the wind blew the dust

so we could hardly see   twas rocky to today   we left the R
R at Corinne.

July the 16   campt on the prairie   had to hall water from
Alben [Albion]   came through canion half a mile long   twas
rough

> July 16th camped on a little stream near a range of mountains
> staid all day washed and baked.   sent letter home. AFS
> traded horses for pony. Paid $40 Boot   Came in Idaho.

July the 17   we take dinner on good [Goose] creek   no
more water for 18 miles   came on to spring creek   July the
16 bought hay   July the 17 came to rock creek 8 miles
came to it 2 or 3 times before we cross it   tis a worthles peice
of country we went over 16 and 17th   tis level but covered
with sage   no rain   cant eregate   AFS waggon whele ran
off   campt at Spring Creek   July the 17 campt on rock
creek   herded horses along the stream

> July the 17th camped by raft river   tis a pretty country we
> like Idaho best of any place weve seen yet.   But not so well
> as kansas. We came through a ceder grove the most timber
> we have seen in a body yet.

> July 18th camped on kizer creek   we saw some nice country
> but they have to erragate   we saw some curious stone hills
> one looked like old rusty stone pipes standing on end, and
> one like plates standing edgeways   great hills of them.   we
> passed thru Albino town.   every thing is vary high   noth-
> ing less than 5 cts   no pennies in use here. We come over
> spring creek and rock creek   same old names continually
> Delia Tingley helps me to learn the names of places and
> streams. She laughs and sayes Mrs Surfus no use to ask the
> names of these streams   just put down spring or rock creek
> two thirds of the time.

July 19   Halled water   campt on prairie

> July 19th hauled water and camped on prairie.   came to
> Salman creek. We saw sand springs from here   they run
> down over high banks and make a nice falls

July the 20   came to salman creek   we can see the sand
springs from here   they run down over the high banks at
snake river & make a nice water fall   Came to snake river to
day   tis a big one for this country   the rivers are not any
larger than creeks in Iowa   salman river emties in snake
river here
        July 20th came to Snake River   tis a large river for this
        country   the most of the rivers are small but swift
July the 21   we are still on snake river   we stop to wash and
bake   I had a big washing to do & baked 12 loaves of light
bread   campt the 20 on snake river   July the 21th We came
to the falls   oh how beautiful   nicer than anything I ever
saw in echo canion Weber canion rivers mountains lakes trees
flowers gap slide springs all combined cant compare with the
water falls nature can & does go far ahead of art   the salman
falls are terabley grand but the falls that run down out & over
the banks of the snake river is just sublime   thare is a river
running on the right of snake they call blind river which runs
under the ground part of the time and part along through it
as others do & it is higher up than the Snake & makes its way
through the ground & rock & runs down the banks of Snake
river   the banks on that side are 60 or 75 feet high & the
water runs down in hundreds of little streams as large as my
arm & larger   counted 20 hills where it runs out of   they
look pritier than any water in any other shape I ever saw
salman falls is the snake river its selfe that falls down a high
place   thare is a store post office & 3 or 4 houses in the town
/Sent a card July 20th home/ We came to sage plains or desert
tis 20 miles acrost the plain and there is no water till we get
through   it was past 10 oclock & we could not reach water at
night nor hall enough so we camp till morning
        July 21 camped on Snake River   stoped to wash and bake
        I had a big wash this time   have been sick so long   hitched

up about 3 oclock P.M.   the men had been hunting   came
in to tell us of a falls.   the Salman Falls tis the river that
runs down in the Snake   tis wonderfully grand. Ribbon
Falls is just sublime   there is a river called blind river on the
right of snake and part of it runs underground and part
through it as other Rivers do.   it is higher up than the
Snake and makes its way under ground near the Snake and
runs down the banks of Snake.   the banks on that side are
60 & 75 feet high and almost strait, and the water runs down
in hundreds of little streams the size of a knitting needle to
that of a stove pipe   the sun shone on the falls and the green
trees above and the foliage beneath made the colors of the
rainbow.   the streams come out in all shapes and we all
voted it the prettiest sight we had yet seen.   is a little town
here.   July 21st We camped at Edge of sage desart   tis 20
miles acrost and no water they tell us till we get through   in
the middle of the desart is a man By a well & sells water   we
took dinner on the plain or desert   tis dry sandy and sage
brush and grease wood is all that growes on it.   they both
emit a sickening oder it seemed along 20 miles. We came
over it in the one day tho it was a hard drive just a dead pull
thru the sand   the sand makes the hardest wheeleing of any
thing else.

July the 22   we took dinner on plain it is not like learmies
[Laramie] plains   it is not level here & it has grass   the
grass is all dry but is good   we got fruit cheaper than at all
before   tame plums dryed for 10 cts lb & peaches apples the
same   We follow Snake river all day but not near enough to
get water   it is vary crocked that why it is called Snake
river   We killed a rattle snake today   saw wild geese to   we
came through sand   the roads was bad & steep hills to pull
up

July 22 we came to habitations   got fruit here dryed for 10
cts lb   killed a rattlesnake   sent letters home.   we follow
snake river   found grass and water.

July 23   We came over the worst roads weve seen at all   We
stop to dinner on Snake river   follow it 30 miles   the grass
is salt grass is not good   We found a number of fish skeletons
they mesured 3 feet in lenght   the Oregon short line RR
runs along this river   tis hot to day   Alvaretta Martin is
sick   We killed a rattle snake to day   So far saw 7 deer   We
campt near a large rock that looks like a torr [tower] & near
Snake river   we passed to places on Snake river where men
was diging gold   they say one of the mines brings his owner
$30 per day   tom Martin caut 10 fish out Snake river

> July 23rd camped   camped near Snake R again   followed
> it 30 miles   the grass is salt not fit for the horses. We found
> some fish skellitons   they mesured 3 feet in length   Alva-
> retta Martin is sick   we killed another ratler to day   saw 7
> deer

July the 24th   We stoped to get dinner on a biyow & the
moscetoes drove us out   they were as thick all over as I ever
saw knats   the horses run out of the grass & would not
eat   We drove out on hill   We camp to night by Branew
[Bruneau] creek   it emties in snake river near here   We
have had bad roads the last three days   had to double twice
up hill & the sand ran over the rim of the waggon whele   July
the 24 sent a card home to

> July 24th camped by bruno creek   stoped to get dinner on a
> Biou and the mosketoes really drove us out   the horses ran
> up on the hill and refused to eat   the children screamed and
> twas out of the question to keep the mosketos off of us so the
> men hitched up and drive up the hill   saw bear and two
> cubs on a log playing   Sent a card home to day

July the 25th   We stop to rest Abes horses   one of them
give out yesterday   We are by snake river in sage or alkilie
desert   no grass for our horses   no way to get hay & some of
company short of provesian & money   thare was 25 teams
campt on branno [Bruneau] river last night

July 25 stoped to rest   AFS horse gave out. We saw tower rock today   passed two places on snake river where men were diging gold   Tom Martin caught 10 fish. July 25 camped on brouren creek   it emties in the Snake.   had bad roads to day had to double twice up hills   we camp on Snake R again   are in Alkilie plain   some of the co are out of Provesion and means   the rest of us are helping them thru.   was 25 teams camped here last night.

July the 26   We came over a vary dusty road   We came to kizer creek   stop to let our horses eat awhile   tis 15 miles to water so we will fill up our kegs & go on 8 or 10 miles   I am most sick   We went 2 miles & found plenty grass & good water   it was the same creek kizer   we camped

July 26 camped on Burrough [Bruneau] River   came to kizer creek   let our horses eat awhile   cannot find feed now every day   we by hay and put it in the waggon   tis bailed and when we find grass we stop and let them eat for sometimes we cannot get neither grass or hay. Will fill up our kegs and drive 8 or 10 miles   tis 15 miles to water.

July the 27th   We have found bad roads   sand was 8 or 10 inches deep   it rained last night & is sprinkling now   We can get plenty new potatoes 3 cts lb

July 27th camped on Snake River   found bad roads to day got new potatoes for 3 cts lb   AFS horse gave out again   tis sandy roads   tis a dead pull   our mules stand it fine   are much better to travil with than horses.   we can see silver mts on our left   are in foot hills   the country here is bare or covered with sage. We see some of the prettiest hills and curious rocks standing up like trunks of trees,   tis nice and cool   we can in morning see snow on the mts but hot in middle of day. The dust is mixed with Alkilie and hurts us to Breathe it and tis so deep. and rools up so we cant help it   Snake R runs thru Sage at Alkilie desert.   it is 60 75 & 100 feet down to the its waters   we have drove dayes along its banks and not got one drop of water   no trees or bushes

grows along it only vary rairly.   it has islands ocasionly and
people live on them and eragate and fish.   they stretch lines
big ropes or wire from one island to another and fasten
smaller lines with big hooks on them on the ropes and catch
the biggest fish. What a life away from church or school &
civalizatoin

July the 28   We came to snake river again   campt at
night   AFS horse gave out again   We can see silver mountains on our left   we are in this foot hills   the country here
is level but bare or covered with sage brush   We have seen
some of the pritiest hills lately & great curious rock standing
up like trunks of trees   it nice & cool this morning   We
can see Mount Snowan   tis vary hot in midle of day   the
salt is mixt with alkalie & is hard on man or beast   Snake
river runs through sage or alkilie desert   it has the highest
banks of any river I ever seen & not much shrubery grod
along it & no trees at all   people live on its banks & its
Ilands in fraim houses   they have little patches iregated &
rais potatoes & vegetables & catch fish   they fish with lines
stretch clear acrost the river or from one iland to another &
the line is fixet with hooks & little fish for bait   28 campt on
Snake river

 July 28 camped on Snake again.   found a salty hot spring
 we got some fine turnips to day but could not get any thing
 else   Floar is $7.- per hund $1. for 3 doz eggs   potatoes
 3 cts lb   we have been where we could not get any thing but
 onions and potatoes for 8 or 10 days at a time

July the 29   campt on Snake river   saw a hot salt spring in
the grass   We stoped near a house & they gave us all turnips
we wanted   could get no butter or meat or flour & some of
our copany is out of all of them   3 doz eggs cost $1   floiur
$7 per hund   potatoes 2 cts ½ lb   We have been where we
could not get any thing but onions and potatoes for 8 or 10
days   it is cold nights & hot dayes   the roads are bad & our

horses are falling away & part of the time we cant find grass for
them nor hay to buy   We take dinner to day by the Snake
again   Isaac catched a fish & killed 3 rabbits   he has killed
26   the grass that growes along the Snake is salt grass   it is
not good   you can see the salt on it & taste it   oh it is
hot   we came to sinker creek   it emties into the snake
here   Could get rosenears [roasting ears] for 35 cts a doz

> July 29 cmped by sinker creek   isant that a name for a
> creek. Isaac caught 4 nice fish & killed 3 hairs   we eat them
> to. We would not eat them at tall at first but travelers cannot
> be choice hah   the drinking is worse than the eating but the
> fine sceanry pays for it all   we got 12 ears of green corn for
> 36 cts

July 30   campt on Snake

> July 30 camped on Snake R   AFS horse gave out   Taylor
> H [W.T. Henderson] put his spare horse in and we went on

July the 31th   took dinner on Snake   came through some
bad sandy roads   AFS horse gave out   Taylor had him put
calenel in & drive in afternoon   Saw some of the pritiest
sand hills   they were drab culler & laid in waves   I walked
over them   dont sink in them but a little

> July 31 camped on snake again   saw some of the cutest sand
> hills   they were drab color and lay in waves like water
> waves   we walked over them   dont sink in much   July 31
> camped on snake   the snake river gets larger as we go North
> west   tis a muddy looking river   reminds me of the
> Missouri

August 1th   We came to the Owyhee   tis a nice big river
the Snake river gets larger as we go northwest   the Owyhee
emties in Snake here   the country is dry all through   it
don't rain here either   We are just in Oregon but so far we
have seen no Co we could swap decatur Co for in kan   Some
of our company are intirley out of provesion and money but
wont give contract or security for it & have went on without

it   5 of our teams went on   AFS horse cant go the 18 miles
drive we have to go before we find water   So Mr. Tinglies
Taylors Abes & us stay till tomorrow & put our horses in the
pasture   give 25 cts a team for puting them in one day &
night he did not charge   kansas goes far ahead of anything
we have seen yet I think & know

> August the 1st we came to the Owyhee   tis a nice big river it
> emties into the snake here. We are just in Oregon   we like
> Decatur Co Kansas best yet.   we will have to go 18 miles
> before we find water and tis nearly noon so Mr Tingly
> Taylors Abes and us will put our teams in the pasture and
> stay till morning   give 25 cts a team and can overtake the co
> tomorrow   August 1st camped on Malhure River   tis a
> nice big river   tis vary dry here   reminds us of Kansas
> when there is drougth   did not overtake the other teams
> AFS traded horses again

August the 2   campt on Willow Creek   August the 2 we
came to Malhue river   it is quite a nice river   came to a
stone store

> August 2nd camped in a valley   are in Baker Co Oregon.
> The vally is green with grass but tis salty   can see the salt on
> the blades and taste it   We dont want to stop here

August the 3   we came in baker Co   did not overtake the
others   AFS traded old bill for a grey pony   he paid $40
difference   We have come to the niceest valley we seen
yet   tis green with grass but tis salt grass most of it   the
Willow Creek is dry   Most all the streams have white willow
in them   took dinner at grove springs & picked goosberries
on shares   I picked 3 quarts   campt by a house at Willow
Creek   put horses in pasture   Wind & dust blew offal in
night

> August 3rd camped at Groves Springs   overtook the other
> teams   the water is good here and the grass also   I sent
> letter home   We picked goosberries on shares here at ranch
> I got 3 quarts,

August the 4   took dinner at a mining camp   thare is a
gold mine near hear & they are diging ditches to run water to
wash gold   thay have a ditch dug from burnt river to Willow
Creek the distance of one hundred & 30 miles   We can see
the gold in the sand   Where there is a reveane they make
troughs to run acrost & where they want to turn it up hill
they run pipe up   We seen one pipe 90 or 100 yards
long   We have seen some bunch grass today   the sage gets
thinner   We found lots of wild berries today   they are
larger than those of kansas but not as good, are more bitter
We are on what they call the duly road   it is a told road

    August 4th. camped near a mining camp. There is a gold
    mine near and they are diging ditches to run water to wash
    gold   have ditches from burnt river to willow creek the
    distance of 130 miles. We seen some bunch grass to day   the
    sage bush gets thiner   found lots of choke cherries   they
    are larger than those of Kansas but not so good.

August the 5   came where they was diging gould in 3
places   they had along rubber pipe as thick as a man & 100
rods long   it was fixt so as to throw the water with great force
& they was washing the gold out of the mountain way down
thare   Was a lader to go down & it was open at top   I went
most down but the rest was afraid so I came back   We came
to the Duly [Dooley] mountains   they are a spur from the
blue mts   We went over them most the higest place it was 7
miles from the base till the summit & 7 miles down & it was
covered with fir & pine trees   it was the bigest & most
timber I ever saw   the trees was from 100 to 125 feet high &
so strate   it was the pritiest sight I ever saw to run up on the
highest point & look down between the mountains   the rest
of the women said it made them dizy but it did not me   We
found rasberries currents cherries & sarves berries   the currents are just like the tame red ones & thare is black ones just
like the red except the culler   the strawberries were all gone

& most all of the berries   We campt at the Mountain
house   We came through Malhue town & several Mining
camps & over burnt river & some mountains streams   it
rained   the mountains are covered with grass so beautiful &
geen   there is strawberrie vines on Mo-ts

August 5 we camped at the foot of the duly mts   they are a
spur from the blue mts   we went over them   it was 7 miles
from the base to the summit.   we saw the first big trees
here   they were fir from 125 to 200 feet   oh what beauties

Aughust the 6   came down west side of M & 12 miles to
baker city   it is as larger than oberlin   tis situated in a
vally   tis vary pritty here   We met the rest of our co & the
best thing that happened to us on the road came to us   it was
a letter from home   Aldridges & Jonies got letters from
Oregon   Jony got $20 from his father and Al $20 of george
they write very incurrageing to us   We are campt to night
by powder river in as pritty a vally as I ever saw   We got a
letter from SED Aughust 6   tis Isaac berth day   he is 31
years old   20 teams campt here

August 6th came down west side of mts. Camped at mountain
house. We came thru Malhure town and several mining
camps over burnt river and mountain streams cold swift and
lovely   tis 12 miles from mts to baker city   tis large as
Oberlin [Kansas] situated in a lovely vally.   a happy event
awaited us here   letters from home   it had been nearly 3
mo. since we heard from there. When we left mother was
prostrated with grief and we left with vary sore hearts but the
letters said she was well. Isaac was 31 years old that day   20
teams camped with us last night   Some going east but most
of them west   A Mr James wife and baby came in our co at
baker city

August the 7   came over north powder & several mountain
streams through powder vally & powder town   it is a pritty
vally   the water was yellow or clayey & some the culler of

water which a gun has been washed with but the wells water is good to drink

August 7th we came over North Powder river and several mts streams and thru powder vally and Powder ville.   the vally is very pretty   the water vary bad in powder springs they looked and smelled like water which a gun has been washed in. But the well water is good   there is no grass to speak of in this vally but the soil is vary black and loose.   we are hunting homes in Oregon but dont want any here. camped in vally.

August the 8   We stoped to wash & bake   We emtied a waggon & went 2 miles to gether berries on the shares but when we got there thay had none for to pick   Some people told us they had but we bought some cabbage & got some milk   Alldridge Jonie Lawns gripheffs stoped a mile or to back   Jonies came in our company at baker city the 6th August & sent a letter 8th in offace for father

August 8th stoped to wash and bake   the people there told us there was berries to pick on shares 2 miles off. So we emtied a waggon and went to pick or buy some but they were all gone.   but we got some cabage and milk   I put letter in office to day for fathers.

August the 9th   we came through bad canion over several streams & in grand round vally   it is the nicest vally weve seen   We took dinner near a house in vally   the vally is 25 through   came through legrand   tis a nice town   turned off mane road took a new road   it is not good is very rocky   came to house on mountain at 1 m   stop & taylor & abe went to find right road   Isaac & tom went back & followed a road till it gave out   We are all getting gum spruce & fir   tis like that we buy   we could get pounds of it   part of our company went the pendelton road   We went over some bad roads   came to the old road   came over the blue mountains   it was vary steep & rocky   We came to

where they was building R R   the ground was covered with
tents & chinemen   We came campt on a mountain   AFS
waggon whele run off again

August 9 we came thru bad canion and into Grand round
vally to day.   the people told us not to stop in city for the
children there had Diptheria in a vary bad form so we went a
mile out of town and stoped near a house so as to get
water.   the vally is 25 miles thru it   we came to Legrand
tis a beautifull town   August 10 we took a short cut road.
Some man told us we'd save 5 miles by doing so   4 waggons
of us   the rest took the Pendelton road.   well our road was
terable and dangerous   we stoped and Isaac Tom went to
look ahead and found the old government road   we gethered
spruce gum and some juniper berries   neither is vary good.
well the men came back in an hour and what a time we
had   we could not turn back   the road was up on a high
bluff and just room enough for a waggon so the men unhitched
and partly emptied the waggons   locked the wheeles tight
tied ropes to them and got them over the bluffs into the old
road   it took a good half day and a lot of hard work   We
will not try any more short cuts.   We camped in blue mts at
foot

August the 11th   came over mountain   came through a
stateon   they are working RR here   We came the free
road   thare is a tole road   the roads are 6 or 8 inches
deep   the mountains are heavy with timber juniper spruce
& 3 or 4 other kind I dont know   AFS horses are gone
Isaac is helping hunt them   we find some black haws that is
good and mealy   not like the black haws of Iowa but like the
red ones   the afternoon nearly gone & no horses yet   We

---

[9]Could it be that she meant the Meacham Stage Station, built by Harvey J. and Alfred
B. Meacham in 1863? The broad mountain meadow had been Lee's Encampment, not
for Jason Lee the missionary, but for one Henry A.G. Lee. Meacham enlarged his station
in 1865. One wonders just how Mary Surfus managed to call it "Meter" or "Meeter."
The best new study of this region is the newly published book, *Powerful Rocky: The Blue
Mountains and the Oregon Trail*, by John W. Evans (LaGrande, Oregon, 1990).

campt here tis Meter[9] station   AFS horses came back early
Sun Morning

August 11 we came over the Blue mts   it was vary steep and
rocky   oh how pretty the trees and streams. Ina and I
walked a great deal   wanted to see the sights   the mts
streams were numerous and the trees so tall and the mts so
straight   not like any we had come over but prittier by far.
We would go on top   they are bare on top down quite a
peice too.   the trees cannot grow above the friezeing point
freizes every night I supose. We could look down between
the mts and see the streams rushing over rocks and the trees
stood up tall and strait   their tops coming up on the mountain sides & such a lovely green   Ina would clap her hands
and say oh if grandma and uncle Jim could see this Id be so
glad.   they were working R R in here   we camped at
station Aug 11

August the 12th   We start for pendelton   tis a R R town 28
miles from Meter Station   tis cold   We came at Umatilla
vally   tis pritty but vary dry   We pass large schoolhouse
Indian School   We came through the Umatilla reservation
or a part of it   saw a good meny Indians & ponies

August 12   We camped by meeter station   AFS horses
ran off   he and Isaac are hunting them   we are injoying
ourselves picking haws black and red. Hawthorn trees grow
in abundance here   AFS children are sick with sore throats
we fear tis Diptheria   well here comes the men and horses
Sunday morning August 12 we start for Pendelton   tis 28
miles from meeter station   Ina is sick, Johny Surfus quite
sick, he rides with us   some of them ride most of the way
with us they have such a load. We took dinner in Umatilla
Vally   tis a pretty vally but dry and hot.   we pass a large
schoolhouse   tis an Indian school

August 13th came thru umatilla reservation   saw a good
many Indians & ponies   they wont allow us to tuch the
timber not even pick up the dead limbs   we have to twist up
hay to bake with   there is lots of dead grass here

August the 14   came to Pendelum   campt   came up on
high land   level & it was fenced all in lanes   they was
harvesting   it was a nice scene after so long a barren country
We campt on the umatilla

> August 14th came to Pendelton.   camped on high level
> land in lane   tis all fenced in   they are harvesting   tis
> refreshing to see big fields of grain after traveling so much in
> a barren country   the children are nearly all sick Ina is
> bad   we got some medicine at Pendelton for her.

August the 15   We came along the river   found some of
the red alderberries   they are sour & are larger than them
east   We came through echo town   a small town on the
umatilla   We take dinner near some houses   lillie & Johny
Surfus is sick & Dealy & Jame tingly   thare is all of us
campt here   it is very dusty   we cant see the teams next us
sometimes & tis rocky in places   we see some nice apples
in orchards   all vegetables growd good here & small grain
& ear corn growes to   people have rosenears [roasting ears]
We haul water & take dinner on the prairie   the bunch grass
is good   tis 30 miles acrost the prairie without timber & 14
miles without water   the prairie is nice & raised good small
grain & some early corn   . the timber was 40 miles through &
water plenty   campt on prairie   it was a regular sand storm
We had to stop traveling

> Aug 15th camped on the umatilla   came along the river
> found some Oregon Elderberries   they are biger than those
> in Iowa and are sour quite good.   came thru Arlington
> [Echo] town

August the 16th   We came through wind & sand & take
dinner on willow creek   traveled part afternoon and had to
stop   campt on prairie

> August 16th camped on prairie   had a hard dust storm
> We could not see even our horses   they refused to face the
> storm   turned around. We had to camp   the wind blowed
> so hard it lifted the waggon covers bows and all off of the

waggons.   but A.F.S. neiled his on   two of his children are
sick   Ina seems some better

August the 17   came to willow creek   Wind & sand is vary
bad   came to rock creek   followed it down   had to stop
again on account of wind & dust   We could not see our
horses   We had to drive back half or quarter mile to get
behind bluffs   the country is vary rough & some places
vary rocky & sandy   We dont like it here   We got some of
the best haws we ever saw   got some sweet corn 15 cts
doz   We camp to night near rock creek   we came through
canion   crost toll bridge John Day River paid $1.00   take
dinner on prairie   water in draw half mile away   wind blows
yet same   tis cold we ware hoods & shalls   has been cold 3
days

August 17th came to Willow Creek   wind and dust vary
bad   we get green corn here 15 cts per doz. We came to rock
creek   have to follow it down and had to stop again on
account of wind and dust   could not see where to drive and
horses would not face it   everything is completely covered
with dust   cannot see our faces they are the color of wood
ashes, hard wood   We find different wood makes different
colored ashes. We had to turn back a half mile to get behind
bluffs to camp. We dont want any of this part of Oregon.
Camp by rock creek   came thru Canyon crost tole bridge on
John Day River   paid $1. tole   tis so cold we ware hoods
and shawls   We are in foot hills tho comming to Cascades.
Ina vary vary bad   oh We are where we cannot get a docter
or any help   tis so far back to a town and on to Oregon
City   here my diary ceased   it took all my time and attention to care for Ina

We came thru foot hills and it was cold and we came to some
little vallys and I remember they fetched Ina apples and blue
and red Hucklel berries but she would not eat them her
throat was so sore   3 days passed and it was August 20 at 3
oclock in afternoon her nose began to bleed and it continued
to bleed untill 3 in the night   we done all in our power but

could not stop it.   the next day we stayed all day in camp
she was so bad could scarcly breath and the lineing of her
stomach came out   she would strangle and sink away then
revive again   We could not get feed for teams and the next
morning we emtied our waggon and intended to only stop
long enough to let the horses eat grain without unhitching
them and drive to some town before we stoped   we fixted a
swing bed in the wagon and she lay on it and the jolts did not
hurt her. She was delerious part of the time. I had to fan her
for it seemed she could not get breath enough   we were
coming up the Cascades   it was near 3 oclock AM when she
said to me mama you need not fan me now I can breath
eisier   I said Ina you are better   she said no I will never get
to Oregon City   I tryed to hush her and said oh yes we will
be there before long   we wont unhitch till we get there   She
said oh mama hear me let me tell you dont stop me this time
it hurts me to talk (she had started to tell me before that she
would die but Id try to incourage her so I said well tell us
what you want to and Isaac said let her talk)   She said you
and Papa and Virtie and Ona will to to Oregon City but I will
go to my home that my hymn tells about.   and oh I could
not bear the idea of her dying in the mountains so I cryed out
oh Ina not way up here in the mountains   she said why
Jesus is here to   he knows where I am and will take me from
here as easy as from Oregon City. her father said yes
Darling he can.   then she closed her mouth and Eyes
folded her hands acrost her breast and slept for 15 minits. I
said oh is she not better? Isaac shook his head.   then she
awoke with a gaspe and said oh mother   we saw she was
dying and called Taylor Henderson   he came in our waggon
and put her head in his lap and said now till be quiet   let her
go in peace.   and a few breaths she was gone   oh the
anguish of that, our god alone knows.   but she has gone
home as she said   her hymn was this, I will sing you a song
of that beautifull land the faraway home of the soul where no
storms ever beat on its glittering strand while the years of

Eternity roll ect.   tis found in gospell hymns No 20   We sang a great deal on the road and at night and that hymn was her favorette   she was 8 years lakeing 11 days. We drove on untill we came to a camping place. (Camping places are cut out in the woods on mts sides) so we stayed there till morning then drove on up to the summit house   twas 10 oclock August 23rd   it was our 10th weding anaversery just 10 years on that day we were married. We stayed all day at the summit   made a coffin of the top side boards of our waggon it was a new waggon   the boards were oak and well painted Isaac took some mesures of her coffin so as to make one when we got to Oregon City thinking he could come right back and put her coffin in it and bring her to the cemetry at Oregon City but we burried her at Mount Hood in an Emegrant grave yard by another little girl who was laid there.   and Vert and Ona were both sick   Ona soon got well but Vert was not expected to live for 6 weeks.   and did not get well for 5 years.   he had sinking spells for 5 years, then he got stout.   and when Isaac wanted a pass in fall to go to Mount Hood to get Ina the roads were closed and he did not get to go till the next August just the year from the day she was laid there   Isaac and Taylor took her up and brought her to Oregon City grave yard and laid her there Roy our first child died when he was 6 months old is burried Iowa Butlar Co   Isaac is buried in Elwood Oregon   mary M Surfus's diary kept while coming to Oregon in 1883

ROSTER OF 1883 TREK

Abraham Franklin Surfus   Till's brother-in-law
   wife: Sarah Margarette (Boylan)   Till's first cousin "Sade"
   children: William, Myrta, Eldora

Isaac Delong Surfus   Till's husband
   wife: Mary Matilda (Park)   the diarist, "Till"
   children: Ina (died on Trek),
       Vert, Ona

William Taylor Henderson   Till's "stepbrother-in-law"
   wife: Martha Ann (Park)   Till's sister "Mattie"
   children: William, Bert,
       Wesley, Della

Thomas Martin
   wife: Alvaretta (Surfus)   Till's "stepsister-in-law"
   children: Orvid, Garrett, Curtis

William Aldredge
   wife: Martha
   children: John, Dube, William,
       Joseph

Alonzo Aldredge ·
   wife: Lydia (Boylan)   Till's first cousin
   children: Anna, Clara, Joseph,
       Clarence

Edward Dibble
   wife: Margarette (Park)   Till's sister
   children: Floyd, Elmer

Jonah Boylan   Till's first cousin
   wife: Nola (Adams)
   children: Grace, Allen

John Matthew Park   Till's brother
   (stopped in Idaho awhile)
   wife: Lydia (Dibble)
   children: Susie, Evelyn, Matthew, Ed

Isaac Marvin Park   Till's brother
   (stopped in Idaho awhile)
   wife: Katherine (Howard)
   children: John, Rosa

Rennard - two families

Griffith family

Chute family

Tingley - two families

INA ELIZABETH SURFUS
About age 3, before the trek on
which she died at age 7, near the
end of the journey in 1883

ONA AND VERT SURFUS
About 1883, at ages 3 and 5, after
the trek. Vert still recovering from
diphtheria.

Both photos from the *Composite
Diary* of Mary Matilda Surfus.

*The final volume of the series will provide
an index, bibliography, gazetteer and other
reference material pertaining to
all volumes of the work.*

The Series

Covered Wagon Women: Diaries and Letters from the Western Trails, 1840-1890, is a projected series of eleven volumes. Each volume will contain documents which are either unpublished, or very rare, from a certain time period of our history. They will be transcribed as written, without internal editing, and will be introduced and footnoted by the editor.

All volumes are produced in Caslon type, with Centaur hand-set display type. Great care has been taken to assure their durability, and only the finest of materials have been chosen for printing and binding.

Subscriptions to the series are welcomed by the publisher, although each volume is available individually. The publisher will furnish descriptive material or other detailed information on request.

The Arthur H. Clark Company
P.O. Box 14707
Spokane, WA 99214